MW00959086

WALKING
IN
FREEDOM
FOR WOMEN

A YEAR OF DAILY ENCOURAGEMENT

Pastor Dennis J. Cummins

WALKING
IN
FREEDOM
FOR WOMEN

About the Author

Dennis J. Cummins is the lead pastor of Experiencechurch.tv. He has faithfully shepherded since 2004, ordained under the mentorship of Pastor Gerald Brooks of Grace Outreach Center in Plano, Texas, Dennis brings a wealth of spiritual insight and pastoral care to his congregation. With over three decades of experience as a leadership expert, he has devoted his life to equipping others to grow in their faith and become effective leaders in their families, communities, and ministries. Dennis's ministry is centered on instilling hope, strengthening faith, and guiding people to focus on their God-given purpose rather than their past failures.

As an author, Dennis expands his pastoral mission through his writing, including his 365-day devotional book for women. This book is a practical and inspiring guide designed to encourage men in their daily walk with Christ, offering wisdom and biblical insights to navigate the challenges of life. With a heartfelt passion for helping others win in their relationship with God, Dennis uses his devotional writings to provide readers with daily encouragement, actionable reflections, and transformative spiritual growth. His writing reflects his commitment to helping people deepen their faith and live out their God-ordained purpose with confidence and integrity.

A New Year, A New Heart

"Create in me a clean heart, O God.
Renew a loyal spirit within me."

— **PSALM 51:10 (NLT)**

Additional Scripture References:

Ezekiel 36:26 - *"And I will give you a new heart, and I will put a new spirit in you. I will take out your stony, stubborn heart and give you a tender, responsive heart."*

2 Corinthians 5:17 - *"This means that anyone who belongs to Christ has become a new person. The old life is gone; a new life has begun!"*

Devotional Thought:

The new year is a time for new beginnings, a chance to reset and renew. Ask God today to cleanse your heart from any worries or regrets of the past year, inviting Him to fill you with peace and purpose. Let this be a season to trust His plans and embrace a fresh perspective on your role as a woman of faith.

Reflection Questions

What are your hopes and intentions for this year?

How can you invite God to shape them?

Are there past struggles you're ready to release?

Prayer for the Day

Lord, create in me a heart that is open and renewed. Help me to trust You with this new year, knowing Your plans are good. Amen.

January 2

Seeking God's Vision for Your Year

*"Trust in the Lord with all your heart;
do not depend on your own understanding."*
— PROVERBS 3:5 (NLT)

Additional Scripture References:

Jeremiah 17:7-8 (NLT): "*But blessed are those who trust in the Lord and have made the Lord their hope and confidence. They are like trees planted along a riverbank, with roots that reach deep into the water. Such trees are not bothered by the heat or worried by long months of drought. Their leaves stay green, and they never stop producing fruit.*"

Isaiah 26:4 (NLT): "*Trust in the Lord always, for the Lord God is the eternal Rock.*"

Devotional Thought:

It's natural to want control over plans, but God's vision for us is often greater than we can imagine. Invite Him to direct your path, trusting that His guidance will lead you toward growth and peace. As a mother, wife, or daughter, seek His wisdom as you step into new responsibilities and seasons.

Reflection Questions

What do you feel God is calling you to focus on this year?

How can you release control and embrace His guidance?

Are there areas where you need to trust Him more fully?

Prayer for the Day

Father, show me the path You have for me this year. Help me to trust in Your vision and release my own need for control. Amen.

January 3

Embracing Peace in Every Season

"And the peace of God, which transcends all understanding, will guard your hearts and your minds in Christ Jesus."

— PHILIPPIANS 4:7 (NLT)

Additional Scripture References:

John 14:27: *"I am leaving you with a gift — peace of mind and heart. And the peace I give is a gift the world cannot give. So don't be troubled or afraid."*

Isaiah 26:3: *"You will keep in perfect peace all who trust in you, all whose thoughts are fixed on you."*

Devotional Thought:

Peace is a gift that anchors us amid all seasons — whether in joy or challenge. As a godly woman, allow His peace to settle your heart and mind, especially when life feels overwhelming. Reflect on how you can bring this peace into your home, impacting your family with a calm, Christ-centered spirit.

Reflection Questions

Where do you need God's peace the most right now?

How can you practice inviting peace into your day?

Are there routines you can adjust to create a more peaceful environment?

Prayer for the Day

Lord, let Your peace fill my heart and home. Help me to rest in Your presence and bring Your calmness to those around me. Amen.

Setting Intentional Goals with God

"Commit to the Lord whatever you do, and he will establish your plans."
— **PROVERBS 16:3 (NLT)**

Additional Scripture References:

Psalm 37:5: "Commit everything you do to the Lord. Trust him, and he will help you."

Jeremiah 29:11: "For I know the plans I have for you," says the Lord. "They are plans for good and not for disaster, to give you a future and a hope."

Devotional Thought:

Setting goals can be powerful, especially when they are aligned with God's purpose. Rather than creating a list of goals on your own, invite God into the process. Whether it's a personal goal, a family goal, or a faith-based goal, commit it to Him and trust that He will guide your steps.

Reflection Questions

What goals do you want to commit to God this year?

How can these goals strengthen your walk with Him?

Are there any goals you feel God is leading you to pursue?

Prayer for the Day

Father, I commit my goals and plans to You. Lead me toward what is best, and let my life reflect Your purpose. Amen.

January 5

Being Present in God's Purpose

"For we are God's masterpiece. He has created us anew in Christ Jesus, so we can do the good things he planned for us long ago."

— **EPHESIANS 2:10 (NLT)**

Additional Scripture References:

2 Corinthians 5:17: "This means that anyone who belongs to Christ has become a new person. The old life is gone; a new life has begun!"

Romans 12:2: "Don't copy the behavior and customs of this world, but let God transform you into a new person by changing the way you think. Then you will learn to know God's will for you, which is good and pleasing and perfect."

Devotional Thought:

As God's masterpiece, you have been created with a unique purpose. Let today be about being present in His plan for you right now, resisting the urge to compare yourself to others. Whether you're nurturing children, working in your career, or caring for loved ones, know that each role is valuable in His eyes.

Reflection Questions

How can you embrace your role without comparing yourself to others?

What gifts or talents has God given you that you can use to bless those around you?

How can you lean into God's purpose for this season of life?

Prayer for the Day

Lord, thank You for creating me with purpose. Help me to focus on being present and use my gifts to glorify You. Amen.

Building Strong Foundations

*"Anyone who listens to my teaching and follows it is wise,
like a person who builds a house on solid rock."*

— MATTHEW 7:24 (NLT)

Additional Scripture References:

Luke 6:48: *"It is like a person building a house who digs deep and lays the foundation on solid rock. When the floodwaters rise and break against that house, it stands firm because it is well built."*

James 1:22: *"But don't just listen to God's wor*

Devotional Thought:

Strong foundations are essential not only for our faith but for our families and homes. Begin this year by strengthening your foundation on God's truth. Let His Word be the rock upon which you build your marriage, raise your children, and nurture your relationships.

Reflection Questions

How can you build a stronger foundation in your faith this year?

What are some ways you can make God's Word more central in your home?

Are there practices you can adopt that will help reinforce these foundations?

Prayer for the Day

Lord, let my life and home be built on the solid rock of Your Word. Help me to listen to Your teachings and follow them with faithfulness. Amen.

Letting Go of Past Regrets

*"Forget the former things; do not dwell on the past.
See, I am doing a new thing!"*

— ISAIAH 43:18-19 (NLT)

Additional Scripture References:

2 Corinthians 5:17: "This means that anyone who belongs to Christ has become a new person. The old life is gone; a new life has begun!"

Revelation 21:5: "And the one sitting on the throne said, 'Look, I am making everything new!' And then he said to me, 'Write this down, for what I tell you is trustworthy and true.'"

Devotional Thought:

Regret can be a heavy burden, but God offers a fresh start. Embrace His forgiveness and release past mistakes, allowing Him to do something new in your life. This year, trust in His grace, knowing that He can transform every setback into growth.

Reflection Questions

Are there regrets from last year that you need to release?

How does God's promise to do a "new thing" bring hope to your life?

What steps can you take to let go of past mistakes?

Prayer for the Day

Father, help me to let go of any regrets that hold me back. Thank You for offering me a fresh start, and may I walk forward in Your grace. Amen.

January 8

Walking in God's Strength

"But those who trust in the Lord will find new strength.
They will soar high on wings like eagles."
— ISAIAH 40:31 (NLT)

Additional Scripture References:

Psalm 27:14: "Wait patiently for the Lord. Be brave and courageous. Yes, wait patiently for the Lord."

2 Corinthians 12:9: "But he said to me, 'My grace is sufficient for you, for my power is made perfect in weakness.' Therefore I will boast all the more gladly about my weaknesses, so that Christ's power may rest on me."

Devotional Thought:

Life's challenges can drain us, but God offers strength that renews us daily. When we rely on Him instead of our own abilities, we find the energy to persevere. As you walk through your roles as a wife, mother, daughter, or friend, lean into God's strength, knowing He will sustain you.

Reflection Questions

Are there areas where you feel drained or overwhelmed?

How can you invite God's strength into your daily routines?

What steps can you take to prioritize rest and renewal in Him?

Prayer for the Day

Lord, thank You for being my strength. Help me to lean on You and find renewal as I navigate my responsibilities each day. Amen.

Embracing God's Plan Over Perfection

"My grace is all you need. My power works best in weakness."
— **2 CORINTHIANS 12:9 (NLT)**

Additional Scripture References:

Romans 8:28: *"And we know that God causes everything to work together for the good of those who love God and are called according to his purpose for them."*

Philippians 4:13: *"For I can do everything through Christ, who gives me strength."*

Devotional Thought:

Striving for perfection can often leave us feeling inadequate. God reminds us that His power shines through our weaknesses. Instead of pursuing an impossible standard, let God's grace carry you, trusting that His plan is greater than any ideal of perfection.

Reflection Questions

Are there areas where you struggle with perfectionism?

How can you allow God's grace to bring peace into those areas?

What steps can you take to rely more on God's strength and less on your own?

Prayer for the Day

Father, help me to let go of perfectionism and embrace Your grace. Teach me to find peace in Your plan, knowing that Your power is made perfect in my weaknesses. Amen.

Living with Purpose in the Present

"This is the day the Lord has made.
We will rejoice and be glad in it."
— PSALM 118:24 (NLT)

Additional Scripture References:

1 Thessalonians 5:16-18: *"Always be joyful. Never stop praying. Be thankful in all circumstances, for this is God's will for you who belong to Christ Jesus."*

Psalm 100:4: *"Enter his gates with thanksgiving; go into his courts with praise. Give thanks to him and praise his name."*

Devotional Thought:

Each day is a gift, and God has a purpose for you in it. Embrace the present, finding joy and purpose in your daily routines. Instead of focusing on what lies ahead or behind, ask God to reveal His plan for you in each moment, living intentionally as a reflection of His love.

Reflection Questions

Are there ways you can be more present with loved ones today?

How does finding joy in each day strengthen your faith?

What steps can you take to appreciate the present moment more fully?

Prayer for the Day

Lord, thank You for today. Help me to live with purpose, finding joy in each moment and being present with those around me. Amen.

January 11

Prioritizing Your Faith

*"Seek the Kingdom of God above all else,
and live righteously, and he will give you everything you need."*

— MATTHEW 6:33 (NLT)

Additional Scripture References:

Philippians 4:19: *"And this same God who takes care of me will supply all your needs from his glorious riches, which have been given to us in Christ Jesus."*

Proverbs 3:5-6: *"Trust in the Lord with all your heart; do not depend on your own understanding. Seek his will in all you do, and he will show you which path to take."*

Devotional Thought:

It's easy to let faith slip to the background as life gets busy, but keeping God first transforms everything. When you prioritize your relationship with Him, you're able to love and serve others more fully. Make time today to connect with God, asking Him to guide you and provide what you need.

Reflection Questions

Are there distractions that keep you from prioritizing your faith?

How can putting God first impact other areas of your life?

What steps can you take to make time with God a regular habit?

Prayer for the Day

Father, help me to seek You above all else. Let my relationship with You be the foundation of everything I do. Amen.

Finding Joy in Small Moments

"Always be joyful. Never stop praying.
Be thankful in all circumstances."

— 1 THESSALONIANS 5:16-18 (NLT)

Additional Scripture References:

Philippians 4:4: "Always be full of joy in the Lord. I say it again — rejoice!"

Colossians 3:17: "And whatever you do or say, do it as a representative of the Lord Jesus, giving thanks through him to God the Father."

Devotional Thought:

Life is filled with small moments that often go unnoticed. Choosing joy in these moments, even amid routine tasks, shifts our perspective and fills us with gratitude. Look for ways to celebrate the little things today, finding God's presence in the ordinary.

Reflection Questions

Are there small moments or blessings you can appreciate today?

How does choosing joy in the everyday affect your mindset?

What steps can you take to focus on gratitude throughout the day?

Prayer for the Day

Lord, thank You for the beauty in small moments. Help me to see and celebrate Your presence in the ordinary parts of my day. Amen.

Renewing Your Mind Daily

"Don't copy the behavior and customs of this world, but let God transform you into a new person by changing the way you think."

— ROMANS 12:2 (NLT)

Additional Scripture References:

Ephesians 4:23-24: "Instead, let the Spirit renew your thoughts and attitudes. Put on your new nature, created to be like God — truly righteous and holy."

Colossians 3:2: "Think about the things of heaven, not the things of earth."

Devotional Thought:

Renewing your mind in God's truth is essential for a godly life. With so many competing voices, it's easy to be swayed by worldly values. Take time each day to meditate on God's Word, allowing His wisdom to shape your thoughts and guide your actions.

Reflection Questions.

Are there thoughts or influences you need to release to God?

How can renewing your mind daily help you stay grounded in faith?

What steps can you take to incorporate more of God's Word into your daily life?

Prayer for the Day

Father, transform my mind with Your truth. Let my thoughts be focused on what is pure, good, and aligned with Your will. Amen.

Building a Life of Faithfulness

*"Let love and faithfulness never leave you; bind them
around your neck, write them on the tablet of your heart."*
— PROVERBS 3:3 (NLT)

Additional Scripture References:

Micah 6:8: *"No, O people, the Lord has told you what is good, and this is what
he requires of you: to do what is right, to love mercy, and to walk humbly with
your God."*

Ephesians 4:32: *"Instead, be kind to each other, tenderhearted, forgiving one
another, just as God through Christ has forgiven you."*

Devotional Thought:

Faithfulness isn't just about loyalty to God but also reflects in our
relationships and responsibilities. Being a woman of faith means
showing consistency in love, kindness, and commitment to others. As
you go about your day, consider how you can live faithfully, making
love and integrity a foundation in all you do.

Reflection Questions

How can you show faithfulness in your relationships today?

Are there areas where you struggle with consistency?

What steps can you take to keep love and faithfulness at the center of
your actions?

Prayer for the Day

Lord, help me to be faithful in all areas of my life. Let my love and
actions reflect Your unwavering faithfulness to me. Amen.

January 15

Embracing God's Forgiveness

"But if we confess our sins to him, he is faithful and just to forgive us our sins and to cleanse us from all wickedness."

— 1 JOHN 1:9 (NLT)

Additional Scripture References:

Psalm 32:5: "Finally, I confessed all my sins to you and stopped trying to hide my guilt. I said to myself, 'I will confess my rebellion to the Lord.' And you forgave me! All my guilt is gone."

Romans 10:9: "If you openly declare that Jesus is Lord and believe in your heart that God raised him from the dead, you will be saved."

Devotional Thought:

God's forgiveness is a gift that renews us, washing away guilt and regret. Embrace His forgiveness today, allowing His grace to set you free from any past mistakes or burdens. Let go of self-criticism, knowing God's love and mercy are greater than any shortcomings.

Reflection Questions

Are there regrets or burdens you need to release to God?

How does embracing His forgiveness bring peace to your life?

What steps can you take to accept God's grace more fully?

Prayer for the Day

Lord, thank You for Your forgiveness and mercy. Help me to let go of past mistakes and live in the freedom of Your grace. Amen.

January 16

Trusting God with Your Family

"Cast all your anxiety on him because he cares for you."
— 1 PETER 5:7 (NLT)

Additional Scripture References:

Philippians 4:6-7: "Don't worry about anything; instead, pray about everything. Tell God what you need, and thank him for all he has done. Then you will experience God's peace, which exceeds anything we can understand."

Matthew 11:28: "Come to me, all of you who are weary and carry heavy burdens, and I will give you rest."

Devotional Thought:

Entrusting your family to God's care can bring peace and reassurance, especially in times of worry. Remember, He loves your family members even more than you do and desires the best for them. Release any anxieties about your loved ones to Him, trusting that He is faithfully watching over them.

Reflection Questions

Are there family concerns you need to entrust to God?

How does trusting God with your loved ones bring you peace?

What steps can you take to pray over your family each day?

Prayer for the Day

Father, I place my family in Your hands. Help me to trust that You are working in their lives, guiding and protecting them each day. Amen.

Relying on God's Provision

"And my God will meet all your needs according to the riches of his glory in Christ Jesus."

— PHILIPPIANS 4:19 (NLT)

Additional Scripture References:

Matthew 6:31-33: "So don't worry about these things, saying, 'What will we eat? What will we drink? What will we wear?' These things dominate the thoughts of unbelievers, but your heavenly Father already knows all your needs. Seek the Kingdom of God above all else and live righteously, and he will give you everything you need."

2 Corinthians 9:8: "And God will generously provide all you need. Then you will always have everything you need and plenty left over to share with others."

Devotional Thought:

God promises to provide for every need, even when circumstances seem uncertain. By trusting in His provision, you can find contentment and peace, knowing He will care for you and your family. Today, release any financial or material concerns, trusting in God's faithful supply.

Reflection Questions

Are there needs or worries you need to bring before God?

How does trusting in God's provision free you from worry?

What steps can you take to rely more on God's provision daily?

Prayer for the Day

Lord, thank You for being my provider. Help me to trust that You will meet all my needs, and let my heart rest in Your faithfulness. Amen.

Renewing Your Strength in Christ

"The Lord gives his people strength.
The Lord blesses them with peace."

— PSALM 29:11 (NLT)

Additional Scripture References:

Isaiah 26:3: *"You will keep in perfect peace all who trust in you, all whose thoughts are fixed on you."*

Philippians 4:13: *"For I can do everything through Christ, who gives me strength."*

Devotional Thought:

In times of exhaustion, God offers His strength and peace to sustain you. As a mother, wife, daughter, or friend, you carry many responsibilities, but God is with you in each one. Turn to Him for strength, allowing His peace to refresh your heart and mind.

Reflection Questions

Are there areas where you feel physically or emotionally drained?

How does relying on God's strength renew your energy and peace?

What steps can you take to rest in God's presence more often?

Prayer for the Day

Father, renew my strength and fill me with Your peace. Let Your presence restore me, enabling me to carry out my responsibilities with joy. Amen.

Setting Healthy Boundaries

"Guard your heart above all else,
for it determines the course of your life."

— **PROVERBS 4:23 (NLT)**

Additional Scripture References:

Matthew 15:18: "But the words you speak come from the heart — that's what defiles you."

James 1:14-15: "Temptation comes from our own desires, which entice us and drag us away. These desires give birth to sinful actions. And when sin is allowed to grow, it gives birth to death."

Devotional Thought:

Setting boundaries is a way to honor yourself and God, allowing you to protect your heart and energy. Healthy boundaries help you avoid burnout, enabling you to serve others with a joyful spirit. Consider where you need boundaries in your life, inviting God's wisdom to guide you in preserving balance.

Reflection Questions

Are there areas where you need stronger boundaries?

How can setting boundaries help you honor God in your relationships and responsibilities?

What steps can you take to create healthy boundaries today?

Prayer for the Day

Lord, help me to establish boundaries that honor You and protect my heart. Give me the wisdom to say "no" when needed and the courage to guard my well-being. Amen.

God's Guidance for Your Path

*"The Lord says, 'I will guide you along the best pathway for your life.
I will advise you and watch over you.'"*

— PSALM 32:8 (NLT)

Additional Scripture References:

Proverbs 3:5-6: *"Trust in the Lord with all your heart; do not depend on your own understanding. Seek his will in all you do, and he will show you which path to take."*

Isaiah 30:21: *"Your own ears will hear him. Right behind you a voice will say, 'This is the way you should go,' whether to the right or to the left."*

Devotional Thought:

God promises to guide us, leading us along paths that align with His purpose. As you look ahead, invite Him to be your counselor and protector, knowing He will steer you in the right direction. Trust that His guidance is perfect, even when the way forward isn't entirely clear.

Reflection Questions

Are there areas in your life where you need God's guidance?

How does trusting in His direction bring peace to your heart?

What steps can you take to seek God's wisdom in your daily decisions?

Prayer for the Day

Father, guide my steps according to Your wisdom. Let me follow Your counsel, trusting that You know the best path for my life. Amen.

January 21

Growing Through Difficulties

*"Dear brothers and sisters, when troubles of any kind come your way,
consider it an opportunity for great joy."*

— JAMES 1:2 (NLT)

Additional Scripture References:

*Romans 5:3-4: "We can rejoice, too, when we run into problems and trials, for
we know that they help us develop endurance. And endurance develops strength
of character, and character strengthens our confident hope of salvation."*

*1 Peter 1:6-7: "So be truly glad. There is wonderful joy ahead, even though
you must endure many trials for a little while. These trials will show that your
faith is genuine. It is being tested as fire tests and purifies gold — though your
faith is far more precious than mere gold."*

Devotional Thought:

Challenges are a part of life, but they also hold opportunities for growth. God uses difficult seasons to strengthen our faith and deepen our relationship with Him. Instead of focusing on the hardship, look for ways God is growing you through it, trusting that His grace is enough to carry you through.

Reflection Questions

Are there challenges you're currently facing where God may be teaching you?

How can looking for growth in trials strengthen your faith?

What steps can you take to trust God's purpose in difficult times?

Prayer for the Day

Lord, thank You for using challenges to grow me. Help me to trust in Your purpose, knowing that You are with me in every trial. Amen.

Finding Balance in Every Season

"For everything there is a season,
a time for every activity under heaven."

— ECCLESIASTES 3:1 (NLT)

Additional Scripture References:

Isaiah 60:22: "When the time is right, I, the Lord, will make it happen."

Galatians 6:9: "So let's not get tired of doing what is good. At just the right time, we will reap a harvest of blessing if we don't give up."

Devotional Thought:

Life's demands often change with different seasons, and balancing them all can be challenging. Rather than trying to do everything perfectly, ask God to help you recognize what is most important in each season. Trust that He will guide you to focus on what matters, giving you peace as you seek balance.

Reflection Questions

Are there responsibilities you need to adjust for this season?

How can finding balance help you focus on what's truly important?

What steps can you take to prioritize God's guidance over perfection?

Prayer for the Day

Lord, help me to find balance in every season of life. Guide me to focus on what truly matters, trusting that You will provide the wisdom I need. Amen.

January 23

Practicing Kindness in the Small Moments

"Be kind to each other, tenderhearted, forgiving one another,
just as God through Christ has forgiven you."

— EPHESIANS 4:32 (NLT)

Additional Scripture References:

Colossians 3:12-13: "Since God chose you to be the holy people he loves, you must clothe yourselves with tenderhearted mercy, kindness, humility, gentleness, and patience. Make allowance for each other's faults and forgive anyone who offends you. Remember, the Lord forgave you, so you must forgive others."

Matthew 6:14-15: "If you forgive those who sin against you, your heavenly Father will forgive you

Devotional Thought:

Kindness has the power to change atmospheres and brighten someone's day, even in the smallest of moments. Whether it's a kind word, a gentle smile, or a helping hand, let today be a chance to reflect Christ's love in all you do. Embrace the small acts of kindness that bring His light into your world.

Reflection Questions

Are there small acts of kindness you can share today?

How does kindness in small moments impact those around you?

What steps can you take to be more intentional in showing kindness?

Prayer for the Day

Father, let my actions be filled with kindness and compassion. Help me to show Your love through small acts of care and tenderness. Amen.

Seeking Joy in the Everyday

"The joy of the Lord is your strength!"
— **NEHEMIAH 8:10 (NLT)**

Additional Scripture References:

Psalm 16:11: "You will show me the way of life, granting me the joy of your presence and the pleasures of living with you forever."

John 15:11: "I have told you these things so that you will be filled with my joy. Yes, your joy will overflow!"

Devotional Thought:

Joy is more than a feeling; it's a source of strength that God provides, even in ordinary moments. Finding joy in simple things — whether in family, work, or daily routines — reminds you of God's goodness. Seek out moments of joy today, letting God's presence fill your heart and renew your spirit.

Reflection Questions

Are there small joys you can celebrate in your everyday life?

How does seeking joy strengthen your relationship with God?

What steps can you take to make joy a regular part of your day?

Prayer for the Day

Lord, thank You for the gift of joy. Help me to find it in the ordinary moments and let it be my strength today. Amen.

Walking in Faith, Not Fear

*"For God has not given us a spirit of fear and timidity,
but of power, love, and self-discipline."*

— 2 TIMOTHY 1:7 (NLT)

Additional Scripture References:

Romans 8:15: "So you have not received a spirit that makes you fearful slaves. Instead, you received God's Spirit when he adopted you as his own children. Now we call him, 'Abba, Father.'"

Philippians 4:13: "For I can do everything through Christ, who gives me strength."

Devotional Thought:

Fear can sometimes hold us back from living fully in God's purpose. He calls us to walk in faith, trusting in His strength instead of succumbing to worry or doubt. Today, let go of any fears that limit you, and step forward in the power, love, and confidence that God provides.

Reflection Questions

Are there fears holding you back from what God has planned?

How does walking in faith rather than fear change your perspective?

What steps can you take to lean into God's strength and let go of fear?

Prayer for the Day

Father, help me to walk in faith, free from fear. Remind me of the power, love, and self-discipline You have given me, and help me to trust in You fully. Amen.

Cultivating Patience with God's Timing

"But if we look forward to something we don't yet have,
we must wait patiently and confidently."

— ROMANS 8:25 (NLT)

Additional Scripture References:

Hebrews 11:1: "Now faith is confidence in what we hope for and assurance about what we do not see."

James 1:3-4: "For you know that when your faith is tested, your endurance has a chance to grow. So let it grow, for when your endurance is fully developed, you will be perfect and complete, needing nothing."

Devotional Thought:

Waiting on God's timing is often challenging, but it builds trust and patience. Sometimes we can't see the full picture, yet God knows what's best for us. Today, embrace the patience that comes from trusting in His perfect timing, knowing that He will fulfill His promises in the right season.

Reflection Questions

Are there areas where you need patience in waiting on God's timing?

How does trusting God's timing bring peace to your life?

What steps can you take to grow in patience and confidence in His promises?

Prayer for the Day

Lord, give me patience to trust in Your timing. Help me to wait confidently, knowing that Your plans for me are good and perfect. Amen.

January 27

Renewing Hope for the Future

"For I know the plans I have for you… plans for good and not for disaster, to give you a future and a hope."

— JEREMIAH 29:11 (NLT)

Additional Scripture References:

Proverbs 19:21: *"You can make many plans, but the Lord's purpose will prevail."*

Romans 8:28: *"And we know that God causes everything to work together for the good of those who love God and are called according to his purpose for them."*

Devotional Thought:

God's promises give us hope for the future, even when the present is uncertain. Let this truth encourage you today, reminding you that God has a plan filled with purpose and hope. Release any worries about what lies ahead, trusting that God's future for you is good and full of potential.

Reflection Questions

Are there worries about the future you need to give to God?

How does God's promise of hope and purpose encourage you?

What steps can you take to renew your trust in God's plan for your life?

Prayer for the Day

Father, thank You for the hope You give me for the future. Help me to let go of worry and trust that Your plans for me are good. Amen.

Reflecting God's Love to Your Family

"We love each other because he loved us first."
— 1 JOHN 4:19 (NLT)

Additional Scripture References:

John 15:12: "This is my commandment: Love each other in the same way I have loved you."

Romans 5:8: "But God showed his great love for us by sending Christ to die for us while we were still sinners."

Devotional Thought:

God's love is the foundation of every meaningful relationship. When you reflect His love to your family, you create a home filled with grace and peace. Let today be a time to express love in practical ways, showing those closest to you how deeply God cares for them through your words and actions.

Reflection Questions

How can you reflect God's love to your family today?

What impact does showing God's love have on your relationships?

What steps can you take to make love the center of your family life?

Prayer for the Day

Lord, thank You for loving me so completely. Help me to show that same love to my family, creating a home that reflects Your grace and kindness. Amen.

Choosing Gratitude Every Day

*"Be thankful in all circumstances, for this is God's will
for you who belong to Christ Jesus."*
— 1 THESSALONIANS 5:18 (NLT)

Additional Scripture References:

*Ephesians 5:20: "And give thanks for everything to God the Father in the
name of our Lord Jesus Christ."*

*Colossians 3:17: "And whatever you do or say, do it as a representative of the
Lord Jesus, giving thanks through him to God the Father."*

Devotional Thought:

Gratitude transforms our hearts, even in difficult times. By choosing
to be thankful, we shift our focus from what we lack to what
God has provided. Let today be an opportunity to look around and
appreciate the blessings in your life, big or small, and let gratitude
bring you closer to God.

Reflection Questions

Are there blessings you've overlooked in your daily life?

How does practicing gratitude change your outlook?

What steps can you take to make gratitude a regular habit?

Prayer for the Day

Father, help me to be thankful in all circumstances. Open my eyes to the
blessings around me and let my heart be filled with gratitude. Amen.

Seeing Yourself Through God's Eyes

"I praise you because I am fearfully and wonderfully made;
your works are wonderful, I know that full well."

— PSALM 139:14 (NLT)

Additional Scripture References:

Ephesians 2:10: "For we are God's masterpiece. He has created us anew in Christ Jesus, so we can do the good things he planned for us long ago."

Isaiah 43:7: "Bring all who claim me as their God, for I have made them for my glory. It was I who created them."

Devotional Thought:

God sees you as His unique, beloved creation. Embracing your worth in His eyes allows you to live confidently, free from comparison or self-doubt. Reflect on how God made you intentionally and let His love affirm your identity today, giving you courage to live authentically as His daughter.

Reflection Questions

Are there areas where you struggle to see yourself as God does?

How does knowing you are "fearfully and wonderfully made" impact your confidence?

What steps can you take to embrace your worth in Christ?

Prayer for the Day

Lord, help me to see myself through Your eyes. Remind me that I am wonderfully made, and let Your love be my foundation and strength. Amen.

January 31

Embracing God's Purpose for the Year Ahead

"And I am certain that God, who began the good work within you, will continue his work until it is finally finished."

— PHILIPPIANS 1:6 (NLT)

Additional Scripture References:

2 Corinthians 5:17: "This means that anyone who belongs to Christ has become a new person. The old life is gone; a new life has begun!"

Romans 8:28: "And we know that God causes everything to work together for the good of those who love God and are called according to his purpose for them."

Devotional Thought:

God has begun a unique work in you, one that He promises to complete. As you close this month, look forward to all He has in store, embracing the journey with faith and anticipation. Trust that He will guide you step-by-step as you seek to fulfill His purpose in your life this year.

Reflection Questions

Are there specific hopes or goals you want to bring to God for this year?

How does knowing God's promise to finish His work bring peace?

What steps can you take to align yourself with God's purpose as you move forward?

Prayer for the Day

Father, thank You for the work You have begun in me. Guide me each day as I seek Your purpose, trusting that You will bring it to completion in Your time. Amen.

February 1

The Foundation of Godly Love

"We love each other because he loved us first."
— 1 JOHN 4:19 (NLT)

Additional Scripture References:

John 15:12: *"This is my commandment: Love each other in the same way I have loved you."*

Romans 5:8: *"But God showed his great love for us by sending Christ to die for us while we were still sinners."*

Devotional Thought:

God's love for us is the foundation of all genuine love. When we love from a place of knowing we are fully loved by Him, we are free to care for others without expecting anything in return. Let today be a reminder to root your love for others in God's love for you, allowing His kindness to flow through your actions.

Reflection Questions

How does knowing God loves you unconditionally impact your relationships?

Are there ways you can reflect God's love in your family today?

What steps can you take to rest in His love more fully?

Prayer for the Day

Father, thank You for loving me first. Help me to love others with the same selfless, unconditional love that You show to me. Amen.

February 2

Love That Serves

"For even the Son of Man came not to be served but to serve others."

— MARK 10:45 (NLT)

Additional Scripture References:

Philippians 2:5-7: *"You must have the same attitude that Christ Jesus had. Though he was God, he did not think of equality with God as something to cling to. Instead, he gave up his divine privileges; he took the humble position of a slave and was born as a human being."*

Matthew 20:28: *"For even the Son of Man came not to be served but to serve others and to give his life as a ransom for many."*

Devotional Thought:

True love is expressed through serving, even in the smallest tasks. Whether it's preparing a meal, caring for children, or simply offering a listening ear, each act of service reflects Christ's heart. Let your love today be expressed through service, honoring those you care for with acts of kindness and humility.

Reflection Questions

Are there ways you can serve your loved ones today?

How does serving others with love strengthen your relationships?

What steps can you take to make service a natural part of how you show love?

Prayer for the Day

Lord, help me to love others by serving with a joyful heart. Let my actions be a reflection of Christ's kindness and humility. Amen.

Loving with Patience

"Love is patient and kind."

— 1 CORINTHIANS 13:4 (NLT)

Additional Scripture References:

Colossians 3:14: "Above all, clothe yourselves with love, which binds us all together in perfect harmony."

1 John 3:18: "Dear children, let us not love with words or speech but with actions and in truth."

Devotional Thought:

Patience is a powerful expression of love, especially in relationships that challenge us. By choosing patience, we reflect God's enduring love, allowing others the grace to grow and learn. Embrace patience today in your interactions, recognizing that each moment of patience is a gift of love.

Reflection Questions

Are there relationships where you need to practice more patience?

How does choosing patience show God's love to others?

What steps can you take to be patient and kind in challenging situations?

Prayer for the Day

Father, help me to be patient and kind in all my interactions. Let my love be a reflection of Your enduring patience with me. Amen.

Forgiving as an Act of Love

*"Make allowance for each other's faults, and
forgive anyone who offends you."*

— COLOSSIANS 3:13 (NLT)

Additional Scripture References:

*Ephesians 4:32: "Instead, be kind to each other, tenderhearted, forgiving one
another, just as God through Christ has forgiven you."*

*Matthew 6:14-15: "If you forgive those who sin against you, your heavenly
Father will forgive you. But if you refuse to forgive others, your Father will
not forgive your sins."*

Devotional Thought:

Forgiveness is an act of love that releases resentment and makes way
for healing. By forgiving others, we show God's grace, recognizing
that we too are in need of forgiveness. Let today be a time to release any
grudges and offer forgiveness as a gift of love and grace.

Reflection Questions

Are there past hurts that you need to release in forgiveness?

How does forgiving others free you to love more fully?

What steps can you take to make forgiveness a regular part of your
relationships?

Prayer for the Day

Lord, help me to forgive those who have hurt me, just as You
have forgiven me. Let forgiveness bring healing and peace in my
relationships. Amen.

February 5

Loving Through Words of Encouragement

"So encourage each other and build each other up."
— 1 THESSALONIANS 5:11 (NLT)

Additional Scripture References:

Hebrews 10:24-25: "And let us consider how we may spur one another on toward love and good deeds, not giving up meeting together, as some are in the habit of doing, but encouraging one another — and all the more as you see the Day approaching."

Galatians 6:2: "Share each other's burdens, and in this way obey the law of Christ."

Devotional Thought:

Words hold the power to lift, encourage, and strengthen those around us. Today, use your words to build up your family and friends, offering encouragement that shows them their worth and value. Let your speech be filled with kindness, bringing light and love to each conversation.

Reflection Questions

Are there people in your life who need encouragement today?

How does speaking encouragement strengthen your relationships?

What steps can you take to be more intentional with encouraging words?

Prayer for the Day

Father, let my words be filled with encouragement and kindness. Help me to build others up, showing them Your love and care through what I say. Amen.

February 6

Love that Overcomes Selfishness

"Don't be selfish; don't try to impress others.
Be humble, thinking of others as better than yourselves."
— PHILIPPIANS 2:3 (NLT)

Additional Scripture References:

Romans 12:10: *"Love each other with genuine affection, and take delight in honoring each other."*

James 4:6: *"But he gives us more grace. That is why Scripture says: 'God opposes the proud but shows favor to the humble.'"*

Devotional Thought:

Selfless love means putting others' needs above your own, even when it requires sacrifice. By choosing humility over selfishness, we reflect Christ's character in our relationships. Let today be an opportunity to love others with a selfless heart, seeking to serve rather than to be served.

Reflection Questions

Are there areas where selfishness hinders your relationships?

How does loving selflessly change your perspective on serving others?

What steps can you take to practice humility in your relationships?

Prayer for the Day

Lord, help me to put others before myself, choosing love over selfishness. Let my actions reflect Christ's humility and grace. Amen.

Embracing God's Love to Love Yourself

"You must love the Lord your God with all your heart, all your soul, all your mind, and all your strength... Love your neighbor as yourself."
— MARK 12:30-31 (NLT)

Additional Scripture References:

Matthew 22:37-40: "Jesus replied, 'You must love the Lord your God with all your heart, all your soul, and all your mind.' This is the first and greatest commandment. A second is equally important: 'Love your neighbor as yourself.' The entire law and all the demands of the prophets are based on these two commandments."

1 John 4:20: "If someone says, 'I love God,' but hates a fellow believer, that person is a liar; for if we don't love people we can see, how can we love God, whom we cannot see?"

Devotional Thought:

Self-love grounded in God's love allows us to care for ourselves in a healthy, balanced way. When we recognize our worth in God's eyes, we are able to extend that love to others. Take time today to care for yourself, knowing that self-love rooted in God's love is a foundation for healthy relationships.

Reflection Questions

Are there ways you can practice self-love in a healthy, godly way?

How does loving yourself as God does impact your relationships?

What steps can you take to embrace your worth and care for yourself?

Prayer for the Day

Father, help me to see myself through Your love, valuing who I am in You. Let this love be the foundation for how I love and care for others. Amen.

February 8

Loving Your Family Unconditionally

"Above all, clothe yourselves with love, which binds us all together in perfect harmony."

— COLOSSIANS 3:14 (NLT)

Additional Scripture References:

1 Peter 4:8: "Most important of all, continue to show deep love for each other, for love covers a multitude of sins."

Ephesians 4:2-3: "Always be humble and gentle. Be patient with each other, making allowance for each other's faults because of your love. Make every effort to keep yourselves united in the Spirit, binding yourselves together with peace."

Devotional Thought:

Family relationships aren't always easy, yet God calls us to love unconditionally, just as He loves us. When you choose love in moments of frustration or disagreement, you reflect God's peace and unity. Today, let love be the foundation of your interactions with family, seeking harmony and understanding.

Reflection Questions

Are there areas in your family relationships where you need to practice unconditional love?

How does choosing love in difficult moments bring unity?

What steps can you take to show love even in challenging situations?

Prayer for the Day

Lord, help me to love my family unconditionally. Let Your love fill our home with harmony and grace. Amen.

Love in Action

*"Dear children, let's not merely say that we love each other;
let us show the truth by our actions."*

— 1 JOHN 3:18 (NLT)

Additional Scripture References:

*James 2:15-17: "Suppose you see a brother or sister who has no food or clothing
and you say, 'Goodbye and have a good day; stay warm and eat well!' But then
you don't give that person any food or clothing. What good does that do? So
you see, faith by itself isn't enough. Unless it produces good deeds, it is dead
and useless."*

*Galatians 5:13: "For you have been called to live in freedom, my brothers and
sisters. But don't use your freedom to satisfy your sinful nature. Instead, use
your freedom to serve one another in love."*

Devotional Thought:

Love is more than words; it's demonstrated through actions.
Whether through small gestures or acts of service, love is visible
and impactful. Let today be a time to put love into action, serving those
around you in ways that reflect Christ's compassion and kindness.

Reflection Questions

Are there specific ways you can show love through actions today?

How does demonstrating love impact your relationships?

What steps can you take to make love a tangible part of your life?

Prayer for the Day

Father, let my love be seen through my actions. Help me to serve others
with a joyful heart, reflecting Your love in all I do. Amen.

February 10

Loving Your Neighbor as Yourself

"Do to others whatever you would like them to do to you."
— MATTHEW 7:12 (NLT)

Additional Scripture References:

Luke 6:31: "Do to others as you would like them to do to you."

Galatians 5:14: "For the whole law can be summed up in this one command: 'Love your neighbor as yourself.'"

Devotional Thought:

Loving others as we love ourselves is a powerful expression of Christ's teaching. When we treat others with the same care, respect, and kindness we desire, we embody His love. Today, let this perspective shape your interactions, striving to show others the same love and grace you hope to receive.

Reflection Questions

Are there ways you can love others more selflessly?

How does treating others with kindness and respect impact your relationships?

What steps can you take to live out this Golden Rule more fully?

Prayer for the Day

Lord, help me to love others as I love myself. Let my actions reflect Your kindness, bringing hope and encouragement to those around me. Amen.

February 11

Choosing Love Over Judgment

"Do not judge others, and you will not be judged."
— MATTHEW 7:1 (NLT)

Additional Scripture References:

Luke 6:37: *"Do not judge others, and you will not be judged. Do not condemn others, or it will all come back against you. Forgive others, and you will be forgiven."*

James 4:12: *"God alone, who gave the law, is the Judge. He alone has the power to save or to destroy. So what right do you have to judge your neighbor?"*

Devotional Thought:

Love leaves no room for judgment; instead, it seeks to understand, support, and lift others. By choosing love over judgment, you reflect God's grace, allowing others to experience His kindness and patience. Let today be an opportunity to approach others with a spirit of understanding and grace.

Reflection Questions

Are there areas where judgment has affected your relationships?

How does choosing love over judgment reflect God's grace?

What steps can you take to see others through a lens of compassion?

Prayer for the Day

Father, help me to choose love over judgment. Let my interactions be filled with understanding and grace, showing others Your kindness. Amen.

February 12

God's Love Through Hard Times

"The Lord is close to the brokenhearted; he rescues those whose spirits are crushed."

— **PSALM 34:18 (NLT)**

Additional Scripture References:

Isaiah 61:1: "The Spirit of the Sovereign Lord is on me, because the Lord has anointed me to proclaim good news to the poor. He has sent me to bind up the brokenhearted, to proclaim freedom for the captives and release from darkness for the prisoners."

2 Corinthians 1:3-4: "All praise to God, the Father of our Lord Jesus Christ. God is our merciful Father and the source of all comfort. He comforts us in all our troubles, so that we can comfort others."

Devotional Thought:

God's love shines brightest in our hardest moments, offering comfort and peace when we need it most. Remember that God is with you in every struggle, carrying you through with His unwavering love. Let today be a reminder to rely on His presence and extend that comfort to others facing challenges.

Reflection Questions

Are there difficult situations where you need to feel God's love and support?

How can leaning on God's love bring peace to hard times?

What steps can you take to share God's comfort with others?

Prayer for the Day

Lord, thank You for being near to me in hard times. Let Your love be my source of strength and help me to share that comfort with others. Amen.

February 13

Accepting Love and Support from Others

"Carry each other's burdens, and in this way
you will fulfill the law of Christ."

— **GALATIANS 6:2 (NLT)**

Additional Scripture References:

Romans 12:15: "Rejoice with those who rejoice; mourn with those who mourn."

1 Thessalonians 5:14: "Brothers and sisters, we urge you to warn those who are lazy. Encourage those who are timid. Take tender care of those who are weak. Be patient with everyone."

Devotional Thought:

Sometimes accepting help is as important as offering it. God places people in our lives to support and uplift us. Today, embrace the love and support others offer, knowing it is one of the ways God cares for you. Allow others to be part of your journey, lifting one another in faith and friendship.

Reflection Questions

Are there times when you find it hard to accept help from others?

How does accepting support deepen your relationships?

What steps can you take to be open to love and help from those around you?

Prayer for the Day

Father, thank You for the people You've placed in my life to support me. Help me to accept their love and encouragement, trusting that You work through them. Amen.

February 14

Celebrating Love in All Forms

*"And may the Lord make your love for one another and
for all people grow and overflow."*
— 1 THESSALONIANS 3:12 (NLT)

Additional Scripture References:

*Philippians 1:9: "And this is my Prayer for the Day that your love may abound
more and more in knowledge and depth of insight."*

*1 Peter 1:22: "You were cleansed from your sins when you obeyed the truth,
so now you must show sincere love to each other as brothers and sisters. Love
each other deeply with all your heart."*

Devotional Thought:

Valentine's Day is a beautiful opportunity to celebrate love in all its
forms—romantic love, friendship, family, and God's unconditional
love. Take time to express appreciation for those in your life and reflect
on the many ways God's love shines through your relationships. Let
this day be a celebration of love that overflows from a grateful heart.

Reflection Questions

Are there people in your life you can celebrate and appreciate today?

How does recognizing God's love in all forms strengthen your faith?

What steps can you take to show appreciation to loved ones?

Prayer for the Day

Lord, thank You for the gift of love in all its forms. Help me to celebrate
the people You've placed in my life and let my love for them grow and
overflow. Amen.

Love Through Compassion

*"Be kind to each other, tenderhearted, forgiving one another,
just as God through Christ has forgiven you."*

— **EPHESIANS 4:32 (NLT)**

Additional Scripture References:

*Colossians 3:13: "Make allowance for each other's faults and forgive anyone
who offends you. Remember, the Lord forgave you, so you must forgive others."*

*Matthew 6:14-15: "If you forgive those who sin against you, your heavenly
Father will forgive you. But if you refuse to forgive others, your Father will
not forgive your sins."*

Devotional Thought:

Compassion is a powerful form of love, showing others that you care about their feelings and experiences. Being tenderhearted helps you connect with others on a deeper level, offering support and understanding. Today, let your heart be moved by compassion, looking for ways to uplift and care for those around you.

Reflection Questions

Are there people in your life who need compassion today?

How does being tenderhearted strengthen your relationships?

What steps can you take to show compassion to someone who is struggling?

Prayer for the Day

Lord, fill me with compassion. Help me to be kind, tenderhearted, and forgiving, showing Your love to everyone I encounter. Amen.

February 16

Love That Builds Up

"Encourage one another and build each other up."

— 1 THESSALONIANS 5:11 (NLT)

Additional Scripture References:

Hebrews 10:24-25: "And let us consider how we may spur one another on toward love and good deeds, not giving up meeting together, as some are in the habit of doing, but encouraging one another — and all the more as you see the Day approaching."

Galatians 6:2: "Share each other's burdens, and in this way obey the law of Christ."

Devotional Thought:

Love should lift others up, helping them see their worth and purpose. By offering encouragement and support, you reflect God's love, bringing hope to those who need it. Today, be intentional about building others up, especially in moments where they may feel discouraged.

Reflection Questions

Are there people in your life who could use encouragement?

How does building others up bring them closer to God?

What steps can you take to make encouragement a daily habit?

Prayer for the Day

Father, help me to be a source of encouragement. Let my words and actions build others up, reflecting Your love and strength. Amen.

February 17

Loving with Boundaries

"Let your 'Yes' be yes, and your 'No,' no."
— MATTHEW 5:37 (NLT)

Additional Scripture References:

James 5:12: "But above all, my brothers and sisters, never take an oath by heaven or earth or anything else. Just say a simple 'Yes' or 'No,' so that you will not sin and be condemned."

Proverbs 10:19: "Too much talk leads to sin. Be sensible and keep your mouth shut."

Devotional Thought:

Healthy love often includes setting boundaries, allowing you to love others without feeling overwhelmed or taken advantage of. By being honest about what you can and cannot do, you protect your well-being while still caring for others. Let today be a reminder that saying "no" when necessary is an act of love for yourself and those around you.

Reflection Questions

Are there areas where you need to set boundaries?

How does setting boundaries allow you to love more effectively?

What steps can you take to communicate your boundaries with kindness?

Prayer for the Day

Lord, give me wisdom to set healthy boundaries. Help me to love others in a way that is honest and sustainable, honoring You in my relationships. Amen.

February 18

Enduring Love in Difficult Times

*"Love never gives up, never loses faith, is always hopeful,
and endures through every circumstance."*

— 1 CORINTHIANS 13:7 (NLT)

Additional Scripture References:

*Romans 8:39: "No power in the sky above or in the earth below – indeed,
nothing in all creation will ever be able to separate us from the love of God that
is revealed in Christ Jesus our Lord."*

*Hebrews 10:23: "Let us hold tightly without wavering to the hope we affirm,
for God can be trusted to keep his promise."*

Devotional Thought:

Godly love remains steadfast, even in challenging times. When difficulties arise, true love continues to hope, support, and believe. Let today encourage you to hold onto love in difficult circumstances, trusting that God will sustain you and bring healing to your relationships.

Reflection Questions

Are there challenging relationships where you need to practice enduring love?

How does God's love for you help you to persevere in loving others?

What steps can you take to nurture hope and faith in your relationships?

Prayer for the Day

Father, help me to love with endurance and patience. Let my love be unwavering, reflecting Your faithfulness in every circumstance. Amen.

Love That Brings Healing

"A gentle answer deflects anger, but harsh words make tempers flare."
— **PROVERBS 15:1 (NLT)**

Additional Scripture References:

James 1:19: "Understand this, my dear brothers and sisters: You must all be quick to listen, slow to speak, and slow to get angry."

Proverbs 25:15: "Patience can persuade a prince, and soft speech can break bones."

Devotional Thought:

L ove has the power to heal wounds and ease conflicts. By responding with gentleness and kindness, you can bring peace to difficult situations, reflecting God's grace. Today, choose words that heal rather than hurt, allowing love to soften hearts and strengthen relationships.

Reflection Questions

Are there situations where you need to respond with gentleness?

How does choosing gentle words bring healing to relationships?

What steps can you take to create peace in challenging conversations?

Prayer for the Day

Lord, help me to speak with gentleness and love. Let my words bring healing and reflect Your grace in all situations. Amen.

February 20

Love That Seeks Reconciliation

"Blessed are the peacemakers,
for they will be called children of God."
— MATTHEW 5:9 (NLT)

Additional Scripture References:

Romans 12:18: "Do all that you can to live in peace with everyone."

James 3:18: "And those who are peacemakers will plant seeds of peace and reap a harvest of righteousness."

Devotional Thought:

Love often requires us to seek reconciliation, mending relationships that may have been broken or strained. God calls us to be peacemakers, working toward unity and understanding. Let today be an opportunity to reach out, extend forgiveness, or offer an olive branch to someone you may be at odds with.

Reflection Questions

Are there relationships where you need to seek reconciliation?

How does being a peacemaker bring you closer to God?

What steps can you take to bring peace and healing to strained relationships?

Prayer for the Day

Father, make me a peacemaker. Help me to seek reconciliation and bring healing to my relationships, reflecting Your love and unity. Amen.

Loving with Integrity

"The Lord detests lying lips,
but he delights in those who tell the truth."

— PROVERBS 12:22 (NLT)

Additional Scripture References:

Proverbs 19:5: "A false witness will not go unpunished, and a liar will be destroyed."

Ephesians 4:25: "So stop telling lies. Let us tell our neighbors the truth, for we are all parts of the same body."

Devotional Thought:

Love is rooted in honesty and integrity. When we are truthful and transparent, we build trust and show respect for those we care about. Let today be a reminder to approach your relationships with integrity, creating a foundation of trust that honors God.

Reflection Questions

Are there ways you can bring more honesty into your relationships?

How does loving with integrity strengthen your connections?

What steps can you take to ensure transparency in your interactions?

Prayer for the Day

Lord, help me to love with honesty and integrity. Let my words and actions build trust and honor You in all my relationships. Amen.

February 22

Love That Reflects Christ

*"Your love for one another will prove
to the world that you are my disciples."*

— JOHN 13:35 (NLT)

Additional Scripture References:

1 John 4:7: *"Dear friends, let us continue to love one another, for love comes from God. Anyone who loves is a child of God and knows God."*

Galatians 5:13: *"For you have been called to live in freedom, my brothers and sisters. But don't use your freedom to satisfy your sinful nature. Instead, use your freedom to serve one another in love."*

Devotional Thought:

Jesus taught that our love for one another is the greatest witness of our faith. By loving others selflessly, we show the world a glimpse of Christ's love. Let today be a reminder to let your love be genuine, drawing others to God by the way you care for them.

Reflection Questions

Are there ways you can let Christ's love shine through you today?

How does selfless love witness to others about your faith?

What steps can you take to be a light in someone's life?

Prayer for the Day

Father, let my love be a reflection of Christ. Help me to love others in a way that points them to You and strengthens their faith. Amen.

Love That Leads by Example

"Don't let anyone look down on you because you are young, but set an example for the believers in speech, in conduct, in love."

— 1 TIMOTHY 4:12 (NLT)

Additional Scripture References:

Titus 2:7-8: "And you yourself must be an example to them by doing good works of every kind. Let everything you do reflect the integrity and seriousness of your teaching. Teach the truth so that your teaching can't be criticized."

Philippians 3:17: "Dear brothers and sisters, pattern your lives after mine, and learn from those who follow our example."

Devotional Thought:

Setting an example of love means leading with kindness, respect, and integrity. When you love others well, you become a model of Christ's love, inspiring those around you. Today, let your actions be an example, showing others what it means to live out God's love.

Reflection Questions

Are there ways you can set an example of love for others?

How does leading with love inspire those around you?

What steps can you take to be a role model in your relationships?

Prayer for the Day

Lord, help me to set an example in love. Let my actions inspire others to know and seek You, reflecting Your love in all I do. Amen.

February 24

Strengthening Bonds Through Prayer

*"Confess your sins to each other and
pray for each other so that you may be healed."*

— JAMES 5:16 (NLT)

Additional Scripture References:

*1 John 1:9: "If we confess our sins, he is faithful and just to forgive us our sins
and to cleanse us from all unrighteousness."*

*Matthew 18:19-20: "I also tell you this: If two of you agree here on earth
concerning anything you ask, my Father in heaven will do it for you. For
where two or three gather together as my followers, I am there among them."*

Devotional Thought:

Praying for others strengthens the bonds of love, bringing healing
and unity. When you pray for family and friends, you invite God's
presence into their lives and open doors for His grace to work. Today,
lift up those you care about in prayer, letting God's love strengthen
your connections.

Reflection Questions

Are there people in your life who need prayer today?

How does praying for others bring healing to relationships?

What steps can you take to make prayer a regular part of your
relationships?

Prayer for the Day

Father, I lift up my loved ones to You. Strengthen our bonds through
prayer and let Your love bring healing and unity to our relationships.
Amen.

February 25

Gratitude for God's Unfailing Love

"Give thanks to the Lord, for he is good!
His faithful love endures forever."

— PSALM 136:1 (NLT)

Additional Scripture References:

1 Chronicles 16:34: *"Give thanks to the Lord, for he is good; his love endures forever."*

Psalm 107:1: *"Give thanks to the Lord, for he is good! His faithful love endures forever."*

Devotional Thought:

God's love is unwavering, offering comfort and security in all circumstances. Take time today to thank God for His faithful love, letting gratitude fill your heart and remind you of His goodness. As you embrace His love, allow it to shape how you love others.

Reflection Questions

How does God's unfailing love bring comfort to your life?

Are there ways you can express gratitude for His love?

What steps can you take to love others with the same faithfulness?

Prayer for the Day

Lord, thank You for Your unfailing love. Let my heart be filled with gratitude, and may Your love be the foundation of how I care for others. Amen.

February 26

Faithfulness in Love

"Let love and faithfulness never leave you; bind them around your neck,
write them on the tablet of your heart."

— PROVERBS 3:3 (NLT)

Additional Scripture References:

Proverbs 16:6: "Unfailing love and faithfulness make atonement for sin. By
fearing the Lord, people avoid evil."

Colossians 3:12: "Since God chose you to be the holy people he loves, you must
clothe yourselves with tenderhearted mercy, kindness, humility, gentleness,
and patience."

Devotional Thought:

Faithfulness is the foundation of lasting love. Being reliable and consistent in your love for others builds trust and deepens connections. Today, let faithfulness guide your actions and words, showing those around you that they can rely on your steady, unwavering love.

Reflection Questions

Are there ways you can show more faithfulness in your relationships?

How does being reliable and steadfast reflect God's love?

What steps can you take to deepen your commitment to others?

Prayer for the Day

Lord, help me to be faithful in my love, showing steadiness and commitment in all my relationships. Let my love reflect Your unchanging faithfulness. Amen.

Humility in Love

Be completely humble and gentle;
be patient, bearing with one another in love."

— **EPHESIANS 4:2 (NLT)**

Additional Scripture References:

Colossians 3:12: "So, as those who have been chosen of God, holy and beloved, put on a heart of compassion, kindness, humility, gentleness, and patience."

Philippians 2:3: "Do nothing out of selfish ambition or vain conceit. Rather, in humility value others above yourselves."

Devotional Thought:

Humility in love means putting others before yourself, allowing room for growth and grace. When we love with humility, we release the need to be right and embrace patience. Let today be an opportunity to practice humility in your relationships, reflecting Christ's gentle, patient love.

Reflection Questions

Are there areas in your life where you need to practice more humility?

How does humility strengthen your relationships?

What steps can you take to love with gentleness and patience?

Prayer for the Day

Father, help me to love with humility, being gentle and patient in all my interactions. Let Your love guide me to put others first. Amen.

February 28

Growing in God's Love

"And may you have the power to understand...how wide, how long, how high, and how deep his love is."

— **EPHESIANS 3:18 (NLT)**

Additional Scripture References:

Romans 8:39: "No power in the sky above or in the earth below – indeed, nothing in all creation will ever be able to separate us from the love of God that is revealed in Christ Jesus our Lord."

Psalm 103:11: "For his unfailing love toward those who fear him is as great as the height of the heavens above the earth."

Devotional Thought:

God's love is beyond measure, and growing in His love brings fulfillment and joy. As we deepen our understanding of His love, we're better able to share it with others. Today, reflect on the vastness of God's love for you and let it inspire you to grow in love for others.

Reflection Questions

How does understanding God's love for you help you to love others?

Are there areas where you want to grow in your love for others?

What steps can you take to deepen your understanding of God's love?

Prayer for the Day

Lord, help me to grow in my understanding of Your love. Let it fill me completely, guiding me to love others with the same depth and compassion. Amen.

The Power of Words

"The tongue can bring death or life;
those who love to talk will reap the consequences."

— PROVERBS 18:21 (NLT)

Additional Scripture References:

James 3:5-6: "In the same way, the tongue is a small thing that makes grand speeches. But a tiny spark can set a great forest on fire. And among all the parts of the body, the tongue is a flame of fire."

Proverbs 21:23: "Watch your tongue and keep your mouth shut, and you will stay out of trouble."

Devotional Thought:

Our words have the power to uplift or tear down, to bring life or harm. Being mindful of what we say can help us reflect God's love and wisdom in our conversations. Today, let your words be intentional, choosing to build others up and bring life to those around you.

Reflection Questions

Are there ways you can be more intentional with your words?

How does speaking life into others reflect God's love?

What steps can you take to be more mindful of what you say?

Prayer for the Day

Lord, help me to use my words wisely, choosing to speak life and encouragement. Let my speech be a reflection of Your love and truth. Amen.

Speaking Truth in Love

"Instead, we will speak the truth in love,
growing in every way more and more like Christ."

— EPHESIANS 4:15 (NLT)

Additional Scripture References:

Colossians 3:9-10: "Don't lie to each other, for you have stripped off your old sinful nature and all its wicked deeds. Put on your new nature, and be renewed as you learn to know your Creator and become like him."

2 Timothy 2:15: "Work hard so you can present yourself to God and receive his approval. Be a good worker, one who does not need to be ashamed and who correctly explains the word of truth."

Devotional Thought:

Speaking truth is essential, but delivering it with love is what makes it Christ-like. When we share the truth with compassion and understanding, we strengthen our relationships and help others grow. Let today be a reminder to speak truth gently, allowing love to guide your words.

Reflection Questions

Are there situations where you need to speak the truth in love?

How does balancing truth with love impact your relationships?

What steps can you take to communicate truth more compassionately?

Prayer for the Day

Father, guide me to speak the truth with love. Let my words be honest yet gentle, helping others grow closer to You. Amen.

Choosing Kindness in Speech

"Kind words are like honey — sweet to the soul and healthy for the body."
— PROVERBS 16:24 (NLT)

Additional Scripture References:

Proverbs 15:4: "Gentle words are a tree of life; a deceitful tongue crushes the spirit."

Colossians 4:6: "Let your conversation be gracious and attractive so that you will have the right response for everyone."

Devotional Thought:

Kind words bring comfort, healing, and encouragement to those who hear them. Choosing kindness in speech, even in challenging situations, reflects Christ's gentleness and grace. Today, let your words be sweet and uplifting, showing love and care to everyone you meet.

Reflection Questions

Are there opportunities to speak with more kindness in your daily life?

How does choosing kind words affect those around you?

What steps can you take to be more intentional about kindness in speech?

Prayer for the Day

Lord, fill my heart with kindness so that my words may be a source of encouragement and healing. Let my speech reflect Your love and grace. Amen.

March 4

Avoiding Gossip

"A gossip betrays a confidence,
but a trustworthy person keeps a secret."

— PROVERBS 11:13 (NLT)

Additional Scripture References:

Proverbs 20:19: "A gossip goes around telling secrets, so don't hang around with chatterers."

James 1:26: "If you claim to be religious but don't control your tongue, you are fooling yourself, and your religion is worthless."

Devotional Thought:

Gossip can easily harm others and damage trust, often turning small matters into large conflicts. By choosing not to gossip, you create an atmosphere of trust and respect. Let today be a reminder to protect others with your words, being mindful of what you share.

Reflection Questions

Are there situations where gossip is a temptation for you?

How does avoiding gossip build trust and respect in relationships?

What steps can you take to steer clear of gossip and speak positively?

Prayer for the Day

Father, help me to avoid gossip and speak only words that build up. Let my words protect and honor others, reflecting Your love. Amen.

Words That Build Up

*"So encourage each other and build each other up,
just as you are already doing."*

— 1 THESSALONIANS 5:11 (NLT)

Additional Scripture References:

Hebrews 10:24-25: "And let us consider how we may spur one another on toward love and good deeds, not giving up meeting together, as some are in the habit of doing, but encouraging one another — and all the more as you see the Day approaching."

Galatians 6:2: "Share each other's burdens, and in this way obey the law of Christ."

Devotional Thought:

God calls us to build one another up, offering encouragement and hope through our words. When we speak in a way that uplifts others, we bring light to their lives. Today, look for ways to use your words to strengthen and encourage those around you.

Reflection Questions

Are there people in your life who need encouragement today?

How does using your words to build others up bring glory to God?

What steps can you take to make encouragement a natural part of your speech?

Prayer for the Day

Lord, help me to use my words to encourage and uplift. Let my speech bring strength and hope, reflecting Your love and grace. Amen.

March 6

Speaking with Grace

*"Let your conversation be gracious and attractive
so that you will have the right response for everyone."*

— COLOSSIANS 4:6 (NLT)

Additional Scripture References:

Proverbs 15:23: "Everyone enjoys a fitting reply; it is wonderful to say the right thing at the right time."

Ephesians 4:29: "Don't use foul or abusive language. Let everything you say be good and helpful, so that your words will be an encouragement to those who hear them."

Devotional Thought:

Grace in conversation means responding with patience, kindness, and understanding. When we speak graciously, we reflect Christ's compassion and wisdom. Let today be a reminder to let grace guide your words, offering others the same kindness and patience that God shows you.

Reflection Questions

Are there areas where you need to respond with more grace?

How does speaking with grace change the tone of your conversations?

What steps can you take to ensure your words reflect God's grace?

Prayer for the Day

Father, let my words be filled with grace and kindness. Help me to respond with patience and understanding, reflecting Your love in all my conversations. Amen.

Quick to Listen, Slow to Speak

"Understand this, my dear brothers and sisters: You must all be quick to listen, slow to speak, and slow to get angry."

— JAMES 1:19 (NLT)

Additional Scripture References:

Proverbs 18:13: "Spouting off before listening to the facts is both shameful and foolish."

Ecclesiastes 7:9: "Control your temper, for anger labels you a fool."

Devotional Thought:

Listening is a powerful act of love and respect. By being slow to speak, we give others the space to be heard and understood. Today, practice listening fully before responding, allowing God's wisdom to guide your words.

Reflection Questions

Are there moments when you find it difficult to listen fully before speaking?

How does being quick to listen deepen your relationships?

What steps can you take to become a better listener?

Prayer for the Day

Lord, help me to listen with an open heart. Let my words be thoughtful and kind, reflecting Your wisdom and patience. Amen.

Avoiding Harsh Words

"A gentle answer deflects anger,
but harsh words make tempers flare."

— PROVERBS 15:1 (NLT)

Additional Scripture References:

James 1:19: "Understand this, my dear brothers and sisters: You must all be quick to listen, slow to speak, and slow to get angry."

Proverbs 25:15: "Patience can persuade a prince, and soft speech can break bones."

Devotional Thought:

Harsh words can escalate conflict, while gentleness often diffuses tension. By choosing a gentle response, we bring peace and show respect to others. Let today be a time to practice gentleness, allowing your words to bring calmness and understanding.

Reflection Questions

Are there situations where you tend to respond harshly?

How does choosing gentleness affect your relationships?

What steps can you take to respond with gentleness rather than harshness?

Prayer for the Day

Father, help me to respond with gentleness. Let my words bring peace and understanding, reflecting Your kindness in all situations. Amen.

March 9

Words That Reflect God's Wisdom

"The mouth of the righteous is a fountain of life."
— PROVERBS 10:11 (NLT)

Additional Scripture References:

Proverbs 18:4: "A person's words can be life-giving water; words of true wisdom are as refreshing as a bubbling brook."

Proverbs 12:18: "Some people make cutting remarks, but the words of the wise bring healing."

Devotional Thought:

When our words are guided by God's wisdom, they become a source of life and encouragement for others. Allow His Word to fill your heart so that your speech reflects His truth and wisdom. Let today be an opportunity to share words that uplift and inspire, bringing God's life into every conversation.

Reflection Questions

Are there ways you can seek God's wisdom more in your speech?

How does speaking wisely impact those around you?

What steps can you take to fill your heart with God's wisdom?

Prayer for the Day

Lord, let my words be a reflection of Your wisdom. Help me to speak with discernment, bringing life and encouragement to those around me. Amen.

March 10

Guarding Your Heart and Speech

"Guard your heart above all else,
for it determines the course of your life."

— PROVERBS 4:23 (NLT)

Additional Scripture References:

Matthew 12:34: "For whatever is in your heart determines what you say."

Philippians 4:7: "And the peace of God, which surpasses all understanding, will guard your hearts and minds in Christ Jesus."

Devotional Thought:

Our words often reveal the state of our hearts. When we guard our hearts, we protect our words from being influenced by negative emotions or thoughts. Let today be a time to examine your heart, asking God to fill it with His peace and love so that your words reflect His goodness.

Reflection Questions

Are there influences in your life that impact your words negatively?

How does guarding your heart affect what you say?

What steps can you take to keep your heart filled with God's love and peace?

Prayer for the Day

Father, guard my heart and fill it with Your love. Let my words reflect Your goodness and be a source of blessing to others. Amen.

Words that Bring Healing

"Some people make cutting remarks,
but the words of the wise bring healing."

— **PROVERBS 12:18 (NLT)**

Additional Scripture References:

Proverbs 15:4: "Gentle words are a tree of life; a deceitful tongue crushes the spirit."

Ephesians 4:29: "Don't use foul or abusive language. Let everything you say be good and helpful, so that your words will be an encouragement to those who hear them."

Devotional Thought:

Words can hurt, but they can also heal. When we choose words carefully, we have the power to bring comfort and encouragement to those who are hurting. Today, let your speech be a source of healing, offering kindness and empathy to those who may need it.

Reflection Questions

Are there people in your life who need healing words today?

How does speaking with empathy and kindness bring comfort?

What steps can you take to make your words a source of healing?

Prayer for the Day

Lord, help me to speak words that heal. Let my conversations reflect Your compassion and bring comfort to those who are struggling. Amen.

March 12

Stewarding Your Words Wisely

"The heart of the godly thinks carefully before speaking."
— **PROVERBS 15:28 (NLT)**

Additional Scripture References:

Proverbs 18:21: "The tongue can bring death or life; those who love to talk will reap the consequences."

James 1:19: "Understand this, my dear brothers and sisters: You must all be quick to listen, slow to speak, and slow to get angry."

Devotional Thought:

Stewarding your words wisely means taking time to think before speaking, choosing words that are helpful and true. By practicing thoughtfulness in speech, you honor God and show respect to others. Let today be a reminder to pause before speaking, allowing God's wisdom to guide your words.

Reflection Questions

Are there moments when you could benefit from pausing before speaking?

How does careful speech show respect and love to others?

What steps can you take to steward your words more thoughtfully?

Prayer for the Day

Father, help me to think carefully before I speak. Let my words reflect Your wisdom and bring honor to Your name. Amen.

The Value of Silence

"Even fools are thought wise when they keep silent;
with their mouths shut, they seem intelligent."

— PROVERBS 17:28 (NLT)

Additional Scripture References:

Ecclesiastes 3:7: "A time to tear and a time to mend, a time to be quiet and a time to speak."

Proverbs 10:19: "Too much talk leads to sin. Be sensible and keep your mouth shut."

Devotional Thought:

Silence can be a powerful tool, allowing us to listen, observe, and reflect. Sometimes, the most impactful thing we can say is nothing at all. Today, embrace the value of silence, using it as a way to respect others and give space for God's wisdom.

Reflection Questions

Are there situations where silence might be more powerful than words?

How does practicing silence help you to listen and understand more deeply?

What steps can you take to embrace the value of silence in your daily interactions?

Prayer for the Day

Lord, teach me to value silence. Help me to know when to speak and when to stay quiet, allowing Your wisdom to guide my actions. Amen.

March 14

Letting Go of Critical Speech

"Do everything without complaining and arguing."
— PHILIPPIANS 2:14 (NLT)

Additional Scripture References:

1 Peter 4:9: "Cheerfully share your home with those who need a meal or a place to stay."

James 5:9: "Don't grumble about each other, brothers and sisters, or you will be judged. For look – the Judge is standing at the door!"

Devotional Thought:

Critical speech can easily lead to negativity and division. By choosing to let go of complaints and arguments, you foster a positive environment and reflect a Christ-like attitude. Let today be a time to practice gratitude and encouragement, letting go of any critical or negative speech.

Reflection Questions

Are there situations where you tend to be critical or negative?

How does choosing positivity strengthen your relationships?

What steps can you take to avoid complaining and focus on gratitude?

Prayer for the Day

Father, help me to let go of complaints and criticisms. Let my words reflect gratitude and bring encouragement to others. Amen.

March 15

Apologizing with Sincerity

*"Confess your sins to each other and pray for each other
so that you may be healed."*

— JAMES 5:16 (NLT)

Additional Scripture References:

*1 John 1:9: "If we confess our sins, he is faithful and just to forgive us our sins
and to cleanse us from all unrighteousness."*

*Matthew 18:19-20: "I also tell you this: If two of you agree here on earth
concerning anything you ask, my Father in heaven will do it for you. For
where two or three gather together as my followers, I am there among them."*

Devotional Thought:

Apologizing sincerely when you've hurt someone demonstrates
humility and strengthens relationships. A genuine apology opens
the door to healing and reconciliation. Today, let your words reflect
humility, offering sincere apologies where needed and embracing the
healing power of forgiveness.

Reflection Questions

Are there people you need to apologize to for past words or actions?

How does a sincere apology strengthen trust and connection?

What steps can you take to make apologies a regular part of your
relationships?

Prayer for the Day

Lord, give me the humility to apologize sincerely. Let my words bring
healing and forgiveness, restoring broken relationships. Amen.

Speaking with Integrity

*"The Lord detests lying lips, but he delights
in those who tell the truth."*

— PROVERBS 12:22 (NLT)

Additional Scripture References:

Proverbs 19:5: "A false witness will not go unpunished, and a liar will be destroyed."

Ephesians 4:25: "So stop telling lies. Let us tell our neighbors the truth, for we are all parts of the same body."

Devotional Thought:

Integrity in speech is about being honest and transparent. Speaking with truth and sincerity reflects God's character and builds trust with others. Today, let integrity guide your words, ensuring that what you say is true, trustworthy, and respectful.

Reflection Questions

Are there situations where you struggle to speak with full honesty?

How does speaking with integrity build trust in your relationships?

What steps can you take to ensure your words are truthful and genuine?

Prayer for the Day

Father, help me to speak with integrity. Let my words be honest and trustworthy, reflecting Your truth and building strong relationships. Amen.

March 17

Using Words to Inspire and Encourage

"Let everything you say be good and helpful,
so that your words will be an encouragement
to those who hear them."

— EPHESIANS 4:29 (NLT)

Additional Scripture References:

Colossians 3:8: "But now is the time to get rid of anger, rage, malicious behavior, slander, and dirty language."

Proverbs 10:11: "The words of the godly are a life-giving fountain; the words of the wicked conceal violent intentions."

Devotional Thought:

Encouraging words inspire hope, confidence, and faith. By speaking positively, you can lift others and bring joy to their day. Let today be a chance to inspire those around you, using your words to uplift, motivate, and strengthen their faith.

Reflection Questions

Are there people in your life who could use encouragement today?

How does inspiring others bring you closer to them and to God?

What steps can you take to make encouragement a regular habit in your speech?

Prayer for the Day

Lord, let my words inspire and encourage others. Help me to reflect Your love through positive and uplifting conversations. Amen.

March 18

Avoiding Idle Talk

"And I tell you this, you must give an account on judgment day for every idle word you speak."

— MATTHEW 12:36 (NLT)

Additional Scripture References:

James 3:10: "And so blessing and cursing come pouring out of the same mouth. Surely, my brothers and sisters, this is not right!"

Proverbs 21:23: "Watch your tongue and keep your mouth shut, and you will stay out of trouble."

Devotional Thought:

Idle talk can often lead to gossip or meaningless chatter. By being mindful of what we say, we show respect to others and honor God. Let today be a time to avoid idle conversations, choosing instead to speak with purpose and intentionality.

Reflection Questions

Are there situations where idle talk becomes a habit?

How does being purposeful in your speech show respect for others?

What steps can you take to make your conversations more meaningful?

Prayer for the Day

Father, help me to avoid idle words and choose speech that reflects purpose. Let my conversations honor You and show respect to those around me. Amen.

Words that Reflect Faith and Hope

"Let us hold tightly without wavering to the hope we affirm,
for God can be trusted to keep his promise."
— HEBREWS 10:23 (NLT)

Additional Scripture References:

Romans 15:13: "I pray that God, the source of hope, will fill you completely with joy and peace because you trust in him. Then you will overflow with confident hope through the power of the Holy Spirit."

1 Thessalonians 5:24: "The one who calls you is faithful, and he will do it."

Devotional Thought:

Speaking words of faith and hope reminds us of God's promises and encourages others to trust in Him. Today, let your words reflect the hope you have in Christ, affirming His goodness and faithfulness to those around you.

Reflection Questions

Are there situations where you can share words of faith and hope?

How does speaking hopefully affect your outlook and relationships?

What steps can you take to keep faith and hope at the center of your speech?

> ### Prayer for the Day

Lord, help me to speak words of faith and hope. Let my words remind others of Your promises and strengthen their trust in You. Amen.

March 20

Praying Before Speaking

*"Set a guard over my mouth, Lord; keep watch
over the door of my lips."*

— PSALM 141:3 (NLT)

Additional Scripture References:

*Proverbs 13:3: "Those who control their tongue will have a long life; opening
your mouth can ruin everything."*

*James 1:26: "If you claim to be religious but don't control your tongue, you are
fooling yourself, and your religion is worthless."*

Devotional Thought:

Taking a moment to pray before speaking allows God to guide your
words, especially in challenging situations. By inviting Him into
your conversations, you ensure that your words align with His will.
Today, make it a habit to pause and pray, allowing God's wisdom to
influence your speech.

Reflection Questions

Are there conversations where you need God's guidance before
speaking?

How does pausing to pray shape your perspective and response?

What steps can you take to make prayer a part of your daily
conversations?

Prayer for the Day

Lord, guard my mouth and guide my words. Help me to pause and
pray before speaking, letting Your wisdom direct my conversations.
Amen.

Responding with Wisdom

"If you are wise and understand God's ways, prove it by living an honorable life, doing good works with the humility that comes from wisdom."

— JAMES 3:13 (NLT)

Additional Scripture References:

Proverbs 11:2: "Pride leads to disgrace, but with humility comes wisdom."

Philippians 2:3: "Do nothing out of selfish ambition or vain conceit. Rather, in humility value others above yourselves."

Devotional Thought:

Responding with wisdom requires humility and a desire to honor God with our words. Wisdom allows us to see the bigger picture, helping us respond thoughtfully rather than impulsively. Today, ask God to fill you with His wisdom, guiding your responses in every interaction.

Reflection Questions

Are there situations where you struggle to respond with wisdom?

How does seeking God's wisdom help you honor Him in your speech?

What steps can you take to respond thoughtfully and with humility?

Prayer for the Day

Father, fill me with Your wisdom. Let my responses reflect Your love and humility, bringing honor to You in every conversation. Amen.

March 22

Gracious Words in Conflict

"A gentle answer deflects anger, but harsh words make tempers flare."
— PROVERBS 15:1 (NLT)

Additional Scripture References:

James 1:19: *"Understand this, my dear brothers and sisters: You must all be quick to listen, slow to speak, and slow to get angry."*

Proverbs 25:15: *"Patience can persuade a prince, and soft speech can break bones."*

Devotional Thought:

Conflict is inevitable, but our words can either calm or escalate it. By choosing gentle responses, we bring peace and show respect for others, even in difficult conversations. Let today be a reminder to respond with grace, allowing God's peace to influence your speech in times of tension.

Reflection Questions

Are there conflicts where you could use gentler words?

How does responding graciously impact tense situations?

What steps can you take to bring peace to difficult conversations?

Prayer for the Day

Lord, help me to respond with gentleness and grace. Let my words deflect anger and reflect Your peace, especially in times of conflict. Amen.

March 23

Speaking with Gratitude

"Always be joyful. Never stop praying.
Be thankful in all circumstances."

— 1 THESSALONIANS 5:16-18 (NLT)

Additional Scripture References:

Philippians 4:4: "Always be full of joy in the Lord. I say it again — rejoice!"

Colossians 3:17: "And whatever you do or say, do it as a representative of the Lord Jesus, giving thanks through him to God the Father."

Devotional Thought:

Gratitude has a way of transforming our speech and perspective. When we speak from a place of thankfulness, our words become a reflection of the blessings God has given us. Today, let your speech be filled with gratitude, acknowledging God's goodness in every conversation.

Reflection Questions

Are there things you can be more grateful for in your life?

How does speaking with gratitude affect your outlook?

What steps can you take to make gratitude a part of your daily speech?

Prayer for the Day

Father, fill my heart with gratitude. Let my words be a reflection of thankfulness, acknowledging Your blessings in all circumstances. Amen.

Encouraging Others in Faith

*"Let us think of ways to motivate one another
to acts of love and good works."*

— HEBREWS 10:24 (NLT)

Additional Scripture References:

*1 Thessalonians 5:11: "So encourage each other and build each other up, just
as you are already doing."*

*Galatians 6:2: "Share each other's burdens, and in this way obey the law of
Christ."*

Devotional Thought:

Encouraging others in their faith is a powerful way to show love.
When we speak words of encouragement, we help build one
another up and inspire each other to continue growing in Christ. Today,
find ways to uplift others in their faith, reminding them of God's love
and strength.

Reflection Questions

Are there people in your life who need encouragement in their faith?

How does encouraging others strengthen your own faith?

What steps can you take to make encouragement a part of your daily
interactions?

Prayer for the Day

Lord, help me to be an encourager. Let my words inspire others in their
faith and remind them of Your love and power. Amen.

Words That Reflect Forgiveness

"Make allowance for each other's faults,
and forgive anyone who offends you."
— COLOSSIANS 3:13 (NLT)

Additional Scripture References:

Ephesians 4:32: "Instead, be kind to each other, tenderhearted, forgiving one another, just as God through Christ has forgiven you."

Matthew 6:14: "If you forgive those who sin against you, your heavenly Father will forgive you."

Devotional Thought:

Forgiveness can be challenging, but it's essential for healthy relationships. Speaking words of forgiveness, even when it's difficult, allows God's love to work through you. Let today be an opportunity to extend forgiveness, using your words to heal and restore broken relationships.

Reflection Questions

Are there relationships where you need to speak words of forgiveness?

How does forgiving others free you and bring healing?

What steps can you take to make forgiveness a regular part of your life?

Prayer for the Day

Father, help me to forgive as You have forgiven me. Let my words reflect a heart of forgiveness, bringing healing to my relationships. Amen.

Speaking Life Over Your Loved Ones

"The words of the godly encourage many."
— PROVERBS 10:21 (NLT)

Additional Scripture References:

Proverbs 11:30: "The seeds of good deeds become a tree of life; a wise person wins friends."

Proverbs 12:25: "Worry weighs a person down; an encouraging word cheers a person up."

Devotional Thought:

Speaking life means using words that bring hope, joy, and encouragement to those we love. When we speak positively and pray for those around us, we reflect God's love and bring strength to our relationships. Today, be intentional about speaking life over your loved ones, affirming their value and purpose.

Reflection Questions

Are there ways you can speak life into your loved ones today?

How does encouraging those you care about strengthen your relationships?

What steps can you take to make speaking life a daily habit?

Prayer for the Day

Lord, let my words bring life and encouragement to those I love. Help me to affirm their value and remind them of Your purpose for their lives. Amen.

Speaking with Hope

"For I know the plans I have for you… plans for good and not for disaster, to give you a future and a hope."

— JEREMIAH 29:11 (NLT)

Additional Scripture References:

Proverbs 19:21: "You can make many plans, but the Lord's purpose will prevail."

Romans 8:28: "And we know that God causes everything to work together for the good of those who love God and are called according to his purpose for them."

Devotional Thought:

Words of hope inspire us to trust in God's future, even when we face challenges. By speaking with hope, we remind others—and ourselves—that God's plans are good and filled with promise. Today, let your words reflect this hope, trusting in God's faithfulness for the days ahead.

Reflection Questions

Are there people who need words of hope and encouragement today?

How does speaking with hope influence your outlook on life?

What steps can you take to make hope a central theme in your conversations?

Prayer for the Day

Father, fill my heart with hope. Let my words inspire faith and remind others of Your good plans for the future. Amen.

March 28

Avoiding Flattery and Insincerity

"A lying tongue hates its victims,
and a flattering mouth works ruin."

— **PROVERBS 26:28 (NLT)**

Additional Scripture References:

Proverbs 12:22: "The Lord detests lying lips, but he delights in those who tell the truth."

Proverbs 20:19: "A gossip goes around telling secrets, so don't hang around with chatterers."

Devotional Thought:

Flattery can be harmful when it's insincere, leading to distrust and hurt. Genuine encouragement, on the other hand, builds trust and brings true comfort. Let today be an opportunity to speak with honesty, offering encouragement that comes from a sincere heart.

Reflection Questions

Are there times when you're tempted to use insincere words?

How does being genuine in your speech build stronger relationships?

What steps can you take to ensure your words are sincere and truthful?

Prayer for the Day

Lord, help me to speak with sincerity. Let my words be genuine and uplifting, reflecting a heart that honors You. Amen.

Blessing Others Through Words

"Bless those who curse you.
Pray for those who hurt you."

— LUKE 6:28 (NLT)

Additional Scripture References:

Matthew 5:44: "But I say, love your enemies! Pray for those who persecute you!"

Romans 12:14: "Bless those who persecute you. Don't curse them; pray that God will bless them."

Devotional Thought:

Choosing to bless others, even those who may not treat us kindly, reflects God's grace and love. By speaking blessings over others, we become a vessel of God's goodness and mercy. Today, choose to speak blessings, especially in situations that challenge your patience or kindness.

Reflection Questions

Are there people who have wronged you whom you can bless today?

How does blessing others in difficult situations reflect God's love?

What steps can you take to make blessing others a regular practice?

Prayer for the Day

Father, help me to bless others with my words, even when it's difficult. Let my speech reflect Your love and mercy in all circumstances. Amen.

March 30

Speaking with Compassion

"Be kind to each other, tenderhearted, forgiving one another."
— EPHESIANS 4:32 (NLT)

Additional Scripture References:

Colossians 3:13: "*Make allowance for each other's faults and forgive anyone who offends you. Remember, the Lord forgave you, so you must forgive others.*"

Matthew 6:14: "*If you forgive those who sin against you, your heavenly Father will forgive you.*"

Devotional Thought:

Compassion in speech means being sensitive to the needs and emotions of others. Speaking with a tender heart brings comfort and healing, helping those who are hurting feel God's love. Today, let your words be filled with compassion, bringing peace and support to those around you.

Reflection Questions

Are there people in your life who need compassionate words today?

How does speaking with compassion strengthen your relationships?

What steps can you take to be more tenderhearted in your speech?

Prayer for the Day

Lord, fill my heart with compassion. Help me to speak words that bring comfort, peace, and encouragement to others. Amen.

Reflecting Christ's Love in All You Say

"Let everything you say be good and helpful, so that your words will be an encouragement to those who hear them."

— EPHESIANS 4:29 (NLT)

Additional Scripture References:

Colossians 4:6: "Let your conversation be gracious and attractive so that you will have the right response for everyone."

Proverbs 15:4: "Gentle words are a tree of life; a deceitful tongue crushes the spirit."

Devotional Thought:

Our words should always reflect Christ's love and encouragement. When we speak with kindness, respect, and empathy, we show the world what it means to follow Jesus. Let today be a reminder to let your words shine with God's love, bringing hope and joy to everyone you encounter.

Reflection Questions

Are there areas where you can better reflect Christ's love in your speech?

How does speaking with love and kindness impact your daily life?

What steps can you take to make Christ's love the foundation of your words?

Prayer for the Day

Father, let my words always reflect the love of Christ. Help me to speak with kindness, encouragement, and grace, bringing glory to You in all I say. Amen.

April 1

Seeking God's Wisdom First

*"If you need wisdom, ask our generous God,
and he will give it to you."*

— JAMES 1:5 (NLT)

Additional Scripture References:

Proverbs 2:6: "For the Lord grants wisdom! From his mouth come knowledge and understanding."

1 Corinthians 1:30: "God has united you with Christ Jesus. For our benefit, God made him to be wisdom itself. Christ made us right with God; he made us pure and holy, and he freed us from sin."

Devotional Thought:

God's wisdom is always available, but we must seek it first, trusting that He will provide the guidance we need. When faced with decisions, large or small, make it a habit to seek God's wisdom before your own understanding. Let today be a reminder to rely on His knowledge, asking Him for direction.

Reflection Questions

Are there areas where you need God's wisdom today?

How does seeking God's guidance first change your perspective on decisions?

What steps can you take to make asking for wisdom a regular part of your decision-making?

Prayer for the Day

Lord, I seek Your wisdom in every decision I face. Help me to trust in Your guidance, knowing that You will lead me in the right direction. Amen.

Trusting in God's Plans Over Your Own

"Trust in the Lord with all your heart;
do not depend on your own understanding."
— PROVERBS 3:5 (NLT)

Additional Scripture References:

Jeremiah 17:7: "But blessed are those who trust in the Lord and have made the Lord their hope and confidence."

Isaiah 26:3: "You will keep in perfect peace all who trust in you, all whose thoughts are fixed on you."

Devotional Thought:

Trusting God's plans requires us to release control, knowing that He sees the bigger picture. Sometimes His path may not align with what we expect, but His wisdom is perfect. Today, let go of any need to control and trust that God's plans are greater than your own.

Reflection Questions

Are there areas where you struggle to trust in God's plans?

How does trusting in God's wisdom bring peace to your life?

What steps can you take to let go and fully trust in His guidance?

Prayer for the Day

Father, help me to trust in Your plans, even when I don't understand them fully. Let my heart rest in Your wisdom, knowing You lead me with love and purpose. Amen.

April 3

Making Decisions with Integrity

"People with integrity walk safely,
but those who follow crooked paths will be exposed."

— PROVERBS 10:9 (NLT)

Additional Scripture References:

Proverbs 11:3: "Honesty guides good people; dishonesty destroys treacherous people."

Proverbs 12:22: "The Lord detests lying lips, but he delights in those who tell the truth."

Devotional Thought:

Godly decisions are made with integrity, valuing honesty and truth. When we choose integrity, we walk in alignment with God's will, bringing peace and stability to our lives. Today, let integrity guide your choices, allowing God's truth to direct each step.

Reflection Questions

Are there decisions where integrity needs to be a stronger focus?

How does choosing integrity impact your relationships and trust with others?

What steps can you take to ensure your decisions are made with honesty?

Prayer for the Day

Lord, help me to make decisions with integrity, valuing honesty and truth above all. Let my choices reflect Your character, bringing honor to You. Amen.

April 4

The Patience to Wait on God's Timing

"But if we look forward to something we don't yet have,
we must wait patiently and confidently."

— ROMANS 8:25 (NLT)

Additional Scripture References:

Hebrews 11:1: "Faith shows the reality of what we hope for; it is the evidence of things we cannot see."

Galatians 6:9: "So let's not get tired of doing what is good. At just the right time we will reap a harvest of blessing if we don't give up."

Devotional Thought:

God's timing is perfect, but waiting can be difficult. Patience in decision-making allows us to move forward in God's time rather than rushing ahead. Today, embrace the peace that comes from waiting on God, trusting that He will reveal the right path in His perfect timing.

Reflection Questions

Are there decisions you're facing where patience is required?

How does waiting on God's timing bring a sense of peace?

What steps can you take to embrace patience as you await His guidance?

Prayer for the Day

Father, grant me the patience to wait on Your timing. Help me to trust that You know what's best and will reveal it at the right moment. Amen.

April 5

Clarity Through Prayer

"Don't worry about anything; instead,
pray about everything."

— PHILIPPIANS 4:6 (NLT)

Additional Scripture References:

1 Peter 5:7: "Give all your worries and cares to God, for he cares about you."

Matthew 6:34: "So don't worry about tomorrow, for tomorrow will bring its own worries. Today's trouble is enough for today."

Devotional Thought:

Prayer brings clarity, helping us focus on God's will rather than our worries. When we pray before making decisions, we invite God's peace and wisdom into our choices. Let today be a reminder to seek clarity through prayer, allowing God's presence to guide you.

Reflection Questions

Are there areas of decision-making where you need more clarity?

How does prayer provide peace and understanding in uncertain times?

What steps can you take to make prayer a daily part of your decision process?

Prayer for the Day

Lord, bring clarity to my decisions through prayer. Let Your peace fill my heart and guide my thoughts, helping me to focus on Your will above all. Amen.

April 6

Walking by Faith in Uncertain Times

"For we live by believing and not by seeing."

— 2 CORINTHIANS 5:7 (NLT)

Additional Scripture References:

Hebrews 11:1: "Faith shows the reality of what we hope for; it is the evidence of things we cannot see."

Romans 4:18: "Even when there was no reason for hope, Abraham kept hoping — believing that he would become the father of many nations. For God had said to him, 'That's how many descendants you will have!'"

Devotional Thought:

Some decisions require us to step out in faith, trusting God's wisdom even when we can't see the full picture. Walking by faith means relying on God's promises and character, knowing He will guide us. Today, let faith be your foundation, trusting God with every step.

Reflection Questions

Are there decisions where you need to rely more on faith than certainty?

How does walking by faith bring peace in uncertain times?

What steps can you take to trust God more fully with the unknown?

Prayer for the Day

Father, help me to walk by faith, trusting You with every unknown. Let my decisions be rooted in Your promises, knowing that You lead me faithfully. Amen.

April 7

Godly Counsel in Decision-Making

"Plans go wrong for lack of advice;
many advisers bring success."

— PROVERBS 15:22 (NLT)

Additional Scripture References:

Proverbs 11:14: "Without wise leadership, a nation falls; there is safety in having many advisers."

Ecclesiastes 4:9-10: "Two people are better off than one, for they can help each other succeed. If one person falls, the other can reach out and help. But someone who falls alone is in real trouble."

Devotional Thought:

Seeking counsel from godly friends or mentors can provide valuable insight, offering perspective that aligns with God's wisdom. Today, if you face a decision, seek advice from those who walk closely with God, allowing their wisdom to guide your steps.

Reflection Questions

Are there decisions where you could benefit from godly counsel?

How does seeking advice help you align with God's will?

What steps can you take to build a support network of godly advisers?

Prayer for the Day

Lord, surround me with wise counsel. Let the advice of those who follow You guide me in truth and help me make decisions that honor You. Amen.

April 8

Discernment to Recognize God's Voice

"My sheep listen to my voice; I know them, and they follow me."
— JOHN 10:27 (NLT)

Additional Scripture References:

Psalm 95:7: "For he is our God, and we are the people of his pasture, the sheep under his care. If only you would listen to his voice today!"

Isaiah 30:21: "Your own ears will hear him. Right behind you a voice will say, 'This is the way you should go,' whether to the right or to the left."

Devotional Thought:

Recognizing God's voice brings clarity and confidence to our choices. By spending time in His Word and prayer, we learn to discern His guidance. Today, focus on listening for God's voice, trusting that He will speak and lead you toward His will.

Reflection Questions

Are there ways you can deepen your ability to recognize God's voice?

How does discernment bring peace to your decisions?

What steps can you take to listen more closely to God's guidance?

Prayer for the Day

Father, help me to recognize Your voice among the noise. Let Your guidance be clear, leading me to make decisions that follow Your will. Amen.

Avoiding Hasty Decisions

"The plans of the diligent lead surely to abundance,
but everyone who is hasty comes only to poverty."
— PROVERBS 21:5 (NLT)

Additional Scripture References:

Proverbs 16:3: "Commit your actions to the Lord, and your plans will succeed."

Ecclesiastes 9:10: "Whatever your hand finds to do, do it with all your might, for in the grave, where you are going, there is neither working nor planning nor knowledge nor wisdom."

Devotional Thought:

Rushing into decisions without careful thought can lead to mistakes and missed opportunities. Taking time to plan and consider allows God's wisdom to direct our choices. Today, resist the urge to make hasty decisions, choosing instead to seek God's guidance patiently.

Reflection Questions

Are there situations where you tend to make quick decisions?

How does taking time in decision-making help you align with God's will?

What steps can you take to be more diligent and thoughtful in your choices?

Prayer for the Day

Lord, give me patience to avoid hasty decisions. Help me to take time to seek Your wisdom, letting each choice reflect Your purpose. Amen.

Aligning Your Will with God's Purpose

*"Teach me to do your will, for you are my God.
May your gracious Spirit lead me forward on a firm footing."*

— **PSALM 143:10 (NLT)**

Additional Scripture References:

Isaiah 48:17: "This is what the Lord says — your Redeemer, the Holy One of Israel: 'I am the Lord your God, who teaches you what is good for you and leads you along the paths you should follow.'"

Psalm 25:4-5: "Show me your ways, O Lord; teach me your paths. Lead me in your truth and teach me, for you are the God of my salvation; for you I wait all the day long."

Devotional Thought:

True wisdom in decisions comes from aligning our will with God's purpose. When we seek His will above our own, He leads us on a path that is firm and steady. Let today be a reminder to invite God into every decision, seeking to honor Him with each choice.

Reflection Questions ?

Are there decisions where you need to surrender your own desires to God's will?

How does aligning with God's purpose bring peace and clarity?

What steps can you take to make honoring God your priority in every decision?

Prayer for the Day

Father, teach me to do Your will above my own. Let Your Spirit guide me, helping me to walk steadily in the path You have set for me. Amen.

April 11

The Peace That Follows Wise Decisions

"You will keep in perfect peace all who trust in you,
all whose thoughts are fixed on you!"

— ISAIAH 26:3 (NLT)

Additional Scripture References:

Philippians 4:6-7: "Don't worry about anything; instead, pray about everything. Tell God what you need, and thank him for all he has done. Then you will experience God's peace, which exceeds anything we can understand."

John 14:27: "I am leaving you with a gift — peace of mind and heart. And the peace I give is a gift the world cannot give. So don't be troubled or afraid."

Devotional Thought:

Wise decisions bring peace, especially when they're rooted in trust and faith in God. When our thoughts and choices align with His guidance, we experience His perfect peace, even amid challenges. Today, let God's peace be the confirmation of a wise choice, guiding you to trust Him more deeply.

Reflection Questions

Are there decisions where you need to seek God's peace?

How does trusting in God's guidance bring calm to your choices?

What steps can you take to fix your thoughts on God for peace?

Prayer for the Day

Lord, let Your peace be my guide. Help me to make decisions that align with Your will and bring calm to my spirit. Amen.

April 12

Accepting God's No as Part of His Wisdom

*"For I know the plans I have for you... plans for good and
not for disaster, to give you a future and a hope."*

— JEREMIAH 29:11 (NLT)

Additional Scripture References:

Proverbs 19:21: "You can make many plans, but the Lord's purpose will prevail."

Romans 8:28: "And we know that God causes everything to work together for the good of those who love God and are called according to his purpose for them."

Devotional Thought:

Sometimes God's wisdom is revealed in His "no" answers, which protect us from paths that may not be for our good. Trusting His "no" is an act of faith, acknowledging that His plans are better than our own. Let today remind you that God's answers always work for your benefit, even when they differ from your desires.

Reflection Questions

Are there "no" answers from God that you struggle to accept?

How does trusting God's plan help you let go of disappointment?

What steps can you take to find peace in God's wisdom, even when it means letting go?

Prayer for the Day

Father, help me to trust Your "no" as much as Your "yes." Let me rest in the knowledge that Your plans are for my good, leading me to hope and a future. Amen.

April 13

The Courage to Follow God's Wisdom

"Be strong and courageous, for the Lord your God is with you wherever you go."

— JOSHUA 1:9 (NLT)

Additional Scripture References:

Isaiah 41:10: "Don't be afraid, for I am with you. Don't be discouraged, for I am your God. I will strengthen you and help you. I will hold you up with my victorious right hand."

Deuteronomy 31:6: "So be strong and courageous! Do not be afraid and do not panic before them. For the Lord your God will personally go ahead of you. He will neither fail you nor abandon you."

Devotional Thought:

Following God's wisdom sometimes requires courage, especially when His guidance leads you away from your comfort zone. Embracing His wisdom means trusting that He is with you every step. Today, let courage be your companion, knowing that God's presence is the foundation of your strength.

Reflection Questions

Are there decisions where you need courage to follow God's wisdom?

How does trusting God's presence give you confidence in tough choices?

What steps can you take to embrace courage in following His guidance?

Prayer for the Day

Lord, give me courage to follow Your wisdom, even when it's challenging. Let Your presence strengthen me, guiding each step I take. Amen.

Learning from Past Decisions

"The heart of the discerning acquires knowledge,
for the ears of the wise seek it out."

— PROVERBS 18:15 (NLT)

Additional Scripture References:

Proverbs 1:5: "Let the wise listen to these proverbs and become even wiser. Let those with understanding receive guidance."

James 1:19: "Understand this, my dear brothers and sisters: You must all be quick to listen, slow to speak, and slow to get angry."

Devotional Thought:

Reflection on past decisions offers valuable lessons that can guide future choices. By seeking to understand what God taught you through past experiences, you grow in wisdom and discernment. Today, take time to reflect on past decisions, asking God to reveal insights that will guide you forward.

Reflection Questions

Are there past decisions that offer lessons for your present?

How can understanding past choices help you make wiser decisions now?

What steps can you take to reflect on God's lessons in your life?

Prayer for the Day

Father, help me to learn from my past decisions. Let Your wisdom guide my reflection, growing me in understanding and discernment. Amen.

April 15

Choosing Joy in Every Decision

"Always be full of joy in the Lord. I say it again – rejoice!"
— **PHILIPPIANS 4:4 (NLT)**

Additional Scripture References:

1 Thessalonians 5:16: "Always be joyful."

Nehemiah 8:10: "The joy of the Lord is your strength."

Devotional Thought:

Joy is a choice, and when we invite God into our decision-making, joy becomes a natural result. Even when decisions are difficult, choosing to focus on God's goodness brings hope and peace. Today, let joy guide your decisions, trusting that God's love and grace surround you in every choice.

Reflection Questions

Are there decisions where joy has been lacking?

How does focusing on God's goodness help you choose joy?

What steps can you take to embrace joy in all circumstances?

Prayer for the Day

Lord, fill my heart with joy, even in difficult decisions. Help me to focus on Your goodness and let Your joy be my strength. Amen.

The Humility to Admit When You're Wrong

"Pride goes before destruction, and haughtiness before a fall."
— **PROVERBS 16:18 (NLT)**

Additional Scripture References:

Proverbs 18:12: "Before destruction a man's heart is haughty, but humility comes before honor."

James 4:6: "But he gives more grace. Therefore it says, 'God opposes the proud but gives grace to the humble.'"

Devotional Thought:

Admitting when we're wrong requires humility, a key component of wise decision-making. When we're willing to change course and acknowledge mistakes, God blesses us with growth and insight. Today, ask God for a heart of humility, allowing His wisdom to shape your choices.

Reflection Questions

Are there areas where pride may hinder your decision-making?

How does humility lead to growth and understanding?

What steps can you take to practice humility in your decisions?

Prayer for the Day

Father, grant me the humility to admit when I'm wrong. Help me to rely on Your wisdom, allowing Your truth to guide my heart. Amen.

April 17

Seeing Beyond Immediate Gratification

"Better to be patient than powerful;
better to have self-control than to conquer a city."

— PROVERBS 16:32 (NLT)

Additional Scripture References:

Proverbs 25:28: "A person without self-control is like a city with broken-down walls."

Galatians 5:22-23: "But the fruit of the Spirit is love, joy, peace, forbearance, kindness, goodness, faithfulness, gentleness, and self-control. Against such things, there is no law."

Devotional Thought:

Wise decisions often require patience, especially when immediate gratification tempts us. By looking beyond temporary satisfaction, we align ourselves with God's long-term purpose for our lives. Today, let patience guide you, helping you make choices that reflect lasting values.

Reflection Questions

Are there choices where immediate gratification may not be best?

How does focusing on long-term values change your perspective?

What steps can you take to cultivate patience in your decision-making?

Prayer for the Day

Lord, help me to look beyond immediate rewards and focus on Your lasting purpose. Let patience guide my choices, aligning them with Your will. Amen.

Embracing God's Wisdom Over Worldly Advice

*"Don't copy the behavior and customs of this world,
but let God transform you into a new person
by changing the way you think."*

— ROMANS 12:2 (NLT)

Additional Scripture References:

2 Corinthians 5:17: "This means that anyone who belongs to Christ has become a new person. The old life is gone; a new life has begun!"

Ephesians 4:23-24: "Instead, let the Spirit renew your thoughts and attitudes. Put on your new nature, created to be like God — truly righteous and holy."

Devotional Thought:

Worldly advice often conflicts with God's wisdom, prioritizing temporary gain over eternal values. When we embrace God's way, we align ourselves with His truth and purpose. Let today be a reminder to filter all advice through God's Word, allowing His wisdom to shape your path.

Reflection Questions

Are there areas where worldly advice may be influencing your choices?

How does filtering advice through God's Word give you clarity?

What steps can you take to embrace God's wisdom over the world's?

Prayer for the Day

Father, help me to seek Your wisdom above all else. Let my decisions reflect Your truth, not the influence of the world around me. Amen.

April 19

Finding Peace in Unclear Decisions

"I am leaving you with a gift — peace of mind and heart."
— JOHN 14:27 (NLT)

Additional Scripture References:

Philippians 4:6-7: "Don't worry about anything; instead, pray about everything. Tell God what you need, and thank him for all he has done. Then you will experience God's peace, which exceeds anything we can understand."

Isaiah 26:3: "You will keep in perfect peace all who trust in you, all whose thoughts are fixed on you."

Devotional Thought:

Not every decision will come with complete clarity, yet God promises His peace in every situation. Trust that His peace will guide you, even when the path seems uncertain. Today, let peace be your anchor, trusting that God will lead you step by step.

Reflection Questions

Are there decisions where clarity is lacking, but peace is present?

How does trusting God's peace help you move forward in faith?

What steps can you take to find peace in uncertain situations?

Prayer for the Day

Lord, let Your peace fill my heart, especially in unclear decisions. Help me to trust that You are guiding me, even when I can't see the whole picture. Amen.

April 20

Trusting God in Uncertainty

"Trust in the Lord with all your heart;
do not depend on your own understanding."

— **PROVERBS 3:5 (NLT)**

Additional Scripture References:

saiah 26:3: *"You will keep in perfect peace all who trust in you, all whose thoughts are fixed on you!"*

Philippians 4:6-7: *"Don't worry about anything; instead, pray about everything. Tell God what you need, and thank him for all he has done. Then you will experience God's peace, which exceeds anything we can understand. His peace will guard your hearts and minds as you live in Christ Jesus."*

Devotional Thought:

Life often brings moments of uncertainty where answers seem out of reach. In those moments, God invites us to trust Him completely. When we lean on His wisdom instead of our own, He provides peace and guidance. Today, choose to trust God with the unknown, surrendering every worry into His capable hands.

Reflection Questions

Are there uncertainties in your life you need to entrust to God? How does trusting God bring peace to your heart? What steps can you take to rely on God's wisdom instead of your own?

Prayer for the Day

Lord, in the face of uncertainty, I choose to trust You. Help me to surrender my fears and lean on Your understanding. Fill my heart with peace as I rely on Your wisdom to guide me through every challenge. Amen.

April 21

Seeking Guidance in All Things

*"The Lord says, 'I will guide you along the best pathway for your life.
I will advise you and watch over you.'"*

— PSALM 32:8 (NLT)

Additional Scripture References:

Proverbs 3:5-6: "Trust in the Lord with all your heart; do not depend on your own understanding. Seek his will in all you do, and he will show you which path to take."

Isaiah 30:21: "Your own ears will hear him. Right behind you a voice will say, 'This is the way you should go,' whether to the right or to the left."

Devotional Thought:

God's promise to guide us covers every aspect of our lives, from small daily choices to life-changing decisions. By inviting His guidance into all things, we align ourselves with His best plan. Today, let God's promise bring comfort, knowing He is with you in every decision, watching over you with love.

Reflection Questions

Are there areas where you haven't invited God's guidance?

How does asking for His direction in all things deepen your trust?

What steps can you take to make God's guidance a daily habit?

Prayer for the Day

Lord, guide me in every choice, big and small. Let my life reflect Your path, and help me to rely on Your wisdom each day. Amen.

Listening for God's Voice in Silence

"Be still, and know that I am God!"

— PSALM 46:10 (NLT)

Additional Scripture References:

Exodus 14:14: "The Lord himself will fight for you. Just stay calm."

Isaiah 30:15: "This is what the Sovereign Lord, the Holy One of Israel, says: 'In repentance and rest is your salvation, in quietness and trust is your strength.'"

Devotional Thought:

Amid life's noise, God often speaks in stillness. By setting aside time for quiet reflection, we open our hearts to hear His gentle voice. Let today be a time to listen for God's guidance in silence, trusting that His wisdom will be clear when we seek Him in stillness.

Reflection Questions

Are there areas where you need clarity that may come through quiet reflection?

How does being still help you to recognize God's presence?

What steps can you take to include moments of silence in your day?

Prayer for the Day

Father, help me to find moments of stillness to hear Your voice. Let Your wisdom come to me in silence, guiding me in all I do. Amen.

April 23

Wisdom in Managing Resources

*"Honor the Lord with your wealth and
with the best part of everything you produce."*
— PROVERBS 3:9 (NLT)

Additional Scripture References:

Malachi 3:10: "Bring all the tithes into the storehouse so there will be enough food in my temple. If you do, says the Lord of Heaven's Armies, I will open the windows of heaven for you. I will pour out a blessing so great you won't have enough room to take it in!"

2 Corinthians 9:7: "You must each decide in your heart how much to give. And don't give reluctantly or in response to pressure. For God loves a person who gives cheerfully."

Devotional Thought:

Managing resources with wisdom honors God, as He is the source of all we have. By using our time, energy, and finances with care, we demonstrate stewardship and gratitude. Today, let wisdom guide you in how you manage what God has entrusted to you, reflecting His goodness in every decision.

Reflection Questions

Are there resources where you need God's wisdom to manage them well?

How does honoring God with your resources bring joy and fulfillment?

What steps can you take to practice wise stewardship daily?

Prayer for the Day

Lord, give me wisdom in managing what You have given me. Let my choices honor You, reflecting gratitude and trust in Your provision. Amen.

Guarding Against Impulsiveness

"A person without self-control is like a city with broken-down walls."

— PROVERBS 25:28 (NLT)

Additional Scripture References:

Proverbs 16:32: "Better to be patient than powerful; better to have self-control than to conquer a city."

Galatians 5:22-23: "But the fruit of the Spirit is love, joy, peace, forbearance, kindness, goodness, faithfulness, gentleness, and self-control. Against such things, there is no law."

Devotional Thought:

Impulsiveness often leads to regret, while self-control creates stability and peace. Practicing self-control in decisions protects us from hasty actions that may not align with God's will. Today, let self-control guard your heart and mind, allowing wisdom to shape your responses and choices.

Reflection Questions

Are there areas where impulsiveness affects your decisions?

How does practicing self-control strengthen your relationship with God?

What steps can you take to develop more self-control in daily choices?

Prayer for the Day

Father, grant me self-control in all things. Let my actions reflect Your wisdom, building a life that is grounded in peace and purpose. Amen.

April 25

Using Past Wisdom for Present Choices

"Teach us to realize the brevity of life,
so that we may grow in wisdom."

— PSALM 90:12 (NLT)

Additional Scripture References:

James 4:14: "How do you know what your life will be like tomorrow? Your life is like the morning fog — it's here a little while and then it's gone."

Ecclesiastes 3:1: "For everything there is a season, a time for every activity under heaven."

Devotional Thought:

Lessons from the past shape our present, providing wisdom for current decisions. Reflecting on what God has taught us helps us make better choices, growing in maturity and understanding. Today, let past experiences guide your steps, using the wisdom gained to make choices that honor God.

Reflection Questions

Are there past experiences that can guide you in current decisions?

How does reflecting on past lessons help you grow in wisdom?

What steps can you take to learn from your experiences?

Prayer for the Day

Lord, thank You for the lessons of the past. Help me to use them to guide my choices, growing in wisdom each day. Amen.

April 26

Valuing God's Perspective Over Popular Opinion

"For my thoughts are not your thoughts,
neither are your ways my ways."

— ISAIAH 55:8 (NLT)

Additional Scripture References:

Proverbs 3:5-6: "Trust in the Lord with all your heart; do not depend on your own understanding. Seek his will in all you do, and he will show you which path to take."

Romans 11:33: "Oh, how great are God's riches and wisdom and knowledge! How impossible it is for us to understand his decisions and his ways!"

Devotional Thought:

God's perspective is eternal, often differing from the views of the world. Choosing to value His wisdom above popular opinion helps us make choices rooted in truth. Let today be a reminder to seek God's guidance, placing His will above the influence of others.

Reflection Questions

Are there areas where popular opinion may be conflicting with God's wisdom?

How does valuing God's perspective bring peace and clarity?

What steps can you take to prioritize God's view in your life?

Prayer for the Day

Father, help me to seek Your wisdom above all else. Let my choices be guided by Your truth, not the shifting views of the world. Amen.

April 27

Patience in Decision-Making

"But let patience have its perfect work,
that you may be perfect and complete, lacking nothing."

— JAMES 1:4 (NLT)

Additional Scripture References:

Romans 5:3-4: "We can rejoice, too, when we run into problems and trials, for we know that they help us develop endurance. And endurance develops strength of character, and character strengthens our confident hope of salvation."

1 Peter 1:6-7: "So be truly glad. There is wonderful joy ahead, even though you must endure many trials for a little while. These trials will show that your faith is genuine. It is being tested as fire tests and p

Devotional Thought:

Patience strengthens our character, allowing wisdom to guide us through each decision. Rather than rushing, let patience shape your choices, trusting that God will reveal the right path in His time. Today, let patience be a foundation in all you do, helping you grow in wisdom and faith.

Reflection Questions

Are there decisions where patience could lead to better outcomes?

How does patience help you rely on God's timing?

What steps can you take to cultivate patience in decision-making?

Prayer for the Day

Lord, give me the patience to wait on Your timing. Let my decisions be rooted in wisdom, trusting that You will guide me each step of the way. Amen.

Surrendering Uncertainty to God

"Give all your worries and cares to God, for he cares about you."
— 1 PETER 5:7 (NLT)

Additional Scripture References:

Philippians 4:6-7: "Don't worry about anything; instead, pray about everything. Tell God what you need, and thank him for all he has done. Then you will experience God's peace, which exceeds anything we can understand."

Matthew 11:28: "Then Jesus said, 'Come to me, all of you who are weary and carry heavy burdens, and I will give you rest.'"

Devotional Thought:

Uncertainty can create fear, but surrendering it to God brings peace. Trusting that He cares allows us to let go of anxiety and rest in His faithfulness. Today, release any worries about the future, trusting that God's wisdom will carry you through.

Reflection Questions

Are there uncertainties in your life you need to surrender?

How does trusting God with your worries bring peace?

What steps can you take to release control and embrace trust in Him?

Prayer for the Day

Father, I surrender my uncertainties to You. Help me to trust in Your care, finding peace in knowing You are with me always. Amen.

April 29

Learning to Let Go of What Isn't Right

"Since we are receiving a Kingdom that is unshakable, let us be thankful and please God by worshiping him with holy fear and awe."

— **HEBREWS 12:28 (NLT)**

Additional Scripture References:

Revelation 21:4: "He will wipe every tear from their eyes, and there will be no more death or sorrow or crying or pain. All these things are gone forever."

2 Peter 1:11: "Then God will give you a grand entrance into the eternal Kingdom of our Lord and Savior Jesus Christ."

Devotional Thought:

Sometimes wisdom is knowing when to let go. Letting go of what isn't aligned with God's purpose makes space for His best. Today, ask God for discernment to release anything that holds you back, embracing His perfect plan for your life.

Reflection Questions

Are there things in your life that may be holding you back?

How does letting go allow God's purpose to flourish in your life?

What steps can you take to embrace God's plan by letting go?

Prayer for the Day

Lord, help me to release what isn't right for me. Let Your purpose be my focus, and give me wisdom to let go and trust in Your plan. Amen.

April 30

Moving Forward with Confidence in God's Wisdom

"I will instruct you and teach you in the way you should go;
I will counsel you with my loving eye on you."

— PSALM 32:8 (NLT)

Additional Scripture References:

Proverbs 3:5-6: "Trust in the Lord with all your heart; do not depend on your own understanding. Seek his will in all you do, and he will show you which path to take."

Isaiah 30:21: "Your own ears will hear him. Right behind you a voice will say, 'This is the way you should go,' whether to the right or to the left."

Devotional Thought:

Confidence in God's wisdom allows us to move forward with assurance, knowing He will guide us each step of the way. As you close this month, trust that God's guidance will continue to be with you, helping you make wise and faithful decisions in all areas of life.

Reflection Questions

Are there areas where you need more confidence in God's guidance?

How does trusting in God's wisdom bring peace to your future?

What steps can you take to walk forward confidently in God's direction?

Prayer for the Day

Father, thank You for Your guidance throughout this month. Help me to move forward with confidence in Your wisdom, trusting that You are always by my side. Amen.

The Heart of Service

"For even the Son of Man came not to be served but to serve others."

— MARK 10:45 (NLT)

Additional Scripture References:

Philippians 2:7: "Instead, he gave up his divine privileges; he took the humble position of a slave and was born as a human being. When he appeared in human form,"

John 13:14-15: "And since I, your Lord and Teacher, have washed your feet, you ought to wash each other's feet. I have given you an example to follow. Do as I have done to you."

Devotional Thought:

True service comes from a heart of love and compassion, putting the needs of others before our own. Jesus set the ultimate example by serving selflessly, even when it was difficult. Today, let His example inspire you to serve others with a willing and joyful heart.

Reflection Questions

Are there people in your life who could use your support today?

How does serving others strengthen your relationship with God?

What steps can you take to make service a natural part of your daily life?

Prayer for the Day

Lord, give me a heart of service, willing to put others before myself. Help me to follow Jesus' example of love and compassion in all I do. Amen.

May 2

Serving with a Willing Heart

"Each of you should use whatever gift you have received to serve others."
— 1 PETER 4:10 (NLT)

Additional Scripture References:

Romans 12:6: "In his grace, God has given us different gifts for doing certain things well. So if God has given you the ability to prophesy, speak out with as much faith as God has given you."

1 Corinthians 12:4-5: "There are different kinds of spiritual gifts, but the same Spirit is the source of them all. There are different kinds of service, but we serve the same Lord."

Devotional Thought:

God has blessed each of us with unique gifts, meant to bless and uplift others. By using these gifts with a willing heart, we reflect His love and purpose. Today, think about the talents God has given you, and let Him show you how to use them in service to others.

Reflection Questions

What gifts has God given you to bless others?

How does using your gifts to serve bring joy and fulfillment?

What steps can you take to use your talents for God's purpose today?

Prayer for the Day

Father, thank You for the gifts You've given me. Help me to use them with a willing heart, bringing glory to You and blessing those around me. Amen.

May 3
Service with Compassion

"Be kind to each other, tenderhearted, forgiving one another."
— EPHESIANS 4:32 (NLT)

Additional Scripture References:

Colossians 3:13: "Make allowance for each other's faults, and forgive anyone who offends you. Remember, the Lord forgave you, so you must forgive others."

Matthew 6:14-15: "If you forgive those who sin against you, your heavenly Father will forgive you. But if you refuse to forgive others, your Father will not forgive your sins."

Devotional Thought:

Compassion is at the heart of true service, allowing us to connect deeply with others and offer kindness when it's needed most. Today, let compassion guide your actions, opening your heart to see and respond to the needs of those around you.

Reflection Questions

Are there people in your life who could use a little extra kindness today?

How does compassion impact your ability to serve others?

What steps can you take to show kindness and understanding to those around you?

Prayer for the Day

Lord, fill my heart with compassion. Let my actions reflect Your love and kindness, bringing comfort and encouragement to others. Amen.

The Joy of Generosity

"You must each decide in your heart how much to give. And don't give reluctantly or in response to pressure."

— 2 CORINTHIANS 9:7 (NLT)

Additional Scripture References:

Proverbs 11:25: "The generous will prosper; those who refresh others will themselves be refreshed."

Luke 6:38: "Give, and you will receive. Your gift will return to you in full — pressed down, shaken together to make room for more, running over, and poured into your lap. The amount you give will determine the amount you get back."

Devotional Thought:

Generosity isn't just about material gifts; it's about giving of ourselves with joy and an open heart. When we give freely, we reflect God's abundant love. Today, embrace the joy of generosity, whether it's through time, encouragement, or resources, knowing that your giving brings God's light into the world.

Reflection Questions

Are there areas where you can be more generous with your time or resources?

How does giving freely bring joy to your heart?

What steps can you take to make generosity a regular part of your life?

Prayer for the Day

Father, teach me to give with joy and a willing heart. Let my generosity reflect Your love, blessing others in meaningful ways. Amen.

Serving Others as an Act of Worship

"And so, dear brothers and sisters, I plead with you to give your bodies to God because of all he has done for you."

— ROMANS 12:1 (NLT)

Additional Scripture References:

1 Corinthians 6:19-20: "Don't you realize that your body is the temple of the Holy Spirit, who lives in you and was given to you by God? You do not belong to yourself, for God bought you with a high price. So you must honor God with your body."

Hebrews 13:15-16: "Therefore, let us offer through Jesus a continual sacrifice of praise to God, proclaiming our allegiance to his name. And don't forget to do good and to share with those in need. These are the sacrifices that please God."

Devotional Thought:

Serving others is one way we can worship God, dedicating our actions to Him and letting His love shine through us. When we serve with this mindset, our actions become an offering to God. Today, let your service be an act of worship, honoring Him with all you do.

Reflection Questions

Are there ways you can serve others as an act of worship?

How does dedicating your service to God change your perspective?

What steps can you take to make service a meaningful part of your faith?

Prayer for the Day

Lord, let my service be a form of worship, honoring You in all I do. Help me to see every act of kindness as an offering to You. Amen.

May 6

Serving in Small, Everyday Ways

"Do not despise these small beginnings, for the Lord rejoices to see the work begin."

— ZECHARIAH 4:10 (NLT)

Additional Scripture References:

Job 8:7: "And though you started with little, you will end with much."

Luke 16:10: "If you are faithful in little things, you will be faithful in large ones. But if you are dishonest in little things, you won't be honest with greater responsibilities."

Devotional Thought:

Service doesn't have to be grand to make a difference; often, it's the small, everyday acts that mean the most. God sees every effort and values every act of kindness, no matter how small. Today, look for simple ways to serve, knowing that God rejoices in every effort.

Reflection Questions

Are there small ways you can serve others today?

How does serving in small ways reflect God's love and care?

What steps can you take to make kindness a part of your daily routine?

Prayer for the Day

Lord, help me to see the value in small acts of service. Let my everyday actions reflect Your love and kindness to those around me. Amen.

Serving with a Grateful Heart

"Give thanks to the Lord, for he is good!
His faithful love endures forever." — Psalm 107:1 (NLT)

Additional Scripture References:

Psalm 118:1: "Give thanks to the Lord, for he is good! His faithful love endures forever."

1 Chronicles 16:34: "Give thanks to the Lord, for he is good! His faithful love endures forever."

Devotional Thought:

A grateful heart transforms service, making it a joyful and fulfilling experience. When we serve others with gratitude, we reflect God's goodness and love. Today, let thankfulness fill your heart as you serve, remembering that each opportunity to help others is a gift from God.

Reflection Questions

Are there ways you can bring gratitude into your acts of service?

How does serving with a grateful heart deepen your joy?

What steps can you take to practice thankfulness as you serve others?

Prayer for the Day

Father, fill my heart with gratitude as I serve. Help me to see each opportunity as a blessing, reflecting Your faithful love. Amen.

Serving Others as Jesus Did

"I have given you an example to follow. Do as I have done to you."
— JOHN 13:15 (NLT)

Additional Scripture References:

1 Peter 2:21: "For God called you to do good, even if it means suffering, just as Christ suffered for you. He is your example, and you must follow in his steps."

Philippians 2:5: "You must have the same attitude that Christ Jesus had."

Devotional Thought:

Jesus showed us how to serve selflessly, placing others' needs before His own. Following His example means loving and helping without expecting anything in return. Today, let Christ's example guide your actions, inspiring you to serve with humility and love.

Reflection Questions

Are there ways you can serve others with humility today?

How does following Jesus' example of service impact your relationships?

What steps can you take to make selfless service a habit?

Prayer for the Day

Lord, help me to serve as Jesus did, with humility and love. Let His example be my guide, inspiring me to care for others selflessly. Amen.

Overcoming Barriers to Service

*"Do not withhold good from those who deserve
it when it's in your power to help them."*

— PROVERBS 3:27 (NLT)

Additional Scripture References:

Galatians 6:10: *"Therefore, whenever we have the opportunity, we should do good to everyone — especially to those in the family of faith."*

James 4:17: "Remember, it is sin to know what you ought to do and then not do it."

Devotional Thought:

Sometimes barriers like busyness, fear, or doubt prevent us from serving. Overcoming these barriers requires faith and commitment to doing good. Today, ask God for the courage to overcome any obstacles, opening your heart to serve freely.

Reflection Questions

Are there barriers that keep you from serving others more often?

How does overcoming these barriers strengthen your faith and commitment?

What steps can you take to make serving others a priority?

Prayer for the Day

Father, give me the courage to overcome any barriers to service. Help me to act with kindness and compassion, using my abilities to bless others. Amen.

Serving with Love and Compassion

"Do everything in love."

— 1 CORINTHIANS 16:14 (NLT)

Additional Scripture References:

Galatians 5:13: "For you have been called to live in freedom, my brothers and sisters. But don't use your freedom to satisfy your sinful nature. Instead, use your freedom to serve one another in love."

Colossians 3:14: "Above all, clothe yourselves with love, which binds us all together in perfect harmony."

Devotional Thought:

When we serve with love and compassion, our actions reflect God's heart. Love is the foundation of true service, creating lasting impact and spreading God's grace. Today, let love be at the center of your actions, bringing God's compassion to those you serve.

Reflection Questions

Are there people in your life who need to feel God's love through your service?

How does serving with compassion deepen your relationships?

What steps can you take to let love guide your actions?

Prayer for the Day

Lord, help me to serve with love and compassion. Let my actions reflect Your grace, bringing hope and comfort to those around me. Amen.

May 11

Seeing Jesus in Those We Serve

"And the King will say, 'I tell you the truth, when you did it to one of the least of these my brothers and sisters, you were doing it to me!'"
— MATTHEW 25:40 (NLT)

Additional Scripture References:

James 2:15-16: "Suppose you see a brother or sister who has no food or clothing, and you say, 'Goodbye and have a good day; stay warm and eat well!' but then you don't give that person any food or clothing. What good does that do?"

Proverbs 19:17: "If you help the poor, you are lending to the Lord — and he will repay you!"

Devotional Thought:

When we serve others, we're serving Jesus Himself. Seeing Christ in those we help transforms our actions, reminding us that every person is valuable to God. Today, let this perspective fill your heart as you serve, seeing each act of kindness as a way to honor Him.

Reflection Questions

Are there people in your life you could serve as though you're serving Jesus?

How does seeing Jesus in others change your approach to service?

What steps can you take to make this perspective a habit in your daily life?

Prayer for the Day

Lord, help me to see You in those I serve. Let my actions honor You and show others the love and grace of Christ. Amen.

May 12

Serving with Purpose and Joy

*"Work with enthusiasm, as though you were working
for the Lord rather than for people."*

— COLOSSIANS 3:23 (NLT)

Additional Scripture References:

*Ecclesiastes 9:10: "Whatever you do, do well. For when you go to the grave,
there will be no work or planning or knowledge or wisdom."*

*1 Corinthians 10:31: "So whether you eat or drink, or whatever you do, do it
all for the glory of God."*

Devotional Thought:

Serving with joy and purpose allows us to work as though we're
serving God directly, bringing fulfillment to each task. Today, focus
on serving others with enthusiasm, knowing that every act of kindness
is a way to honor God and bring joy to your heart.

Reflection Questions

Are there ways you can bring more joy and purpose into your acts of
service?

How does serving with enthusiasm deepen your relationship with
God?

What steps can you take to view all your work as service to God?

Prayer for the Day

Father, fill me with joy and purpose as I serve. Let my actions be done
for You, bringing honor to Your name and joy to my heart. Amen.

May 13

Serving Through Listening

"Understand this, my dear brothers and sisters: You must all be quick to listen, slow to speak, and slow to get angry."

— JAMES 1:19 (NLT)

Additional Scripture References:

Proverbs 18:13: "Spouting off before listening to the facts is both shameful and foolish."

Ecclesiastes 7:9: "Control your temper, for anger labels you a fool."

Devotional Thought:

Sometimes the greatest act of service is simply being present and listening. By giving others our undivided attention, we show them respect, compassion, and care. Today, let your service be shown through listening, offering support and understanding to those around you.

Reflection Questions

Are there people in your life who need someone to listen to them today?

How does listening to others show them respect and love?

What steps can you take to practice being a better listener?

Prayer for the Day

Lord, help me to serve others by listening well. Let my presence and attention bring comfort and encouragement to those around me. Amen.

Encouraging Others in Service

"Therefore encourage one another and build each other up."
— 1 THESSALONIANS 5:11 (NLT)

Additional Scripture References:

Hebrews 10:24-25: "Let us think of ways to motivate one another to acts of love and good works, and let us not neglect our meeting together, as some people do, but encourage one another, especially now that the day of his return is drawing near."

Galatians 6:2: "Share each other's burdens, and in this way obey the law of Christ."

Devotional Thought:

Service can also mean offering words of encouragement to uplift those who may be struggling. Sometimes a kind word is enough to inspire someone to keep going. Today, let your words be a source of strength, encouraging and building others up in their journeys.

Reflection Questions

Are there people in your life who could use encouragement today?

How does encouraging others make a difference in their lives?

What steps can you take to make encouragement a regular part of your interactions?

Prayer for the Day

Father, help me to use my words to encourage others. Let my speech bring hope and strength to those who need it, reflecting Your love. Amen.

May 15

Serving Without Expectation of Return

"But when you give to someone in need, don't let your left hand know what your right hand is doing."

— MATTHEW 6:3 (NLT)

Additional Scripture References:

Luke 14:12-14: "Then he turned to his host. 'When you put on a luncheon or a banquet,' he said, 'don't invite your friends, brothers, relatives, and rich neighbors, for they will invite you back, and that will be your only reward. Instead, invite the poor, the crippled, the lame, and the blind. Then at the resurrection of the righteous, God will reward you for inviting those who could not repay you.'"

Proverbs 21:26: "Some people are always greedy for more, but the godly love to give!"

Devotional Thought:

True service comes without expectations of reward or recognition, focusing only on the needs of others. When we give selflessly, we reflect God's grace, asking for nothing in return. Today, serve with a humble heart, finding joy in giving without expecting anything back.

Reflection Questions

Are there times when you've expected recognition for your service?

How does serving selflessly deepen your connection with God?

What steps can you take to give with a humble heart?

Prayer for the Day

Lord, teach me to serve selflessly, asking for nothing in return. Let my heart find joy in giving freely, as You have given to me. Amen.

Serving Through Prayer

"Pray in the Spirit at all times and on every occasion. Stay alert and be persistent in your prayers for all believers everywhere."

— EPHESIANS 6:18 (NLT)

Additional Scripture References:

1 Thessalonians 5:17: "Never stop praying."

Philippians 4:6: "Don't worry about anything; instead, pray about everything. Tell God what you need, and thank him for all he has done."

Devotional Thought:

Serving others through prayer is a powerful way to show love and support. By lifting others in prayer, we invite God's guidance, comfort, and strength into their lives. Today, spend time in prayer for those in need, offering them encouragement and faith through intercession.

Reflection Questions

Are there people in your life who could benefit from your prayers today?

How does praying for others bring you closer to God?

What steps can you take to make praying for others a regular habit?

Prayer for the Day

Father, help me to serve others through prayer. Let my intercessions be a source of strength, hope, and encouragement for those in need. Amen.

Serving with a Heart of Humility

"Don't be selfish; don't try to impress others. Be humble,
thinking of others as better than yourselves."

— PHILIPPIANS 2:3 (NLT)

Additional Scripture References:

James 3:16: "For wherever there is jealousy and selfish ambition, there you will find disorder and evil of every kind."

Romans 12:10: "Love each other with genuine affection, and take delight in honoring each other."

Devotional Thought:

Humility allows us to serve without pride, focusing solely on the needs of others. By putting others first, we honor God and reflect Christ's humility. Today, let humility guide your actions, serving with a heart that seeks to uplift and support those around you.

Reflection Questions.

Are there ways you can serve with greater humility today?

How does humility in service bring you closer to Christ?

What steps can you take to make humility a part of your service?

Prayer for the Day

Lord, grant me a humble heart as I serve. Help me to put others first, seeking only to bring glory to You through my actions. Amen.

May 18

Serving with Gratitude for God's Blessings

"Whatever you do, whether in word or deed, do it all in the name of the Lord Jesus, giving thanks to God the Father through him."

— COLOSSIANS 3:17 (NLT)

Additional Scripture References:

1 Corinthians 10:31: "So whether you eat or drink, or whatever you do, do it all for the glory of God."

Ephesians 5:20: "And give thanks for everything to God the Father in the name of our Lord Jesus Christ."

Devotional Thought:

Gratitude brings joy to our service, reminding us of God's blessings and faithfulness. When we serve with thankfulness, our actions reflect His love and abundance. Today, let gratitude fill your heart, allowing it to guide your service with joy and purpose.

Reflection Questions

Are there blessings you can be grateful for as you serve others?

How does serving with gratitude strengthen your relationship with God?

What steps can you take to let thankfulness guide your actions?

Prayer for the Day

Father, thank You for the blessings You have given me. Let my heart be filled with gratitude, serving others with joy and purpose. Amen.

Serving as a Light to the World

*"You are the light of the world – like a city
on a hilltop that cannot be hidden."*

— MATTHEW 5:14 (NLT)

Additional Scripture References:

*Philippians 2:15: "So that no one can criticize you. Live clean, innocent lives
as children of God, shining like bright lights in a world full of crooked and
perverse people."*

*Isaiah 60:1: "Arise, Jerusalem! Let your light shine for all to see. For the glory
of the Lord rises to shine on you."*

Devotional Thought:

Serving others allows us to be a light, showing God's love to a world in
need. When we serve, we become a reflection of His grace, drawing
others closer to Him. Today, let your service be a light, bringing hope,
kindness, and love to those around you.

Reflection Questions

Are there people in your life who need to see God's light through your
actions?

How does serving with love and kindness make a difference?

What steps can you take to let God's light shine through your service?

Prayer for the Day

Lord, help me to be a light in the world through my service. Let my
actions reflect Your love, bringing hope to those in need. Amen.

Serving in Faithfulness to God's Call

"And whatever you do, do it heartily, as to the Lord and not to men."
— COLOSSIANS 3:23 (NKJV)

Additional Scripture References:

Ecclesiastes 9:10: "Whatever you do, do well. For when you go to the grave, there will be no work or planning or knowledge or wisdom."

1 Corinthians 10:31: "So whether you eat or drink, or whatever you do, do it all for the glory of God."

Devotional Thought:

Faithful service honors God, reflecting our commitment to Him in all we do. When we serve wholeheartedly, we align ourselves with His purpose, knowing that each act of kindness matters. Today, let your service reflect a heart that is dedicated to God's calling, serving with joy and faithfulness.

Reflection Questions

Are there ways you can serve more faithfully in your daily life?

How does serving with a faithful heart bring you closer to God?

What steps can you take to make faithfulness a key part of your service?

Prayer for the Day

Father, let my service be faithful and wholehearted. Help me to honor You in all I do, reflecting my love and dedication to Your call. Amen.

May 21

Strength Through Perseverance

"For when your faith is tested, your endurance has a chance to grow."

— JAMES 1:3 (NLT)

Additional Scripture References:

Romans 5:3-4: "We can rejoice, too, when we run into problems and trials, for we know that they help us develop endurance. And endurance develops strength of character, and character strengthens our confident hope of salvation."

1 Peter 1:6-7: "So be truly glad. There is wonderful joy ahead, even though you must endure many trials for a little while. These trials will show that your faith is genuine. It is being tested as fire tests and purifies gold – though your faith is far more precious than mere gold."

Devotional Thought:

Trials give us a unique opportunity to strengthen our faith and endurance. God uses challenges to refine us, helping us grow stronger in Him. Today, remember that every trial you face has a purpose, building a resilience that draws you closer to God.

Reflection Questions

Are there challenges in your life where you need perseverance?

How does knowing that trials strengthen your faith bring comfort?

What steps can you take to embrace perseverance through life's struggles?

Prayer for the Day

Father, help me to persevere through trials. Strengthen my faith and let my endurance grow as I trust in Your plan. Amen.

Finding Peace in God Amid Trials

*"I have told you all this so that you may have peace in me.
Here on earth you will have many trials and sorrows.
But take heart, because I have overcome the world."*

— JOHN 16:33 (NLT)

Additional Scripture References:

Romans 8:37: "No, despite all these things, overwhelming victory is ours through Christ, who loved us."

1 John 5:4: "For every child of God defeats this evil world, and we achieve this victory through our faith."

Devotional Thought:

Even in the midst of trials, we can find peace in Jesus. His victory over the world gives us assurance that we can face any hardship. Today, focus on finding peace in God, letting His presence bring calm to your spirit as you face life's difficulties.

Reflection Questions

Are there trials where you need God's peace?

How does Jesus' victory bring you comfort in difficult times?

What steps can you take to invite His peace into your life today?

Prayer for the Day

Lord, fill my heart with Your peace. Help me to remember that You have overcome every struggle, allowing me to rest in Your victory. Amen.

May 23

Trusting God's Timing in Hard Seasons

*"Humble yourselves under the mighty hand of God,
that he may exalt you in due time."*

— 1 PETER 5:6 (NKJV)

Additional Scripture References:

*Romans 8:37: "No, despite all these things, overwhelming victory is ours
through Christ, who loved us."*

*1 John 5:4: "For every child of God defeats this evil world, and we achieve this
victory through our faith."*

Devotional Thought:

Waiting for God's timing during trials is difficult, but He promises to lift us up at the right moment. By humbling ourselves and trusting in His timing, we find hope and strength. Today, choose to trust in God's perfect timing, knowing that He is working all things out for your good.

Reflection Questions

Are there struggles where you need to trust in God's timing?

How does patience in trials deepen your relationship with God?

What steps can you take to rely on God's timing in all things?

Prayer for the Day

Father, help me to trust in Your timing, even when it's hard. Let my heart find peace in knowing that You are in control of every season. Amen.

Persevering Through Prayer

*"Devote yourselves to prayer with an alert mind and
a thankful heart."*

— **COLOSSIANS 4:2 (NLT)**

Additional Scripture References:

1 Thessalonians 5:17: "Never stop praying."

*Ephesians 6:18: "Pray in the Spirit at all times and on every occasion. Stay
alert and be persistent in your prayers for all believers everywhere."*

Devotional Thought:

Prayer is a powerful tool for perseverance, keeping us connected to
God during trials. By devoting ourselves to prayer, we invite His
strength, guidance, and comfort into our lives. Today, let prayer be
your anchor, sustaining you with hope and gratitude through every
challenge.

Reflection Questions

Are there trials where you need to pray more fervently?

How does devoting yourself to prayer help you persevere?

What steps can you take to make prayer a part of your perseverance?

Prayer for the Day

Lord, strengthen me through prayer. Let my heart be steadfast and my
mind alert, relying on Your power and presence through every trial.
Amen.

May 25

Persevering in Faith
When Answers Aren't Clear

*"Faith shows the reality of what we hope for; it is the evidence
of things we cannot see."*

— HEBREWS 11:1 (NLT)

Additional Scripture References:

2 Corinthians 5:7: "For we live by believing and not by seeing."

*Romans 4:20-21: "Abraham never wavered in believing God's promise. In
fact, his faith grew stronger, and in this he brought glory to God. He was fully
convinced that God is able to do whatever he promises."*

Devotional Thought:

Faith allows us to persevere, even when we don't see clear answers.
Trusting in God's unseen work gives us hope and strength to
continue forward. Today, let faith guide you, holding onto the reality
of God's promises even when clarity is lacking.

Reflection Questions

Are there areas where you need faith to carry you through uncertainty?

How does trusting in what you can't see help you persevere?

What steps can you take to strengthen your faith in uncertain times?

Prayer for the Day

Father, give me faith to believe in what I cannot see. Help me to
persevere in hope, trusting that You are working even when answers
aren't clear. Amen.

Learning Patience Through Trials

"Let us run with endurance the race God has set before us."

— HEBREWS 12:1 (NLT)

Additional Scripture References:

1 Corinthians 9:24: "Don't you realize that in a race everyone runs, but only one person gets the prize? So run to win!"

Philippians 3:13-14: "No, dear brothers and sisters, I have not achieved it, but I focus on this one thing: Forgetting the past and looking forward to what lies ahead, I press on to reach the end of the race and receive the heavenly prize for which God, through Christ Jesus, is calling us."

Devotional Thought:

Trials teach us patience, helping us develop endurance for the journey ahead. Running with endurance means trusting God's pace and staying faithful in the process. Today, let patience guide you, giving you strength and peace as you continue forward.

Reflection Questions

Are there situations where patience is hard to maintain?

How does patience help you stay grounded during trials?

What steps can you take to practice patience and endurance?

Prayer for the Day

Lord, grant me patience as I walk through trials. Help me to run this race with endurance, relying on Your strength and guidance each day. Amen.

Hope in God's Promises During Trials

*"Let us hold tightly without wavering to the hope we affirm,
for God can be trusted to keep his promise."*

— HEBREWS 10:23 (NLT)

Additional Scripture References:

Romans 4:20-21: "Abraham never wavered in believing God's promise. In fact, his faith grew stronger, and in this he brought glory to God. He was fully convinced that God is able to do whatever he promises."

2 Peter 3:9: "The Lord isn't really being slow about his promise, as some people think. No, he is being patient for your sake. He does not want anyone to be destroyed, but wants everyone to repent."

Devotional Thought:

God's promises are a source of hope in our darkest times. When trials come, holding onto His promises reminds us that He is faithful and trustworthy. Today, cling to God's promises, letting them sustain you with hope and confidence.

Reflection Questions

Are there promises of God you need to hold onto right now?

How does focusing on His promises strengthen your perseverance?

What steps can you take to meditate on God's promises daily?

Prayer for the Day

Father, thank You for Your promises. Help me to hold tightly to them, finding hope and strength in Your faithfulness through every trial. Amen.

Finding Joy Amid Challenges

*"Dear brothers and sisters, when troubles of any kind come your way,
consider it an opportunity for great joy."*

— James 1:2 (NLT)

Additional Scripture References:

*1 Peter 1:6: "So be truly glad. There is wonderful joy ahead, even though you
must endure many trials for a little while."*

*Romans 5:3-4: "We can rejoice, too, when we run into problems and trials, for
we know that they help us develop endurance. And endurance develops strength
of character, and character strengthens our confident hope of salvation."*

Devotional Thought:

Trials can refine us, drawing us closer to God and helping us grow in
faith. Finding joy in challenges doesn't mean ignoring the hardship,
but it means trusting that God is at work. Today, seek joy in your trials,
knowing that God is using them to shape and strengthen you.

Reflection Questions

Are there difficult situations where you can seek joy?

How does choosing joy help you persevere?

What steps can you take to find joy in the midst of trials?

Prayer for the Day

Lord, help me to find joy in every challenge. Let my heart be filled with
trust and hope, knowing that You are refining me through trials. Amen.

Persevering with a Heart of Gratitude

*"Be thankful in all circumstances, for this is God's will
for you who belong to Christ Jesus."*

— 1 THESSALONIANS 5:18 (NLT)

Additional Scripture References:

*Ephesians 5:20: "And give thanks for everything to God the Father in the
name of our Lord Jesus Christ."*

*Colossians 3:15: "And let the peace that comes from Christ rule in your hearts.
For as members of one body you are called to live in peace. And always be
thankful."*

Devotional Thought:

Gratitude brings peace and perspective, even in the toughest times.
When we give thanks in all circumstances, we open our hearts to
God's work in our lives. Today, choose gratitude, allowing it to fuel
your perseverance and bring joy even in hardship.

Reflection Questions

Are there blessings you can be thankful for during your current trials?

How does gratitude help you face challenges with a hopeful heart?

What steps can you take to practice thankfulness each day?

Prayer for the Day

Father, help me to find gratitude in every circumstance. Let my heart
be filled with thankfulness, bringing hope and strength in the face of
trials. Amen.

Drawing Strength from Community

*"Share each other's burdens,
and in this way obey the law of Christ."*

— GALATIANS 6:2 (NLT)

Additional Scripture References:

Romans 12:15: "Rejoice with those who rejoice, and weep with those who weep."

Philippians 2:4: "Don't look out only for your own interests, but take an interest in others, too."

Devotional Thought:

Community strengthens us, offering support and encouragement during trials. By sharing our burdens with others, we find comfort and renewed strength. Today, reach out to those who can support you, and remember that you are not alone in your journey.

Reflection Questions

Are there people in your life who can support you through trials?

How does sharing burdens with others bring comfort and strength?

What steps can you take to build a strong support network?

Prayer for the Day

Lord, thank You for the gift of community. Help me to share my burdens with others and find strength through the love and support of those around me. Amen.

Trusting God's Power to Sustain You

"My grace is all you need. My power works best in weakness."

— 2 CORINTHIANS 12:9 (NLT)

Additional Scripture References:

Isaiah 40:29: "He gives power to the weak and strength to the powerless."

Philippians 4:13: "For I can do everything through Christ, who gives me strength."

Devotional Thought:

God's power is our strength, especially when we feel weak or weary. Trusting in His grace allows us to persevere, knowing that He will sustain us in every trial. Today, rest in God's power, letting His grace carry you through whatever challenges lie ahead.

Reflection Questions

Are there areas where you need God's strength to carry you?

How does relying on His grace help you persevere through weakness?

What steps can you take to invite His power into your life?

Prayer for the Day

Father, thank You for Your sustaining grace. Help me to rely on Your strength, trusting that Your power is enough to carry me through every trial. Amen.

The Power of Forgiveness

"Instead, be kind to each other, tenderhearted, forgiving one another,
just as God through Christ has forgiven you."
— **EPHESIANS 4:32 (NLT)**

Additional Scripture References:

Colossians 3:13: "Make allowance for each other's faults, and forgive anyone who offends you. Remember, the Lord forgave you, so you must forgive others."

Matthew 6:14-15: "If you forgive those who sin against you, your heavenly Father will forgive you. But if you refuse to forgive others, your Father will not forgive your sins."

Devotional Thought:

Forgiveness is a powerful act that releases both you and others from the hold of hurt. When we forgive as God forgave us, we choose grace and compassion over resentment. Today, reflect on the power of forgiveness in your life and allow God's mercy to flow through you to others.

Reflection Questions ?

Are there past hurts you need to forgive?

How does choosing forgiveness bring freedom and peace?

What steps can you take to make forgiveness a regular part of your life?

Prayer for the Day

Lord, help me to forgive as You have forgiven me. Let my heart be filled with kindness and compassion, choosing grace over bitterness. Amen.

June 2

Forgiveness as a Reflection of God's Love

*"For God so loved the world that he gave his one and only Son,
that whoever believes in him shall not perish but have eternal life."*

— JOHN 3:16 (NLT)

Additional Scripture References:

Romans 5:8: "But God showed his great love for us by sending Christ to die for us while we were still sinners."

1 John 4:9-10: "God showed how much he loved us by sending his one and only Son into the world so that we might have eternal life through him. This is real love — not that we loved God, but that he loved us and sent his Son as a sacrifice to take away our sins."

Devotional Thought:

Forgiveness is an expression of love, mirroring the gift of Jesus' sacrifice for us. By choosing to forgive, we reflect the same love that God showed us. Today, let God's love inspire you to release any grudges or anger, embracing forgiveness as an act of love.

Reflection Questions

Are there relationships where forgiveness can bring healing?

How does forgiving others reflect God's love in your life?

What steps can you take to embrace forgiveness as an act of love?

Prayer for the Day

Father, thank You for the gift of forgiveness through Jesus. Help me to show that same love by forgiving those who have hurt me. Amen.

Forgiving Yourself

*"So now there is no condemnation
for those who belong to Christ Jesus."*
— ROMANS 8:1 (NLT)

Additional Scripture References:

John 3:17: *"God sent his Son into the world not to judge the world, but to save the world through him."*

2 Corinthians 5:17: *"This means that anyone who belongs to Christ has become a new person. The old life is gone; a new life has begun!"*

Devotional Thought:

Sometimes forgiving yourself can be harder than forgiving others, but God's grace covers all. Embracing His forgiveness allows you to release guilt and walk in freedom. Today, let go of self-condemnation and accept God's grace fully, forgiving yourself as He has forgiven you.

Reflection Questions

Are there past mistakes you need to forgive yourself for?

How does letting go of self-condemnation bring peace?

What steps can you take to accept God's grace and forgive yourself?

Prayer for the Day

Lord, thank You for Your grace that frees me from guilt. Help me to forgive myself and walk confidently in the freedom You offer. Amen.

Forgiving Those Who Don't Apologize

"But I say, love your enemies!
Pray for those who persecute you!"
— MATTHEW 5:44 (NLT)

Additional Scripture References:

Luke 6:27-28: "But to you who are willing to listen, I say, love your enemies. Do good to those who hate you. Bless those who curse you. Pray for those who hurt you."

Romans 12:20-21: "If your enemies are hungry, feed them. If they are thirsty, give them something to drink. In doing this, you will heap burning coals of shame on their heads. Don't let evil conquer you, but conquer evil by doing good."

Devotional Thought:

Sometimes forgiveness is necessary even when apologies aren't given. Choosing to forgive without expecting an apology frees your heart from bitterness and allows God's love to flourish. Today, let go of any need for an apology and choose forgiveness as a path to peace.

Reflection Questions

Are there people you need to forgive, even if they haven't apologized?

How does forgiving without an apology bring freedom to your life?

What steps can you take to release any expectations and forgive freely?

Prayer for the Day

Father, help me to forgive others, even when they haven't apologized. Let my heart be filled with peace, choosing love over bitterness. Amen.

June 5

Forgiving Seventy Times Seven

"Then Peter came to him and asked, 'Lord, how often should I forgive someone who sins against me? Seven times?' 'No, not seven times,' Jesus replied, 'but seventy times seven!'"

— MATTHEW 18:21-22 (NLT)

Additional Scripture References:

Ephesians 4:32: "Instead, be kind to each other, tenderhearted, forgiving one another, just as God through Christ has forgiven you."

Colossians 3:13: "Make allowance for each other's faults, and forgive anyone who offends you. Remember, the Lord forgave you, so you must forgive others."

Devotional Thought:

Forgiveness isn't a one-time act but a lifestyle of grace. By choosing to forgive repeatedly, we mirror God's endless mercy. Today, let God's call to forgive continually remind you that each moment of forgiveness is a step toward greater freedom and love.

Reflection Questions

Are there situations where you find it hard to forgive repeatedly?

How does embracing continuous forgiveness impact your relationships?

What steps can you take to practice forgiveness as an ongoing act of grace?

Prayer for the Day

Lord, help me to forgive endlessly, as You do. Let my heart be open to forgive over and over, showing others the mercy You've shown me. Amen.

June 6

The Freedom of Letting Go

"Cast all your anxiety on him because he cares for you."

— 1 PETER 5:7 (NLT)

Additional Scripture References:

Philippians 4:6-7: "Don't worry about anything; instead, pray about everything. Tell God what you need, and thank him for all he has done. Then you will experience God's peace, which exceeds anything we can understand."

Matthew 11:28: "Then Jesus said, 'Come to me, all of you who are weary and carry heavy burdens, and I will give you rest.'"

Devotional Thought:

Holding onto resentment can weigh us down, but casting our burdens onto God allows us to walk in freedom. Today, choose to let go of any hurt, trusting that God's care will bring peace and healing to your heart.

Reflection Questions

Are there burdens you need to release to God?

How does letting go bring peace and freedom to your life?

What steps can you take to release bitterness and embrace God's peace?

Prayer for the Day

Father, help me to let go of every hurt and resentment. Let Your peace fill my heart, allowing me to walk in freedom and love. Amen.

June 7

Forgiveness Brings Healing

*"Confess your sins to each other and pray for each other
so that you may be healed."*

— JAMES 5:16 (NLT)

Additional Scripture References:

Galatians 6:2: "Share each other's burdens, and in this way obey the law of Christ."

1 John 1:9: "If we confess our sins, he is faithful and just to forgive us our sins and to cleanse us from all wickedness."

Devotional Thought:

Forgiveness often brings emotional and spiritual healing, releasing the hold of pain and resentment. When we forgive, we invite God's healing presence into our lives. Today, choose to forgive and let healing begin, trusting that God's grace will restore your heart.

Reflection Questions

Are there areas in your heart that need healing through forgiveness?

How does releasing pain and resentment open the door to healing?

What steps can you take to let God's healing flow through forgiveness?

Prayer for the Day

Lord, let Your healing power flow through me as I choose to forgive. Bring restoration to my heart and peace to my spirit. Amen.

June 8

Choosing Love Over Bitterness

"Make allowance for each other's faults,
and forgive anyone who offends you."
— COLOSSIANS 3:13 (NLT)

Additional Scripture References:

Ephesians 4:32: "Instead, be kind to each other, tenderhearted, forgiving one another, just as God through Christ has forgiven you."

Matthew 6:14-15: "If you forgive those who sin against you, your heavenly Father will forgive you. But if you refuse to forgive others, your Father will not forgive your sins."

Devotional Thought:

Love is more powerful than bitterness, allowing us to forgive even the deepest wounds. By choosing love over resentment, we reflect God's grace and bring healing to our lives. Today, let love guide you as you forgive, allowing peace to take the place of pain.

Reflection Questions

Are there areas where bitterness has taken root?

How does choosing love over resentment bring you closer to God?

What steps can you take to embrace love and release bitterness?

Prayer for the Day

Father, help me to choose love over bitterness. Let my heart be filled with Your grace, bringing peace and healing as I forgive. Amen.

June 9

Forgiveness as Freedom for the Future

"Forget the former things; do not dwell on the past."

— ISAIAH 43:18 (NLT)

Additional Scripture References:

2 Corinthians 5:17: "This means that anyone who belongs to Christ has become a new person. The old life is gone; a new life has begun!"

Philippians 3:13-14: "No, dear brothers and sisters, I have not achieved it, but I focus on this one thing: Forgetting the past and looking forward to what lies ahead, I press on to reach the end of the race and receive the heavenly prize for which God, through Christ Jesus, is calling us."

Devotional Thought:

Forgiveness frees us from the past, allowing us to move forward in God's purpose. By releasing grudges, we open the door to a future filled with peace and joy. Today, choose forgiveness as a way to embrace God's plans for your life, free from the weight of past hurts.

Reflection Questions

Are there past hurts that are holding you back from your future?

How does letting go of the past open doors to new possibilities?

What steps can you take to forgive and step into the future with hope?

Prayer for the Day

Lord, help me to release the past and embrace the future. Let forgiveness free my heart, allowing me to walk in Your plans with joy. Amen.

June 10

Forgiveness Brings Clarity and Peace

*"Create in me a clean heart, O God, and
renew a loyal spirit within me."*

— PSALM 51:10 (NLT)

Additional Scripture References:

*Ezekiel 36:26: "And I will give you a new heart, and I will put a new spirit
in you. I will take out your stony, stubborn heart and give you a tender,
responsive heart."*

*2 Corinthians 5:17: "This means that anyone who belongs to Christ has become
a new person. The old life is gone; a new life has begun!"*

Devotional Thought:

A heart filled with forgiveness is clear and open to God's presence. When we let go of resentment, we create space for His peace to dwell in us. Today, seek a clean heart through forgiveness, inviting God's peace to transform your life.

Reflection Questions

Are there areas where resentment clouds your heart?

How does forgiveness bring clarity and peace to your spirit?

What steps can you take to keep your heart open to God's presence?

Prayer for the Day

Father, create in me a clean heart. Help me to forgive and let Your peace dwell within me, renewing my spirit each day. Amen.

The Foundation of Godly Character

*"But you, Timothy, are a man of God; so run from all these evil things.
Pursue righteousness and a godly life, along with faith, love,
perseverance, and gentleness."*

— 1 TIMOTHY 6:11 (NLT)

Additional Scripture References:

2 Timothy 2:22: "Run from anything that stimulates youthful lusts. Instead, pursue righteous living, faithfulness, love, and peace. Enjoy the companionship of those who call on the Lord with pure hearts."

Matthew 6:33: "Seek the Kingdom of God above all else, and live righteously, and he will give you everything you need."

Devotional Thought:

Godly manhood is built on a foundation of character, focusing on righteousness, faith, and love. By pursuing these qualities, we grow into the men God calls us to be. Today, let your actions reflect the character God desires, choosing to honor Him in all you do.

Reflection Questions

Are there areas in your character that you feel called to strengthen?

How does focusing on godly qualities shape your actions?

What steps can you take to live with integrity and godly character?

Prayer for the Day

Father, help me to build a foundation of godly character. Let my life reflect faith, love, and integrity, honoring You in every way. Amen.

June 12

Courage to Stand for What's Right

*"Be on guard. Stand firm in the faith.
Be courageous. Be strong."*

— 1 CORINTHIANS 16:13 (NLT)

Additional Scripture References:

Ephesians 6:10: "A final word: Be strong in the Lord and in his mighty power."

Philippians 1:27: "Above all, you must live as citizens of heaven, conducting yourselves in a manner worthy of the Good News about Christ. Then, whether I come and see you again or only hear about you, I will know that you are standing firm in one spirit, striving together as one for the faith of the gospel."

Devotional Thought:

Godly manhood requires courage to stand for what's right, even when it's difficult. In moments of challenge, God's strength empowers us to uphold truth and integrity. Today, let courage be your guide, standing firm in faith and honoring God in all you do.

Reflection Questions

Are there areas where you need courage to uphold God's truth?

How does standing firm in faith bring strength to your character?

What steps can you take to be courageous in following God's ways?

Prayer for the Day

Lord, give me the courage to stand firm in my faith. Help me to uphold truth and integrity, reflecting Your strength in all situations. Amen.

Leading by Example

"Don't let anyone think less of you because you are young.
Be an example to all believers in what you say,
in the way you live, in your love, your faith, and your purity."

— 1 TIMOTHY 4:12 (NLT)

Additional Scripture References:

Titus 2:7-8: "And you yourself must be an example to them by doing good works of every kind. Let everything you do reflect the integrity and seriousness of your teaching. Teach the truth so that your teaching can't be criticized."

Philippians 2:15: "So that no one can criticize you. Live clean, innocent lives as children of God, shining like bright lights in a world full of crooked and perverse people."

Devotional Thought:

Godly men lead by example, showing others Christ's love, faith, and purity through their actions. By being a role model, we invite others to follow Christ. Today, let your words and actions set a godly example, inspiring others to walk in faith.

Reflection Questions

Are there people in your life who look up to you as an example?

How does leading by example deepen your commitment to God?

What steps can you take to be a godly influence in others' lives?

Prayer for the Day

Father, help me to be an example of Your love and truth. Let my life reflect Christ's character, inspiring others to know and follow You. Amen.

June 14

Strength Through Humility

"Humble yourselves before the Lord,
and he will lift you up in honor."

— JAMES 4:10 (NLT)

Additional Scripture References:

1 Peter 5:6: "So humble yourselves under the mighty power of God, and at the right time he will lift you up in honor."

Proverbs 22:4: "True humility and fear of the Lord lead to riches, honor, and long life."

Devotional Thought:

Humility is a strength, allowing us to rely fully on God and giving Him the glory in all we do. By choosing humility, we honor God and allow His grace to work in our lives. Today, let humility guide your actions, showing others that true strength comes from God.

Reflection Questions

Are there situations where humility could deepen your faith?

How does relying on God strengthen you in times of weakness?

What steps can you take to practice humility in daily life?

Prayer for the Day

Lord, teach me the strength of humility. Help me to rely on Your power and give You glory in all I do, showing others the beauty of a humble spirit. Amen.

June 15

Loving Others as Christ Loves

"A new command I give you: Love one another.
As I have loved you, so you must love one another."

— JOHN 13:34 (NLT)

Additional Scripture References:

1 John 4:7: "Dear friends, let us continue to love one another, for love comes from God. Anyone who loves is a child of God and knows God."

Matthew 22:37-39: "Jesus replied, 'You must love the Lord your God with all your heart, all your soul, and all your mind.' This is the first and greatest commandment. A second is equally important: 'Love your neighbor as yourself.'"

Devotional Thought:

Godly men are called to love others selflessly, reflecting the love of Christ in all relationships. True love is seen in kindness, patience, and forgiveness. Today, let Christ's love fill your heart, allowing you to love others in a way that honors Him.

Reflection Questions

Are there people in your life who need to experience Christ's love through you?

How does loving others deepen your walk with God?

What steps can you take to make love a defining quality of your character?

Prayer for the Day

Father, let my love reflect Christ's compassion and grace. Help me to love others as You love me, bringing kindness and hope to those around me. Amen.

June 16

Living with Purpose and Integrity

"The righteous man walks in his integrity;
his children are blessed after him."

— PROVERBS 20:7 (NKJV)

Additional Scripture References:

Proverbs 11:3 (NKJV): "The integrity of the upright will guide them, but the perversity of the unfaithful will destroy them."

Psalm 112:1-2 (NKJV): "Praise the Lord! Blessed is the man who fears the Lord, who delights greatly in His commandments. His descendants will be mighty on earth; the generation of the upright will be blessed."

Devotional Thought:

Integrity is the foundation of a godly life, creating a legacy that blesses future generations. By living with purpose and honesty, we honor God and influence those around us. Today, let integrity guide your actions, building a legacy of faith and righteousness.

Reflection Questions

Are there areas in your life where integrity needs to be strengthened?

How does living with integrity impact those around you?

What steps can you take to walk consistently in godly integrity?

Prayer for the Day

Lord, let integrity be the foundation of my life. Help me to live with purpose, honoring You in all I do and leaving a legacy of faith. Amen.

Faithfulness in Every Season

*"Now, a person who is put in charge
as a manager must be faithful."*

— **1 CORINTHIANS 4:2 (NLT)**

Additional Scripture References:

Luke 16:10: *"If you are faithful in little things, you will be faithful in large ones. But if you are dishonest in little things, you won't be honest with greater responsibilities."*

Matthew 25:21: *"The master said, 'Well done, my good and faithful servant. You have been faithful in handling this small amount, so now I will give you many more responsibilities. Let's celebrate together!'"*

Devotional Thought:

Godly men are faithful in every season, remaining committed to God's purpose no matter the circumstances. Faithfulness strengthens our relationship with God and builds trust in all areas of life. Today, let faithfulness guide you, showing others the stability and strength found in God.

Reflection Questions

Are there challenges where faithfulness is especially difficult?

How does staying committed to God deepen your faith?

What steps can you take to remain faithful in all you do?

Prayer for the Day

Father, help me to be faithful in every season. Strengthen my commitment to You, allowing my life to reflect stability and trust in Your purpose. Amen.

June 18

Courageous Faith

"Have I not commanded you? Be strong and courageous.
Do not be afraid; do not be discouraged, for the Lord your
God will be with you wherever you go."

— JOSHUA 1:9 (NLT)

Additional Scripture References:

Deuteronomy 31:6: "So be strong and courageous! Do not be afraid and do not panic before them. For the Lord your God will personally go ahead of you. He will neither fail you nor abandon you."

Isaiah 41:10: "Don't be afraid, for I am with you. Don't be discouraged, for I am your God. I will strengthen you and help you. I will hold you up with my victorious right hand."

Devotional Thought:

Godly manhood requires courageous faith, trusting in God's presence and strength through every challenge. By stepping out in faith, we grow in our reliance on Him. Today, embrace courage as you face life's obstacles, knowing that God is with you every step of the way.

Reflection Questions

Are there areas where you need courage to trust God more fully?

How does relying on God's presence give you strength?

What steps can you take to strengthen your courage in faith?

Prayer for the Day

Lord, give me courage to follow Your path. Help me to trust in Your presence and strength, knowing You are with me always. Amen.

Godly Wisdom in Decisions

"If any of you lacks wisdom, let him ask of God,
who gives to all liberally and without reproach,
and it will be given to him."

— James 1:5 (NKJV)

Additional Scripture References:

Proverbs 2:6: "For the Lord grants wisdom! From his mouth come knowledge and understanding."

1 Corinthians 1:30: "God has united you with Christ Jesus. For our benefit God made him to be wisdom itself. Christ made us right with God; he made us pure and holy, and he freed us from sin."

Devotional Thought:

Godly men seek wisdom in every decision, relying on God's guidance rather than their own understanding. Wisdom from God brings peace, clarity, and purpose. Today, ask God for wisdom, allowing His counsel to guide each choice you make.

Reflection Questions

Are there decisions where you need God's wisdom?

How does seeking wisdom bring peace to your heart?

What steps can you take to make seeking God's wisdom a daily practice?

Prayer for the Day

Father, grant me wisdom in all my decisions. Let Your guidance be my foundation, leading me to choices that honor and reflect You. Amen.

Accountability with God and Others

"As iron sharpens iron,
so a friend sharpens a friend."

— PROVERBS 27:17 (NLT)

Additional Scripture References:

Ecclesiastes 4:9-10: "Two are better than one, for they can help each other succeed. If one person falls, the other can reach out and help. But someone who falls alone is in real trouble."

Proverbs 13:20: "Walk with the wise and become wise; associate with fools and get in trouble."

Devotional Thought:

Accountability strengthens godly character, allowing trusted friends to help us grow in faith and integrity. By seeking accountability with others, we open ourselves to guidance, encouragement, and correction. Today, invite godly counsel into your life, letting trusted friends walk alongside you in faith.

Reflection Questions

Are there trusted people in your life who help hold you accountable?

How does accountability strengthen your commitment to God?

What steps can you take to build accountability in your life?

Prayer for the Day

Lord, help me to embrace accountability. Surround me with friends who will encourage, support, and challenge me to grow in faith and integrity. Amen.

The Heart of a Father

*"As a father has compassion on his children,
so the Lord has compassion on those who fear him."*
— PSALM 103:13 (NLT)

Additional Scripture References:

Isaiah 64:8: "And yet, O Lord, you are our Father. We are the clay, and you are the potter. We all are formed by your hand."

Matthew 7:11: "So if you sinful people know how to give good gifts to your children, how much more will your heavenly Father give good gifts to those who ask him."

Devotional Thought:

A father's compassion mirrors God's love for us, offering guidance, comfort, and support. As we grow in compassion, we reflect the heart of God to those around us. Today, let God's example of compassion inspire you to show care, patience, and understanding to others, especially those you lead.

Reflection Questions

Are there ways you can show more compassion to those around you?

How does reflecting God's compassion deepen your relationships?

What steps can you take to embody the heart of a father to others?

Prayer for the Day

Lord, thank You for Your compassionate heart. Help me to reflect that love to others, showing patience, kindness, and care in every interaction. Amen.

June 22

Strength and Guidance as a Father

"For you are my hiding place; you protect me from trouble.
You surround me with songs of victory."

— PSALM 32:7 (NLT)

Additional Scripture References:

| Psalm 91:1-2: *"Those who live in the shelter of the Most High will find rest in the shadow of the Almighty. This I declare about the Lord: He alone is my refuge, my place of safety; he is my God, and I trust him."*

Isaiah 25:4: "For you have been a refuge for the poor, a refuge for the needy in their distress, a shelter from the storm and a shade from the heat."

Devotional Thought:

A godly father offers strength and protection, much like our Heavenly Father. By providing support and guidance, we create an atmosphere of security and encouragement. Today, seek to be a source of strength for others, reflecting God's guidance in all you do.

Reflection Questions

Are there people in your life who look to you for support and guidance?

How does providing strength help others feel secure?

What steps can you take to create an atmosphere of safety and encouragement?

Prayer for the Day

Father, help me to be a source of strength for those around me. Let my words and actions reflect Your protection and care, bringing comfort to those who rely on me. Amen.

Sacrificing for Others

"Greater love has no one than this: to lay down one's
life for one's friends."

— **JOHN 15:13 (NLT)**

Additional Scripture References:

Romans 5:8: "But God showed his great love for us by sending Christ to die for us while we were still sinners."

1 John 3:16: "We know what real love is because Jesus gave up his life for us. So we also ought to give up our lives for our brothers and sisters."

Devotional Thought:

True fatherhood involves self-sacrifice, putting the needs of others above our own. By laying down our desires to support and care for others, we reflect the love of Christ. Today, embrace the power of sacrificial love, letting it deepen your relationships and honor God's call.

Reflection Questions

Are there areas where self-sacrifice could strengthen your relationships?

How does putting others first help you grow in Christ-like love?

What steps can you take to embrace sacrificial love in your daily life?

Prayer for the Day

Lord, give me the strength to put others above myself. Help me to live out Your love through self-sacrifice, reflecting Christ's example to those around me. Amen.

The Role of Discipline in Love

"For the Lord disciplines those he loves,
and he punishes each one he accepts as his child."

— HEBREWS 12:6 (NLT)

Additional Scripture References:

Proverbs 3:11-12: "My child, don't reject the Lord's discipline, and don't be upset when he corrects you. For the Lord corrects those he loves, just as a father corrects a child in whom he delights."

Revelation 3:19: "I correct and discipline everyone I love. So be diligent and turn from your indifference."

Devotional Thought:

Discipline is an act of love, guiding others toward growth and maturity. By setting boundaries and offering correction, we help those we lead become stronger and wiser. Today, let discipline be motivated by love, helping others grow closer to God's purpose for their lives.

Reflection Questions

Are there areas where you need to practice discipline with love?

How does loving discipline strengthen relationships?

What steps can you take to offer guidance with a compassionate heart?

Prayer for the Day

Father, help me to offer discipline with love and compassion. Let my guidance bring growth and strength to those I lead, reflecting Your love in every correction. Amen.

Teaching by Example

*"Direct your children onto the right path, and
when they are older, they will not leave it."*

— PROVERBS 22:6 (NLT)

Additional Scripture References:

*Deuteronomy 6:6-7: "And you must commit yourselves wholeheartedly to
these commands that I am giving you today. Repeat them again and again to
your children. Talk about them when you are at home and when you are on the
road, when you are going to bed and when you are getting up."*

*Ephesians 6:4: "Fathers, do not provoke your children to anger by the way you
treat them. Rather, bring them up in the discipline and instruction that comes
from the Lord."*

Devotional Thought:

A godly father leads by example, showing others the path to follow
through his own actions. By living out God's values, we set a
foundation of faith for future generations. Today, let your life be a
model of integrity, guiding others by example in faith and character.

Reflection Questions

Are there areas where you can lead by example more intentionally?

How does living out your faith influence those around you?

What steps can you take to be a model of integrity and faith?

Prayer for the Day

Lord, help me to lead by example, showing others Your love and truth
through my actions. Let my life be a guide for those seeking to follow
You. Amen.

Embracing Responsibility as a Leader

*"Whoever can be trusted with very little can
also be trusted with much."*

— LUKE 16:10 (NLT)

Additional Scripture References:

*Matthew 25:21: "The master said, 'Well done, my good and faithful servant.
You have been faithful in handling this small amount, so now I will give you
many more responsibilities. Let's celebrate together!'"*

*1 Corinthians 4:2: "Now, a person who is put in charge as a manager must be
faithful."*

Devotional Thought:

Godly leadership requires responsibility and trustworthiness, taking
ownership of what God has entrusted to us. By being faithful in
small things, we grow into greater leadership. Today, let responsibility
guide your actions, knowing that every choice reflects God's calling.

Reflection Questions

Are there responsibilities where you can be more faithful?

How does embracing responsibility strengthen your leadership?

What steps can you take to honor God in all that He has entrusted to
you?

Prayer for the Day

Father, help me to embrace responsibility with a faithful heart. Let my
actions reflect Your trust in me, guiding others through integrity and
care. Amen.

The Strength of a Servant Leader

"But among you it will be different. Whoever wants to be a leader among you must be your servant."

— **MATTHEW 20:26 (NLT)**

Additional Scripture References:

Mark 10:43-44: "But among you it will be different. Whoever wants to be a leader among you must be your servant, and whoever wants to be first among you must be the slave of everyone else."

Philippians 2:5-7: "You must have the same attitude that Christ Jesus had. Though he was God, he did not think of equality with God as something to cling to. Instead, he gave up his divine privileges; he took the humble position of a slave and was born as a human being."

Devotional Thought:

Godly leadership is rooted in service, prioritizing the needs of others above our own. By leading with a servant's heart, we follow Christ's example and inspire others to do the same. Today, let service guide your leadership, reflecting humility and compassion in all you do.

Reflection Questions

Are there areas where you can serve those you lead more intentionally?

How does servant leadership bring you closer to Christ's example?

What steps can you take to make service a foundation of your leadership?

Prayer for the Day

Lord, teach me to lead by serving others. Let my heart be humble and compassionate, following Christ's example in all I do. Amen.

Encouraging and Uplifting Others

*"So encourage each other and build each other up,
just as you are already doing."*
— 1 THESSALONIANS 5:11 (NLT)

Additional Scripture References:

Hebrews 10:24-25: "Let us think of ways to motivate one another to acts of love and good works, and let us not neglect our meeting together, as some people do, but encourage one another, especially now that the day of his return is drawing near."

Galatians 6:2: "Share each other's burdens, and in this way obey the law of Christ."

Devotional Thought:

A godly leader uplifts those around him, offering encouragement and support in times of need. By speaking life and hope into others, we strengthen their faith and confidence. Today, look for ways to encourage others, helping them see their God-given potential.

Reflection Questions

Are there people in your life who need encouragement today?

How does encouraging others build trust and unity?

What steps can you take to make encouragement a regular part of your leadership?

Prayer for the Day

Father, help me to be a source of encouragement. Let my words and actions bring hope and strength, lifting others closer to You. Amen.

Leading with Integrity

"The godly walk with integrity;
blessed are their children who follow them."

— Proverbs 20:7 (NLT)

Additional Scripture References:

Proverbs 11:3: "Integrity guides the upright; wickedness overthrows the sinner."

Psalm 25:21: "May integrity and honesty protect me, for I put my hope in you."

Devotional Thought:

Integrity is the cornerstone of godly leadership, inspiring others to trust and follow with confidence. When we lead with integrity, we build a legacy of faith that impacts future generations. Today, let integrity guide your actions, honoring God in every decision.

Reflection Questions ?

Are there areas in your life where integrity can be strengthened?

How does leading with integrity inspire those around you?

What steps can you take to make integrity a defining part of your leadership?

Prayer for the Day

Lord, let integrity be the foundation of my leadership. Help me to reflect Your truth and honor in all I do, building a legacy that glorifies You. Amen.

June 30

Dependence on God in Leadership

"Trust in the Lord with all your heart;
do not depend on your own understanding."

— PROVERBS 3:5 (NLT)

Additional Scripture References:

Jeremiah 17:7: "But blessed are those who trust in the Lord and have made the Lord their hope and confidence."

Isaiah 26:3: "You will keep in perfect peace all who trust in you, all whose thoughts are fixed on you."

Devotional Thought:

Godly leadership depends on God's wisdom, trusting Him above our own understanding. By relying on God, we lead with confidence, knowing that He will guide us. Today, let dependence on God be your strength, inviting His wisdom into every decision you make.

Reflection Questions

Are there decisions where you need to rely more fully on God's guidance?

How does trusting in God's wisdom strengthen your leadership?

What steps can you take to make dependence on God a daily practice?

Prayer for the Day

Father, help me to depend on You in all I do. Let Your wisdom guide my leadership, reflecting trust and confidence in Your plans. Amen.

Faith Over Fear

"For God has not given us a spirit of fear and timidity,
but of power, love, and self-discipline."

— 2 TIMOTHY 1:7 (NLT)

Additional Scripture References:

Jeremiah 17:7: "But blessed are those who trust in the Lord and have made the Lord their hope and confidence."

Isaiah 26:3: "You will keep in perfect peace all who trust in you, all whose thoughts are fixed on you."

Devotional Thought:

Fear can often paralyze us, but God has given us a spirit of power, love, and sound mind. By trusting in His strength, we can face challenges with confidence. Today, let your faith rise above any fears, knowing that God's spirit is within you, equipping you with everything you need.

Reflection Questions

Are there fears that have been holding you back?

How does embracing God's power help you overcome these fears?

What steps can you take to strengthen your faith and reject fear?

Prayer for the Day

Lord, thank You for giving me a spirit of power and love. Help me to let go of fear, trusting in Your strength to face any challenges. Amen.

July 2

Trusting God's Control

*"The Lord is my light and my salvation
— so why should I be afraid?"*

— PSALM 27:1 (NLT)

Additional Scripture References:

Isaiah 41:10: "Don't be afraid, for I am with you. Don't be discouraged, for I am your God. I will strengthen you and help you. I will hold you up with my victorious right hand."

2 Timothy 1:7: "For God has not given us a spirit of fear and timidity, but of power, love, and self-discipline."

Devotional Thought:

When we place our trust in God's sovereignty, fear begins to lose its grip. He is our light, guiding us through every circumstance. Today, focus on the comfort of God's presence, trusting that He is with you in every situation.

Reflection Questions

Are there areas in your life where fear has crept in?

How does remembering God's control bring you peace?

What steps can you take to let go of control and trust in Him fully?

Prayer for the Day

Father, help me to rest in Your control, releasing any fear that holds me back. Let my trust be rooted in Your strength and salvation. Amen.

July 3

Facing the Unknown with Faith

"So don't worry about tomorrow, for tomorrow
will bring its own worries. Today's trouble is enough for today."

— MATTHEW 6:34 (NLT)

Additional Scripture References:

Philippians 4:6-7: "Don't worry about anything; instead, pray about everything. Tell God what you need, and thank him for all he has done. Then you will experience God's peace, which exceeds anything we can understand."

1 Peter 5:7: "Give all your worries and cares to God, for he cares about you."

Devotional Thought:

Uncertainty can be daunting, but God calls us to trust Him one day at a time. By focusing on today's challenges, we grow in faith and avoid the fear of the unknown. Today, trust that God is already in your future, preparing a way for you.

Reflection Questions

Are there uncertainties that are causing you fear?

How does focusing on today's challenges help you build faith?

What steps can you take to surrender tomorrow's worries to God?

Prayer for the Day

Lord, help me to trust You with my future. Let my heart be filled with peace, knowing that You are already there, guiding my path. Amen.

Confidence in God's Promises

*"I sought the Lord, and he answered me; he delivered
me from all my fears."*

— PSALM 34:4 (NLT)

Additional Scripture References:

*1 John 5:14: "And we are confident that he hears us whenever we ask for
anything that pleases him."*

*Philippians 4:6: "Don't worry about anything; instead, pray about everything.
Tell God what you need, and thank him for all he has done."*

Devotional Thought:

When we seek God and stand on His promises, we find freedom
from fear. His faithfulness provides a foundation of confidence
and peace. Today, let God's promises remind you that He is faithful,
delivering you from every fear.

Reflection Questions

Are there fears you need to surrender to God?

How does recalling God's promises bring you peace?

What steps can you take to remember His faithfulness daily?

Prayer for the Day

Father, thank You for Your promises. Help me to release my fears to
You, trusting in Your power to deliver and guide me. Amen.

July 5

Faith That Moves Mountains

*"I tell you the truth, if you had faith even
as small as a mustard seed, you could say to this mountain,
'Move from here to there,' and it would move."*

— MATTHEW 17:20 (NLT)

Additional Scripture References:

Luke 1:37: "For nothing will be impossible with God."

*Mark 9:23: "What do you mean, 'If I can'?" Jesus asked. "Anything is possible
if a person believes."*

Devotional Thought:

Even the smallest amount of faith has the power to overcome great
challenges. By placing our trust in God, we can face any obstacle
with hope and courage. Today, let faith lead you, believing that God is
able to move every mountain in your path.

Reflection Questions

Are there obstacles in your life that feel overwhelming?

How does trusting God with small faith impact your outlook?

What steps can you take to practice faith in the face of challenges?

Prayer for the Day

Lord, strengthen my faith to believe that nothing is impossible with
You. Let my trust in You move every mountain in my life. Amen.

July 6

God's Perfect Love Casts Out Fear

"Such love has no fear,
because perfect love expels all fear."

— 1 JOHN 4:18 (NLT)

Additional Scripture References:

Romans 3:23: "For everyone has sinned; we all fall short of God's glorious standard."

1 John 1:9: "If we confess our sins, he is faithful and just to forgive us our sins and to cleanse us from all wickedness."

Devotional Thought:

God's love provides perfect security, driving out fear and replacing it with peace. By resting in His love, we find the courage to face every challenge. Today, let His perfect love fill your heart, casting out all fear and bringing comfort.

Reflection Questions

Are there fears that could be lessened by focusing on God's love?

How does accepting God's love change your approach to fear?

What steps can you take to invite His love into every area of your life?

Prayer for the Day

Father, let Your perfect love fill me completely, casting out all fear. Help me to rest in the security of Your love each day. Amen.

Faith Beyond Feelings

"We live by believing and not by seeing."
— 2 CORINTHIANS 5:7 (NLT)

Additional Scripture References:

Hebrews 11:1: "Faith shows the reality of what we hope for; it is the evidence of things we cannot see."

Romans 8:24-25: "We were given this hope when we were saved. (If we already have something, we don't need to hope for it. But if we look forward to something we don't yet have, we must wait patiently and confidently.)"

Devotional Thought:

True faith isn't based on feelings or circumstances; it's rooted in trust in God's character. When fear arises, we choose faith, believing in God's promises even when we can't see the outcome. Today, let faith guide you beyond any fear or doubt.

Reflection Questions

Are there moments where fear tries to influence your faith?

How does trusting beyond feelings bring strength to your life?

What steps can you take to let faith guide you, not fear?

Prayer for the Day

Lord, help me to walk by faith, not by sight. Let my trust be rooted in Your promises, guiding me beyond any fear or doubt. Amen.

July 8

God's Peace in Every Storm

*"Then he got up and rebuked the wind and the waves,
and suddenly there was a great calm."*

— MATTHEW 8:26 (NLT)

Additional Scripture References:

*Mark 4:39: "When Jesus woke up, he rebuked the wind and said to the waves,
'Silence! Be still!' Suddenly the wind stopped, and there was a great calm."*

*Isaiah 41:10: "Don't be afraid, for I am with you. Don't be discouraged, for I
am your God. I will strengthen you and help you. I will hold you up with my
victorious right hand."*

Devotional Thought:

Jesus calmed the storm with a word, reminding us that He holds
authority over every trial. When we face life's storms, we can rest in
the peace He offers, knowing that He is with us. Today, let God's peace
calm your heart, trusting that He is in control.

Reflection Questions

Are there storms in your life that are causing fear?

How does trusting in God's authority over all things bring you peace?

What steps can you take to invite His calm into your heart?

Prayer for the Day

Father, calm every storm in my life with Your peace. Let my heart find
rest in Your presence, knowing that You are in control of all things.
Amen.

Bold Faith Despite Fear

*"So be strong and courageous! Do not be afraid or discouraged.
For the Lord your God is with you wherever you go."*

— JOSHUA 1:9 (NLT)

Additional Scripture References:

Deuteronomy 31:6: "So be strong and courageous! Do not be afraid and do not panic before them. For the Lord your God will personally go ahead of you. He will neither fail you nor abandon you."

Isaiah 41:10: "Don't be afraid, for I am with you. Don't be discouraged, for I am your God. I will strengthen you and help you. I will hold you up with my victorious right hand."

Devotional Thought:

Courage doesn't mean the absence of fear; it means choosing faith even when fear is present. When we trust God's presence, we can boldly face any challenge. Today, let God's promise of companionship give you the strength to be courageous.

Reflection Questions

Are there areas where fear has held you back?

How does trusting God's presence enable you to be courageous?

What steps can you take to face challenges with bold faith?

Prayer for the Day

Lord, help me to be bold and courageous. Let Your presence strengthen me, guiding me through every challenge with faith and confidence. Amen.

The Steadfastness of Faith

"Let us hold tightly without wavering to the hope we affirm,
for God can be trusted to keep his promise."

— HEBREWS 10:23 (NLT)

Additional Scripture References:

Romans 15:13: *"I pray that God, the source of hope, will fill you completely with joy and peace because you trust in him. Then you will overflow with confident hope through the power of the Holy Spirit."*

1 Thessalonians 5:24: *"The one who calls you is faithful, and he will do it."*

Devotional Thought:

Faith means holding onto hope, trusting that God will fulfill His promises. When fear tries to shake us, we stay steadfast, grounded in God's faithfulness. Today, cling to God's promises, trusting that He is unwavering in His love for you.

Reflection Questions

Are there promises from God that you need to hold tightly to?

How does steadfast faith help you overcome fear?

What steps can you take to remind yourself of God's faithfulness daily?

Prayer for the Day

Father, let my faith be steadfast and unshakable. Help me to trust in Your promises, knowing that You are faithful in every way. Amen.

God's Desire to Heal

"He heals the brokenhearted and bandages their wounds."

— PSALM 147:3 (NLT)

Additional Scripture References:

Isaiah 61:1: "*The Spirit of the Sovereign Lord is upon me, for the Lord has anointed me to bring good news to the poor. He has sent me to comfort the brokenhearted and to proclaim that captives will be released and prisoners will be freed."*

Matthew 11:28: "*Then Jesus said, 'Come to me, all of you who are weary and carry heavy burdens, and I will give you rest.'"*

Devotional Thought:

God cares deeply about our pain, and His desire is to bring healing to our hearts and bodies. When we turn to Him with our hurts, He lovingly brings comfort and restoration. Today, trust that God sees your wounds and is ready to bring healing to your life.

Reflection Questions

Are there areas in your life where you need God's healing touch?

How does knowing God's compassion bring peace to your heart?

What steps can you take to invite God's healing into your life?

Prayer for the Day

Lord, thank You for being a healer of my heart and soul. Let Your love bring comfort and restoration to every area that needs healing. Amen.

Healing Through Faith

"Daughter, your faith has made you well. Go in peace.
Your suffering is over."

— MARK 5:34 (NLT)

Additional Scripture References:

Matthew 9:22: "But Jesus turned around and when he saw her, he said,
'Daughter, be encouraged! Your faith has healed you.' And the woman was
healed at that moment."

James 5:15: "Such a prayer offered in faith will heal the sick, and the Lord will
make you well. And if you have committed any sins, you will be forgiven."

Devotional Thought:

Faith has the power to bring healing, not only physically but spiritually and emotionally as well. When we place our trust in God, we invite His power to work in our lives. Today, let faith fill your heart, believing that God's healing is available to you.

Reflection Questions

Are there areas where you need to increase your faith in God's healing power?

How does trusting in God bring peace to your mind and body?

What steps can you take to nurture faith as you seek healing?

Prayer for the Day

Father, strengthen my faith to believe in Your healing power. Help me to trust You fully, knowing that You are able to bring peace and restoration. Amen.

July 13

Healing of the Heart

"Create in me a clean heart, O God, and
renew a right spirit within me."
— PSALM 51:10 (NLT)

Additional Scripture References:

Ezekiel 36:26: "And I will give you a new heart, and I will put a new spirit
in you. I will take out your stony, stubborn heart and give you a tender,
responsive heart."

2 Corinthians 5:17: "This means that anyone who belongs to Christ has become
a new person. The old life is gone; a new life has begun!"

Devotional Thought:

Healing begins in the heart. When we allow God to cleanse and
renew our spirit, we find inner peace and wholeness. Today, open
your heart to God's transformative love, inviting Him to heal any hurts
and bring restoration from within.

Reflection Questions

Are there wounds in your heart that need God's healing touch?

How does inviting God to renew your spirit bring peace to your life?

What steps can you take to allow God to heal you from within?

Prayer for the Day

Lord, renew my heart and bring healing to every hidden hurt. Let my
spirit be refreshed by Your love and filled with peace. Amen.

July 14

Healing Through Forgiveness

*"Forgive us our sins, for we also forgive
everyone who sins against us."*

— **LUKE 11:4 (NLT)**

Additional Scripture References:

Matthew 6:12: "And forgive us our sins, as we have forgiven those who sin against us."

James 1:13: "And remember, when you are being tempted, do not say, 'God is tempting me.' God is never tempted to do wrong, and he never tempts anyone else."

Devotional Thought:

Forgiveness is a powerful act that brings freedom and healing to our souls. By releasing resentment and bitterness, we allow God's peace to fill our hearts. Today, choose to forgive, inviting God to bring healing and wholeness through grace.

Reflection Questions

Are there people in your life you need to forgive for healing to begin?

How does forgiveness free you from the weight of hurt?

What steps can you take to make forgiveness a regular practice?

Prayer for the Day

Father, help me to forgive those who have hurt me. Let forgiveness be a pathway to healing, filling my heart with peace and freedom. Amen.

Resting in God's Healing Presence

"Come to me, all of you who are weary and carry heavy burdens, and I will give you rest."

— MATTHEW 11:28 (NLT)

Additional Scripture References:

Psalm 55:22: "Give your burdens to the Lord, and he will take care of you. He will not permit the godly to slip and fall."

1 Peter 5:7: "Give all your worries and cares to God, for he cares about you."

Devotional Thought:

God invites us to bring our burdens to Him, where we find rest and healing in His presence. When we lay down our worries and cares, His peace fills our hearts. Today, let go of anything weighing you down, trusting that God's presence brings comfort and renewal.

Reflection Questions ?

Are there burdens you need to release to God for healing?

How does resting in God's presence bring peace to your life?

What steps can you take to make resting in God a part of your daily routine?

Prayer for the Day

Lord, help me to release my burdens to You. Let my heart be filled with peace and healing as I rest in Your presence. Amen.

Faith in God's Timing for Healing

"Wait patiently for the Lord. Be brave and courageous.
Yes, wait patiently for the Lord."

— PSALM 27:14 (NLT)

Additional Scripture References:

Isaiah 40:31: "But those who trust in the Lord will find new strength. They will soar high on wings like eagles. They will run and not grow weary. They will walk and not faint."

Lamentations 3:25-26: "The Lord is good to those who depend on him, to those who search for him. So it is good to wait quietly for salvation from the Lord."

Devotional Thought:

Healing sometimes takes time, and trusting God's timing requires patience and courage. By waiting on God, we open ourselves to His perfect work in our lives. Today, let faith give you patience, trusting that God's timing for healing is always best.

Reflection Questions

Are there areas in your life where you need to trust God's timing for healing?

How does patience in God's timing strengthen your faith?

What steps can you take to embrace patience and trust in your healing journey?

Prayer for the Day

Father, help me to wait patiently for Your healing in my life. Strengthen my faith to trust Your perfect timing and work in every area. Amen.

Healing Through God's Word

"He sent out his word and healed them,
snatching them from the door of death."

— PSALM 107:20 (NLT)

Additional Scripture References:

Isaiah 55:11: "*It is the same with my word. I send it out, and it always produces fruit. It will accomplish all I want it to, and it will prosper everywhere I send it.*"

James 5:15: "*Such a prayer offered in faith will heal the sick, and the Lord will make you well. And if you have committed any sins, you will be forgiven.*"

Devotional Thought:

God's Word has the power to heal, bringing comfort, guidance, and strength. By immersing ourselves in Scripture, we invite His healing presence into our lives. Today, let God's Word refresh your soul, bringing peace and restoration to your spirit.

Reflection Questions

Are there Scriptures that bring you comfort and healing?

How does spending time in God's Word renew your spirit?

What steps can you take to make Scripture a part of your daily healing journey?

Prayer for the Day

Lord, thank You for the healing power of Your Word. Let it refresh and restore me, bringing comfort to every area of my life. Amen.

July 18

Healing Through Surrender

"Give all your worries and
cares to God, for he cares about you."
— 1 PETER 5:7 (NLT)

Additional Scripture References:

Philippians 4:6-7: "Don't worry about anything; instead, pray about everything. Tell God what you need, and thank him for all he has done. Then you will experience God's peace, which exceeds anything we can understand."

Matthew 6:25: "That is why I tell you not to worry about everyday life — whether you have enough food and drink, or enough clothes to wear. Isn't life more than food, and your body more than clothing?"

Devotional Thought:

Surrendering our cares to God opens the door for His healing touch. By trusting in His care, we allow Him to bring peace and restoration. Today, let go of anything that burdens your heart, allowing God to bring healing through surrender.

Reflection Questions

Are there worries or hurts you need to surrender to God?

How does releasing your cares to God bring peace and healing?

What steps can you take to practice surrender in your daily life?

Prayer for the Day

Father, help me to surrender every worry and hurt to You. Let my heart be open to Your healing touch as I trust in Your care. Amen.

Healing in God's Grace

"My grace is all you need.
My power works best in weakness."

— 2 CORINTHIANS 12:9 (NLT)

Additional Scripture References:

Isaiah 40:29: "He gives power to the weak and strength to the powerless."

Philippians 4:13: "For I can do everything through Christ, who gives me strength."

Devotional Thought:

God's grace meets us in our weakness, providing strength and healing. By leaning on His grace, we find comfort, courage, and renewal. Today, embrace the gift of God's grace, knowing that His power is made perfect in your weakness.

Reflection Questions

Are there areas where you need God's grace to heal your heart?

How does relying on God's grace bring comfort and strength?

What steps can you take to accept and rely on His grace each day?

Prayer for the Day

Lord, thank You for Your grace that sustains me. Let Your strength be made perfect in my weakness, bringing healing to my heart and life. Amen.

July 20

Faith and Hope in God's Healing

*"But for you who fear my name, the Sun of Righteousness
will rise with healing in his wings."*

— MALACHI 4:2 (NLT)

Additional Scripture References:

*Isaiah 58:8: "Then your salvation will come like the dawn, and your wounds
will quickly heal. Your godliness will lead you forward, and the glory of the
Lord will protect you from behind."*

*Luke 1:78-79: "Because of God's tender mercy, the morning light from heaven
is about to break upon us, to give light to those who sit in darkness and in the
shadow of death, and to guide us to the path of peace."*

Devotional Thought:

God promises healing for those who place their hope in Him. His
love brings light, hope, and restoration to every area of life. Today,
let faith and hope rise in your heart, believing that God's healing is at
work even when you cannot see it.

Reflection Questions

Are there areas where hope in God's healing can bring comfort?

How does placing your hope in God deepen your faith?

What steps can you take to keep hope alive in your healing journey?

Prayer for the Day

Father, let hope fill my heart as I trust in Your healing power. Help
me to believe in Your promises, knowing that You bring restoration to
every area of my life. Amen.

Casting Anxiety on God

*"Give all your worries and
cares to God, for he cares about you."*

— 1 PETER 5:7 (NLT)

Additional Scripture References:

*Philippians 4:6-7: "Don't worry about anything; instead, pray about
everything. Tell God what you need, and thank him for all he has done. Then
you will experience God's peace, which exceeds anything we can understand."*

*Matthew 11:28: "Then Jesus said, 'Come to me, all of you who are weary and
carry heavy burdens, and I will give you rest.'"*

Devotional Thought:

God invites us to release our worries to Him, reminding us that we
are not alone in our struggles. When we place our cares in His
hands, we find peace that surpasses understanding. Today, let go of
any anxieties, trusting that God's care is greater than your worries.

Reflection Questions

Are there anxieties that you need to release to God today?

How does giving your worries to God bring peace to your life?

What steps can you take to make surrendering your anxieties a daily
practice?

Prayer for the Day

Lord, help me to cast my cares upon You. Let Your love bring comfort
and peace to my heart, knowing that You care for me deeply. Amen.

God's Peace in Place of Worry

"Don't worry about anything; instead,
pray about everything."

— **PHILIPPIANS 4:6 (NLT)**

Additional Scripture References:

1 Thessalonians 5:16-18: "Always be joyful. Never stop praying. Be thankful in all circumstances, for this is God's will for you who belong to Christ Jesus."

Matthew 6:25: "That is why I tell you not to worry about everyday life — whether you have enough food and drink, or enough clothes to wear. Isn't life more than food, and your body more than clothing?"

Devotional Thought:

Prayer replaces worry, allowing God's peace to fill our hearts and minds. When we bring our concerns to God, He provides calm in the midst of life's challenges. Today, let prayer guide you through any anxiety, inviting God's peace to cover every concern.

Reflection Questions

Are there worries you need to bring to God in prayer?

How does turning worry into prayer strengthen your faith?

What steps can you take to make prayer your first response to anxiety?

Prayer for the Day

Father, help me to turn every worry into prayer. Let Your peace fill my heart as I trust You with all my concerns. Amen.

Trusting God's Provision

*"And this same God who takes care of me will supply
all your needs from his glorious riches."*

— PHILIPPIANS 4:19 (NLT)

Additional Scripture References:

*Matthew 6:31-33: "So don't worry about these things, saying, 'What will
we eat? What will we drink? What will we wear?' These things dominate
the thoughts of unbelievers, but your heavenly Father already knows all your
needs. Seek the Kingdom of God above all else and live righteously, and he will
give you everything you need."*

*2 Corinthians 9:8: "And God will generously provide all you need. Then you
will always have everything you need and plenty left over to share with others."*

Devotional Thought:

Anxiety often stems from fear about the future, but God promises
to meet our needs according to His riches. By trusting in His
provision, we release our worries and embrace His care. Today, let go
of financial or material anxieties, trusting that God is faithful to provide.

Reflection Questions ?

Are there areas where you struggle to trust God's provision?

How does focusing on God's faithfulness bring peace to your life?

What steps can you take to trust His provision more fully?

Prayer for the Day

Lord, help me to trust in Your provision. Let my heart be at peace,
knowing that You supply all my needs according to Your riches. Amen.

Finding Strength in Weakness

"My grace is all you need.
My power works best in weakness."

— **2 CORINTHIANS 12:9 (NLT)**

Additional Scripture References:

Isaiah 40:29: "He gives power to the weak and strength to the powerless."

Philippians 4:13: "For I can do everything through Christ, who gives me strength."

Devotional Thought:

Anxiety can make us feel weak, but God's grace turns weakness into strength. By leaning on Him, we find courage and resilience. Today, embrace God's strength, allowing His grace to turn your anxieties into a source of deeper trust and dependence.

Reflection Questions

Are there areas of weakness where you need God's strength?

How does accepting your weaknesses open you to God's grace?

What steps can you take to rely on God's strength in times of anxiety?

Prayer for the Day

Father, let Your grace be my strength. Help me to embrace my weaknesses, knowing that Your power works through them for my good. Amen.

Focusing on God's Faithfulness

*"But the Lord is faithful; he will strengthen you
and guard you from the evil one."*

— 2 THESSALONIANS 3:3 (NLT)

Additional Scripture References:

1 Corinthians 10:13: "The temptations in your life are no different from what others experience. And God is faithful. He will not allow the temptation to be more than you can stand. When you are tempted, he will show you a way out so that you can endure."

Psalm 121:7-8: "The Lord keeps you from all harm and watches over your life. The Lord keeps watch over you as you come and go, both now and forever."

Devotional Thought:

God's faithfulness provides a foundation of peace, reminding us that He protects and strengthens us. By focusing on His past faithfulness, we find assurance for today and confidence for tomorrow. Today, let gratitude for God's faithfulness replace any anxious thoughts.

Reflection Questions

Are there memories of God's faithfulness that can bring you peace today?

How does reflecting on God's faithfulness help you overcome anxiety?

What steps can you take to keep gratitude for God's faithfulness at the forefront of your mind?

Prayer for the Day

Lord, thank You for Your unwavering faithfulness. Let my heart be filled with gratitude, replacing anxiety with confidence in Your love. Amen.

July 26

Hope in the Midst of Depression

"Why am I discouraged? Why is my heart so sad?
I will put my hope in God!"

— PSALM 42:11 (NLT)

Additional Scripture References:

Romans 15:13: "I pray that God, the source of hope, will fill you completely with joy and peace because you trust in him. Then you will overflow with confident hope through the power of the Holy Spirit."

Psalm 43:5: "Why am I discouraged? Why is my heart so sad? I will put my hope in God! I will praise him again — my Savior and my God."

Devotional Thought:

Depression can feel overwhelming, but putting our hope in God offers a way forward. By focusing on His promises and presence, we find light even in dark moments. Today, place your hope in God, trusting that He is with you, bringing strength and comfort.

Reflection Questions

Are there areas where hope feels hard to hold onto?

How does placing hope in God bring strength during difficult times?

What steps can you take to nurture hope and faith daily?

Prayer for the Day

Father, help me to hold onto hope, even when it's difficult. Let Your presence be my comfort and strength in every moment of sadness. Amen.

God's Nearness in Times of Trouble

"The Lord is close to the brokenhearted; he rescues those whose spirits are crushed."

— PSALM 34:18 (NLT)

Additional Scripture References:

Isaiah 61:1: "The Spirit of the Sovereign Lord is upon me, for the Lord has anointed me to bring good news to the poor. He has sent me to comfort the brokenhearted and to proclaim that captives will be released and prisoners will be freed."

Matthew 11:28: "Then Jesus said, 'Come to me, all of you who are weary and carry heavy burdens, and I will give you rest.'"

Devotional Thought:

In times of depression, God draws near, offering comfort to the brokenhearted. His presence brings healing and rescue when we feel crushed. Today, let God's nearness fill you with peace, knowing that He is by your side, ready to heal and uplift.

Reflection Questions

Are there burdens on your heart you need to share with God?

How does experiencing God's nearness bring comfort during hard times?

What steps can you take to invite His presence into moments of sadness?

Prayer for the Day

Lord, thank You for being close to me in times of trouble. Let Your presence bring peace and comfort to my heart, healing every broken part. Amen.

Resting in God's Comfort

"Even when I walk through the darkest valley,
I will not be afraid, for you are close beside me."

— PSALM 23:4 (NLT)

Additional Scripture References:

Isaiah 43:2: "When you go through deep waters, I will be with you. When you go through rivers of difficulty, you will not drown. When you walk through the fire of oppression, you will not be burned up; the flames will not consume you."

2 Timothy 1:7: "For God has not given us a spirit of fear and timidity, but of power, love, and self-discipline."

Devotional Thought:

In dark seasons, God's comfort is our source of peace. He walks with us, offering strength and guidance through every valley. Today, rest in the assurance that God is close, carrying you through any hardships and replacing fear with peace.

Reflection Questions

Are there areas of your life where you need God's comfort?

How does knowing God is with you bring peace in difficult times?

What steps can you take to find comfort in God's presence daily?

Prayer for the Day

Father, let Your comfort be my strength. Walk with me through every valley, filling my heart with peace and assurance. Amen.

July 29

Overcoming Despair with God's Joy

"The joy of the Lord is your strength!"
— **NEHEMIAH 8:10 (NLT)**

Additional Scripture References:

Psalm 16:11: "You will show me the way of life, granting me the joy of your presence and the pleasures of living with you forever."

John 15:11: "I have told you these things so that you will be filled with my joy. Yes, your joy will overflow!"

Devotional Thought:

Depression can cloud our joy, but God's presence fills us with strength and hope. His joy renews us, bringing light into dark places. Today, let God's joy be your strength, lifting your spirit and reminding you of His unending love.

Reflection Questions

Are there things that bring you joy and help you connect with God?

How does focusing on God's joy provide strength during struggles?

What steps can you take to invite His joy into your heart daily?

Prayer for the Day

Lord, let Your joy be my strength. Fill my heart with gladness and peace, even in times of difficulty, reminding me of Your unchanging love. Amen.

July 30

Finding Light in Darkness

*"The light shines in the darkness,
and the darkness can never extinguish it."*

— **JOHN 1:5 (NLT)**

Additional Scripture References:

Matthew 5:14: "You are the light of the world — like a city on a hilltop that cannot be hidden."

1 John 1:7: "But if we are living in the light, as God is in the light, then we have fellowship with each other, and the blood of Jesus, his Son, cleanses us from all sin."

Devotional Thought:

No matter how dark our struggles may feel, God's light shines through, bringing hope and comfort. His love is a beacon that guides us out of despair and into His peace. Today, let God's light fill your heart, reminding you that darkness can never overcome His love.

Reflection Questions

Are there dark areas where you need God's light to shine?

How does focusing on God's light provide hope in hard times?

What steps can you take to let His light guide you daily?

Prayer for the Day

Father, let Your light fill my heart, casting out every shadow of despair. Help me to rest in the assurance that Your love is greater than any darkness. Amen.

Renewed Strength for Tomorrow

"But those who trust in the Lord will find new strength.
They will soar high on wings like eagles."

— ISAIAH 40:31 (NLT)

Additional Scripture References:

Psalm 27:14: "Wait patiently for the Lord. Be brave and courageous. Yes, wait patiently for the Lord."

Philippians 4:13: "For I can do everything through Christ, who gives me strength."

Devotional Thought:

Trusting in God renews our strength, allowing us to face each day with hope and courage. As we rely on Him, He lifts us above our troubles and gives us resilience. Today, place your trust fully in God, allowing His strength to carry you forward.

Reflection Questions

Are there areas where you need renewed strength from God?

How does trusting God empower you to face each new day?

What steps can you take to renew your strength in Him daily?

Prayer for the Day

Lord, renew my strength as I trust in You. Let me soar above every challenge, filled with hope, courage, and resilience for the days ahead. Amen.

August 1

Finding Rest in God's Presence

"Come to me, all of you who are weary and carry heavy burdens,
and I will give you rest."

— MATTHEW 11:28 (NLT)

Additional Scripture References:

Psalm 55:22: "Give your burdens to the Lord, and he will take care of you. He will not permit the godly to slip and fall."

1 Peter 5:7: "Give all your worries and cares to God, for he cares about you."

Devotional Thought:

God invites us to lay down our burdens and find true rest in His presence. By bringing our cares to Him, we receive peace and renewal for our souls. Today, let go of your worries, trusting that God's presence provides the rest and comfort you need.

Reflection Questions

Are there burdens you need to release to God?

How does resting in God's presence bring peace to your heart?

What steps can you take to make time for rest in His presence?

Prayer for the Day

Lord, thank You for inviting me into Your rest. Help me to release my burdens and find peace in Your presence, trusting that You care for me. Amen.

Rest for the Body and Soul

"In peace I will lie down and sleep, for you alone,
O Lord, will keep me safe."

— PSALM 4:8 (NLT)

Additional Scripture References:

Philippians 4:6-7: "Don't worry about anything; instead, pray about everything. Tell God what you need, and thank him for all he has done. Then you will experience God's peace, which exceeds anything we can understand."

Isaiah 26:3: "You will keep in perfect peace all who trust in you, all whose thoughts are fixed on you."

Devotional Thought:

Rest is a gift that renews both our bodies and souls, providing strength for each day. When we trust in God's protection, we find true peace and rest. Today, focus on resting in God, letting His peace refresh your body, mind, and spirit.

Reflection Questions

Are there areas of your life where you feel physically or mentally weary?

How does trusting in God's care bring peace to your rest?

What steps can you take to make rest a priority?

Prayer for the Day

Father, thank You for the gift of rest. Let my heart be filled with Your peace, renewing my strength each day. Amen.

August 3

The Sabbath as a Gift of Renewal

*"Then he said to them, 'The Sabbath was made to meet the needs of people,
and not people to meet the requirements of the Sabbath.'"*

— MARK 2:27 (NLT)

Additional Scripture References:

*Matthew 11:28-30: "Come to me, all of you who are weary and carry heavy
burdens, and I will give you rest. Take my yoke upon you. Let me teach you,
because I am humble and gentle at heart, and you will find rest for your souls.
For my yoke is easy to bear, and the burden I give you is light."*

*Luke 6:5: "And Jesus said to them, 'The Son of Man is Lord, even over the
Sabbath.'"*

Devotional Thought:

God designed the Sabbath as a day of rest, allowing us to step back,
renew, and focus on Him. By embracing rest, we honor God and
refresh our spirits. Today, let the Sabbath remind you of the importance
of rest and reflection in God's presence.

Reflection Questions

Are there ways you can incorporate rest into your week?

How does setting aside time for renewal strengthen your relationship
with God?

What steps can you take to make the Sabbath a time of rest and
reflection?

Prayer for the Day

Lord, help me to embrace the Sabbath as a gift of renewal. Let my time
of rest honor You and fill me with peace and strength. Amen.

August 4

Renewing Your Mind Through Rest

"Don't copy the behavior and customs of this world, but let God transform you into a new person by changing the way you think."

— ROMANS 12:2 (NLT)

Additional Scripture References:

2 Corinthians 5:17: "This means that anyone who belongs to Christ has become a new person. The old life is gone; a new life has begun!"

Ephesians 4:23-24: "Instead, let the Spirit renew your thoughts and attitudes. Put on your new nature, created to be like God — truly righteous and holy."

Devotional Thought:

Rest allows us to step away from the world's pressures and renew our minds in God's truth. When we take time to rest, we allow God to transform and refresh our thoughts. Today, make space for quiet reflection, letting God's Word renew and refresh your mind.

Reflection Questions

Are there areas where you feel mentally exhausted?

How does resting in God's presence refresh your mind and heart?

What steps can you take to create moments of reflection each day?

Prayer for the Day

Father, renew my mind and spirit as I rest in You. Let Your Word bring clarity and refreshment to my thoughts, guiding me in Your truth. Amen.

August 5

Resting in God's Provision

"The Lord is my shepherd;
I have all that I need."

— PSALM 23:1 (NLT)

Additional Scripture References:

Philippians 4:19: *"And this same God who takes care of me will supply all your needs from his glorious riches, which have been given to us in Christ Jesus."*

John 10:11: *"I am the good shepherd. The good shepherd sacrifices his life for the sheep."*

Devotional Thought:

When we trust in God's provision, we find peace and rest in His care. Knowing that He provides for every need allows us to let go of worry. Today, rest in the assurance that God is your shepherd, supplying all you need.

Reflection Questions

Are there worries about provision you need to release to God?

How does trusting in God's care bring rest to your heart?

What steps can you take to rely on God's provision daily?

Prayer for the Day

Lord, thank You for being my Shepherd and providing for every need. Help me to find rest in Your care, trusting that You are always with me. Amen.

August 6

Finding Strength Through Rest

*"He gives power to the weak and
strength to the powerless."*

— ISAIAH 40:29 (NLT)

Additional Scripture References:

2 Corinthians 12:9: "Each time he said, 'My grace is all you need. My power works best in weakness.' So now I am glad to boast about my weaknesses, so that the power of Christ can work through me."

Psalm 68:35: "God is awesome in his sanctuary. The God of Israel gives power and strength to his people. Praise be to God!"

Devotional Thought:

Rest restores our strength, allowing us to continue forward with renewed energy. When we embrace rest, we acknowledge our need for God's power. Today, let rest be a source of strength, reminding you that God's power is made perfect in our weakness.

Reflection Questions

Are there areas where you feel weak and in need of God's strength?

How does resting in God renew your energy and focus?

What steps can you take to make rest a source of strength?

Prayer for the Day

Father, thank You for renewing my strength when I am weary. Let rest remind me of Your power, filling my heart with courage and resilience. Amen.

August 7

Rest as a Time to Listen

"Be still, and know that I am God!"
— PSALM 46:10 (NLT)

Additional Scripture References:

Exodus 14:14: "The Lord will fight for you; you need only to be still."

Isaiah 30:15: "This is what the Sovereign Lord, the Holy One of Israel, says: 'In repentance and rest is your salvation, in quietness and trust is your strength.'"

Devotional Thought:

Rest gives us time to be still, quiet our minds, and listen for God's voice. In moments of stillness, we find clarity, direction, and peace. Today, make space for stillness, allowing God's presence to speak to your heart.

Reflection Questions

Are there ways you can quiet your mind to hear God's voice?

How does being still help you connect more deeply with God?

What steps can you take to make stillness a part of your daily routine?

Prayer for the Day

Lord, help me to be still and know that You are God. Let Your presence fill my heart, bringing clarity and peace in every moment. Amen.

The Power of Spiritual Rest

"Return to your rest, my soul, for the Lord has been good to you."
— PSALM 116:7 (NLT)

Additional Scripture References:

Matthew 11:28: "Then Jesus said, 'Come to me, all of you who are weary and carry heavy burdens, and I will give you rest.'"

Psalm 62:1: "I wait quietly before God, for my victory comes from him."

Devotional Thought:

Spiritual rest renews our souls, reminding us of God's goodness and faithfulness. When we pause to rest in Him, our hearts are filled with gratitude and peace. Today, let spiritual rest renew your heart, reflecting on God's blessings and love.

Reflection Questions

Are there spiritual practices that bring rest to your soul?

How does reflecting on God's goodness bring peace to your heart?

What steps can you take to make spiritual rest a regular practice?

Prayer for the Day

Father, let my soul find rest in Your goodness. Help me to remember Your blessings and to trust in Your love each day. Amen.

August 9

Rest as Preparation for Service

*"Then Jesus said, 'Let's go off by ourselves
to a quiet place and rest awhile.'"*

— MARK 6:31 (NLT)

Additional Scripture References:

*Matthew 11:28: "Then Jesus said, 'Come to me, all of you who are weary and
carry heavy burdens, and I will give you rest.'"*

*Psalm 23:2: "He lets me rest in green meadows; he leads me beside peaceful
streams."*

Devotional Thought:

Even Jesus took time to rest, recognizing its importance before
continuing His work. By resting, we prepare ourselves to serve
others with renewed energy and focus. Today, embrace rest as a way to
prepare for the work God has set before you.

Reflection Questions

Are there areas where you need rest before continuing your work?

How does taking time to rest help you serve others more effectively?

What steps can you take to balance rest with service?

Prayer for the Day

Lord, help me to find balance between rest and service. Let rest prepare
my heart, renewing my strength to serve You and others with joy.
Amen.

The Power of Sabbath Rest

*"Observe the Sabbath day by keeping it holy,
as the Lord your God has commanded you."*

— DEUTERONOMY 5:12 (NLT)

Additional Scripture References:

Exodus 20:8: "Remember to observe the Sabbath day by keeping it holy."

Mark 2:27: "Then Jesus said to them, 'The Sabbath was made to meet the needs of the people, and not people to meet the requirements of the Sabbath.'"

Devotional Thought:

The Sabbath is a time to pause, reflect, and find rest in God's presence. By honoring this sacred time, we allow our spirits to be refreshed and focused on His goodness. Today, let Sabbath rest restore your heart, keeping you centered in God's love.

Reflection Questions

Are there ways you can honor the Sabbath as a day of rest and renewal?

How does observing the Sabbath strengthen your connection with God?

What steps can you take to make Sabbath rest a meaningful part of your week?

Prayer for the Day

Lord, help me to honor the Sabbath as a time of rest and renewal. Let my spirit be refreshed in Your presence, focused on Your love and grace. Amen.

God's Gift of Restful Sleep

"In peace I will lie down and sleep, for you alone,
O Lord, will keep me safe."

— PSALM 4:8 (NLT)

Additional Scripture References:

Philippians 4:6-7: "Don't worry about anything; instead, pray about everything. Tell God what you need, and thank him for all he has done. Then you will experience God's peace, which exceeds anything we can understand."

Psalm 127:2: "It is useless for you to work so hard from early morning until late at night, anxiously working for food to eat; for God gives rest to his loved ones."

Devotional Thought:

Sleep is a gift from God, allowing our bodies to rest and recharge. When we trust in His protection, we can sleep peacefully, knowing He watches over us. Tonight, invite God's peace into your rest, letting go of any worries as you sleep.

Reflection Questions

Are there worries keeping you from restful sleep?

How does trusting in God's protection bring peace to your rest?

What steps can you take to make sleep a peaceful time of renewal?

Prayer for the Day

Lord, thank You for the gift of restful sleep. Help me to trust in Your care, letting go of any anxieties as I rest in Your peace. Amen.

August 12

Releasing Worries for a Restful Night

"Give all your worries and cares to God,
for he cares about you."

— 1 PETER 5:7 (NLT)

Additional Scripture References:

Philippians 4:6: "Don't worry about anything; instead, pray about everything. Tell God what you need, and thank him for all he has done."

Matthew 6:25: "That is why I tell you not to worry about everyday life — whether you have enough food and drink, or enough clothes to wear. Isn't life more than food, and your body more than clothing?"

Devotional Thought:

Worry can keep us from sleep, but God invites us to cast every care onto Him. By releasing our concerns, we allow God's peace to fill our hearts and bring restful sleep. Tonight, surrender any lingering worries, trusting that God is in control.

Reflection Questions

Are there worries you need to release before sleep?

How does giving your concerns to God bring peace to your mind?

What steps can you take to practice releasing worries before bed?

Prayer for the Day

Father, help me to release all my worries to You. Let my heart be at peace, knowing that You care for me deeply and guide me through every concern. Amen.

August 13

Finding Renewal Through Sleep

"It is useless for you to work so hard from early morning until late at night, anxiously working for food to eat; for God gives rest to his loved ones."

— PSALM 127:2 (NLT)

Additional Scripture References:

Matthew 11:28: "Then Jesus said, 'Come to me, all of you who are weary and carry heavy burdens, and I will give you rest.'"

Ecclesiastes 3:13: "And people should eat and drink and enjoy the fruits of their labor, for these are gifts from God."

Devotional Thought:

God intends for us to find balance between work and rest, trusting that He provides what we need. When we embrace restful sleep, we receive renewal for the day ahead. Tonight, let sleep refresh you, trusting that God sustains you and provides for your needs.

Reflection Questions

Are there areas of your life where overworking has affected your rest?

How does trusting in God's provision allow you to sleep peacefully?

What steps can you take to prioritize sleep as part of a healthy lifestyle?

Prayer for the Day

Lord, thank You for providing all I need. Help me to rest in Your provision, allowing sleep to renew my strength for each day. Amen.

Strength Through Sleep

"He gives power to the weak and
strength to the powerless."

— ISAIAH 40:29 (NLT)

Additional Scripture References:

2 Corinthians 12:9: "Each time he said, 'My grace is all you need. My power works best in weakness.' So now I am glad to boast about my weaknesses, so that the power of Christ can work through me."

Psalm 68:35: "God is awesome in his sanctuary. The God of Israel gives power and strength to his people. Praise be to God!"

Devotional Thought:

Sleep restores our bodies and minds, giving us strength for the tasks ahead. By prioritizing rest, we acknowledge our dependence on God for renewal and energy. Tonight, let sleep be a source of strength, preparing you to face each day with resilience.

Reflection Questions

Are there ways you can prioritize sleep for better strength and energy?

How does resting in God's care bring peace and strength to your heart?

What steps can you take to make sleep a foundation of strength in your life?

Prayer for the Day

Father, renew my strength through restful sleep. Let my heart and mind be restored, trusting in Your power to sustain me. Amen.

August 15

A Mind at Peace for Restful Sleep

*"You will keep in perfect peace all who trust in you,
all whose thoughts are fixed on you!"*

— ISAIAH 26:3 (NLT)

Additional Scripture References:

Philippians 4:7: "Then you will experience God's peace, which exceeds anything we can understand. His peace will guard your hearts and minds as you live in Christ Jesus."

John 14:27: "I am leaving you with a gift — peace of mind and heart. And the peace I give is a gift the world cannot give. So don't be troubled or afraid."

Devotional Thought:

When our minds are fixed on God, His peace fills our hearts and brings calm to our thoughts. By focusing on Him, we prepare ourselves for restful, uninterrupted sleep. Tonight, let God's peace cover you, allowing every worry to fade as you trust in His love.

Reflection Questions

Are there thoughts or worries that prevent you from sleeping peacefully?

How does focusing on God's presence bring calm to your mind?

What steps can you take to prepare your mind for peaceful sleep?

Prayer for the Day

Lord, let my mind be filled with Your peace. Help me to trust in Your presence, finding rest and calm in Your love. Amen.

Sleep as a Time of Restoration

"Return to your rest, my soul,
for the Lord has been good to you."
— PSALM 116:7 (NLT)

Additional Scripture References:

Psalm 62:1: "I wait quietly before God, for my victory comes from him."

Isaiah 30:15: "This is what the Sovereign LORD, the Holy One of Israel, says: 'Only in returning to me and resting in me will you be saved. In quietness and confidence is your strength.'"

Devotional Thought:

Sleep is a time of restoration, renewing our bodies and souls. By honoring this need, we allow God to replenish our energy and refresh our spirits. Tonight, let sleep restore you, reflecting on God's goodness as you rest.

Reflection Questions

Are there areas of exhaustion where you need God's restoration?

How does reflecting on God's goodness prepare you for peaceful sleep?

What steps can you take to make sleep a time of renewal?

Prayer for the Day

Father, let my soul find rest in Your goodness. Restore my spirit as I sleep, filling me with energy and peace for each new day. Amen.

Trusting God in Our Sleep

"Trust in the Lord with all your heart;
do not depend on your own understanding."
— PROVERBS 3:5 (NLT)

Additional Scripture References:

Jeremiah 17:7: "But blessed are those who trust in the LORD and have made the LORD their hope and confidence."

Psalm 37:5: "Commit everything you do to the LORD. Trust him, and he will help you."

Devotional Thought:

Sleep requires trust, a surrendering of control as we rest in God's care. By trusting Him fully, we let go of the need to handle everything ourselves. Tonight, let trust be your foundation as you sleep, knowing that God is watching over you.

Reflection Questions

Are there areas where you struggle to release control?

How does trusting in God's care allow you to rest more deeply?

What steps can you take to build trust in God as you prepare for sleep?

Prayer for the Day

Lord, help me to trust You fully, releasing all control as I sleep. Let my heart be at peace, knowing You are always near. Amen.

Waking with Gratitude

"This is the day the Lord has made.
We will rejoice and be glad in it."
— PSALM 118:24 (NLT)

Additional Scripture References:

Psalm 16:11: "You will show me the way of life, granting me the joy of your presence and the pleasures of living with you forever."

Philippians 4:4: "Always be full of joy in the Lord. I say it again — rejoice!"

Devotional Thought:

Waking with gratitude for each new day sets the tone for joy and peace. By thanking God for restful sleep and the day ahead, we prepare our hearts for His guidance. Tomorrow morning, let gratitude fill your heart as you rise, ready to embrace the blessings of a new day.

Reflection Questions

Are there blessings you're grateful for as you wake each morning?

How does starting each day with gratitude impact your outlook?

What steps can you take to make gratitude part of your morning routine?

Prayer for the Day

Father, thank You for the gift of each new day. Let my heart be filled with gratitude, rejoicing in the blessings You provide. Amen.

August 19

A Heart Ready to Rest

"The Lord gives his people strength.
The Lord blesses them with peace."

— PSALM 29:11 (NLT)

Additional Scripture References:

Isaiah 40:29: "He gives power to the weak and strength to the powerless."

John 14:27: "I am leaving you with a gift — peace of mind and heart. And the peace I give is a gift the world cannot give. So don't be troubled or afraid."

Devotional Thought:

When our hearts are at peace, we are ready to rest deeply, knowing that God provides strength for each new day. By ending each day with His peace, we prepare ourselves for true rest. Tonight, let God's peace fill your heart, setting you up for a restful night and renewed strength.

Reflection Questions

Are there ways you can end each day with peace and gratitude?

How does trusting in God's strength prepare you for restful sleep?

What steps can you take to make peace a part of your evening routine?

Prayer for the Day

Lord, thank You for Your peace that blesses my heart. Let my rest be filled with calm, trusting in Your strength and care. Amen.

The Power to Fight with God's Strength

*"For the Lord your God is the one who goes with you
to fight for you against your enemies to give you victory."*
— **DEUTERONOMY 20:4 (NLT)**

Additional Scripture References:

Exodus 14:14: "The LORD himself will fight for you. Just stay calm."

Romans 8:31 "If God is for us, who can ever be against us?"

Devotional Thought:

God promises to go before us in every battle, strengthening us and providing victory. When we rely on His power, we find the courage to stand firm. Today, let God's strength guide you in any battles you face, knowing He fights for you.

Reflection Questions

Are there battles you need to surrender to God?

How does trusting in God's strength bring you confidence?

What steps can you take to let God be your strength in difficult times?

Prayer for the Day

Lord, thank You for fighting my battles. Let Your strength fill my heart with courage, giving me victory in all areas of my life. Amen.

Fighting Fear with Faith

"So be strong and courageous! Do not be afraid or discouraged. For the Lord your God is with you wherever you go."

— JOSHUA 1:9 (NLT)

Additional Scripture References:

Deuteronomy 31:6: "So be strong and courageous! Do not be afraid and do not panic before them. For the LORD your God will personally go ahead of you. He will neither fail you nor abandon you."

Isaiah 41:10: "Don't be afraid, for I am with you. Don't be discouraged, for I am your God. I will strengthen you and help you. I will hold you up with my victorious right hand."

Devotional Thought:

Faith is our weapon against fear, reminding us that God is always by our side. By choosing courage over fear, we stand strong in God's promises. Today, let faith replace any fear, knowing that God's presence empowers you in every battle.

Reflection Questions

Are there fears that weaken your courage?

How does faith in God's presence help you overcome fear?

What steps can you take to rely on faith when faced with challenges?

Prayer for the Day

Father, strengthen my faith to overcome any fear. Help me to be courageous, trusting that You are always with me. Amen.

The Armor of God

"Put on all of God's armor so that you will be able to stand firm against all strategies of the devil."
— **EPHESIANS 6:11 (NLT)**

Additional Scripture References:

2 Corinthians 10:4: "We use God's mighty weapons, not worldly weapons, to knock down the strongholds of human reasoning and to destroy false arguments."

Romans 13:12: "The night is almost gone; the day of salvation will soon be here. So remove your dark deeds like dirty clothes, and put on the shining armor of right living."

Devotional Thought:

God equips us with His armor to stand firm against temptation and hardship. By putting on His truth, righteousness, and peace, we are prepared for any spiritual battle. Today, let the armor of God strengthen you, helping you stand firm in faith.

Reflection Questions

Are there areas where you need God's protection and strength?

How does wearing the armor of God prepare you for challenges?

What steps can you take to put on God's armor daily?

Prayer for the Day

Lord, help me to wear Your armor, prepared to stand firm in faith. Let Your truth and righteousness protect me in every situation. Amen.

August 23

Not Ashamed of the Gospel

"For I am not ashamed of this Good News about Christ. It is the power of God at work, saving everyone who believes."

— ROMANS 1:16 (NLT)

Additional Scripture References:

1 Corinthians 1:18: "The message of the cross is foolish to those who are headed for destruction. But we who are being saved know it is the very power of God."

2 Timothy 1:8: "So never be ashamed to tell others about our Lord. And don't be ashamed of me, either, even though I am in prison for him. With the strength God gives you, be ready to suffer with me for the sake of the Good News."

Devotional Thought:

The Gospel is God's gift of salvation, offering hope and truth to all who believe. By embracing it with boldness, we share His love with the world. Today, let the power of the Gospel give you confidence to share your faith without shame.

Reflection Questions

Are there situations where you feel hesitant to share the Gospel?

How does embracing the power of the Gospel strengthen your witness?

What steps can you take to share your faith boldly?

Prayer for the Day

Father, help me to proclaim Your Gospel with confidence. Let my life reflect Your love and truth, bringing hope to those who need it. Amen.

Boldness to Stand for Christ

*"The wicked run away when no one is chasing them,
but the godly are as bold as lions."*

— PROVERBS 28:1 (NLT)

Additional Scripture References:

Psalm 27:1: "The LORD is my light and my salvation — so why should I be afraid? The LORD is my fortress, protecting me from danger, so why should I tremble?"

2 Timothy 1:7: "For God has not given us a spirit of fear and timidity, but of power, love, and self-discipline."

Devotional Thought:

God gives us the courage to stand for truth and righteousness, even when it's challenging. By being bold, we reflect His strength and love to those around us. Today, let your boldness be rooted in God's power, standing firm for Christ.

Reflection Questions

Are there areas where boldness could strengthen your faith?

How does standing for Christ deepen your relationship with God?

What steps can you take to embrace boldness in your daily life?

Prayer for the Day

Lord, grant me the courage to stand for You. Let my life reflect boldness in faith, honoring You in every decision. Amen.

August 25

Standing Against Cultural Pressures

"Do not conform to the pattern of this world,
but be transformed by the renewing of your mind."

— ROMANS 12:2 (NLT)

Additional Scripture References:

2 Corinthians 5:17: "This means that anyone who belongs to Christ has become a new person. The old life is gone; a new life has begun!"

Colossians 3:2: "Think about the things of heaven, not the things of earth."

Devotional Thought:

God calls us to live by His standards, even when they conflict with cultural norms. By aligning our minds with His truth, we find strength to stand firm in faith. Today, let God's Word guide your values, giving you the courage to resist worldly pressures.

Reflection Questions

Are there cultural pressures that challenge your faith?

How does focusing on God's truth empower you to stand firm?

What steps can you take to renew your mind in God's Word daily?

Prayer for the Day

Father, help me to stand firm in Your truth. Let my mind be renewed by Your Word, giving me strength to resist cultural pressures. Amen.

Living by Biblical Standards

*"Your word is a lamp to guide my feet and
a light for my path."*

— PSALM 119:105 (NLT)

Additional Scripture References:

Proverbs 6:23: "For their command is a lamp and their instruction a light; their corrective discipline is the way to life."

John 8:12: "Jesus spoke to the people once more and said, 'I am the light of the world. If you follow me, you won't have to walk in darkness, because you will have the light that leads to life.'"

Devotional Thought:

God's Word provides a foundation of truth and guidance, helping us walk in righteousness. By living according to His standards, we honor Him and reflect His love. Today, let Scripture be your guide, lighting your path and shaping your decisions.

Reflection Questions

Are there areas where you struggle to live by God's standards?

How does relying on God's Word help you stay on His path?

What steps can you take to make Scripture a part of your daily life?

Prayer for the Day

Lord, let Your Word guide my every step. Help me to live according to Your standards, reflecting Your truth in all I do. Amen.

August 27

Building Healthy Disciplines

"Physical training is good, but training for godliness is much better,
promising benefits in this life and in the life to come."

— 1 TIMOTHY 4:8 (NLT)

Additional Scripture References:

1 Corinthians 9:24: "Don't you realize that in a race everyone runs, but only
one person gets the prize? So run to win!"

Hebrews 12:1: "Therefore, since we are surrounded by such a huge crowd of
witnesses to the life of faith, let us strip off every weight that slows us down,
especially the sin that so easily trips us up. And let us run with endurance the
race God has set before us."

Devotional Thought:

Developing spiritual disciplines like prayer, Bible study, and worship builds strength and resilience in our faith. By prioritizing godly practices, we nurture our relationship with God. Today, let discipline guide you, helping you grow in godliness and faith.

Reflection Questions

Are there spiritual disciplines that could strengthen your faith?

How does building healthy routines bring you closer to God?

What steps can you take to incorporate godly practices into your daily life?

Prayer for the Day

Father, help me to build disciplines that nurture my relationship with You. Let my habits reflect a commitment to godliness, growing me in faith. Amen.

August 28

Discipline in Thoughts and Actions

*"We take captive every thought to make
it obedient to Christ."*

— 2 CORINTHIANS 10:5 (NLT)

Additional Scripture References:

Philippians 4:8: "And now, dear brothers and sisters, one final thing. Fix your thoughts on what is true, and honorable, and right, and pure, and lovely, and admirable. Think about things that are excellent and worthy of praise."

Ephesians 4:23: "Instead, let the Spirit renew your thoughts and attitudes."

Devotional Thought:

Discipline starts with our thoughts, shaping how we live and respond to challenges. By taking control of our minds, we align our actions with Christ's teachings. Today, practice discipline in your thoughts, allowing God's truth to guide your mind and behavior.

Reflection Questions

Are there thought patterns that you need to bring under control?

How does aligning your mind with Christ's teachings impact your actions?

What steps can you take to cultivate disciplined thoughts?

Prayer for the Day

Lord, help me to take every thought captive, aligning my mind with Your truth. Let my actions reflect Your love and discipline each day. Amen.

Embracing Change Through God's Power

"And the Spirit of the Lord will transform you
into his image from glory to glory."
— **2 CORINTHIANS 3:18 (NLT)**

Additional Scripture References:

Romans 8:29: "*For God knew his people in advance, and he chose them to become like his Son, so that his Son would be the firstborn among many brothers and sisters.*"

Colossians 3:10: "*Put on your new nature, and be renewed as you learn to know your Creator and become like him.*"

Devotional Thought:

God's power within us allows for transformation, helping us grow closer to His image. By embracing change through His Spirit, we become more like Christ. Today, let God's power work in you, transforming you into His likeness with every step.

Reflection Questions

Are there areas in your life where you need transformation?

How does inviting God's power bring change and growth?

What steps can you take to embrace God's transformation in your life?

Prayer for the Day

Lord, transform my heart to reflect Your image. Let Your Spirit guide me in every change, shaping me to be more like You. Amen.

August 30

The Power to Start Anew

*"Anyone who belongs to Christ has become a new person.
The old life is gone; a new life has begun!"*

— 2 CORINTHIANS 5:17 (NLT)

Additional Scripture References:

*Galatians 2:20: "My old self has been crucified with Christ. It is no longer I
who live, but Christ who lives in me. So I live in this earthly body by trusting
in the Son of God, who loved me and gave himself for me."*

*Ephesians 4:24: "Put on your new nature, created to be like God — truly
righteous and holy."*

Devotional Thought:

In Christ, we have the power to leave behind our old ways and
embrace a new life of purpose and hope. By starting fresh, we walk
in God's grace and embrace His plan for us. Today, let the power of
new beginnings fill you with hope and courage.

Reflection Questions

Are there past habits you need to leave behind for a fresh start?

How does God's gift of a new life inspire you to walk in His purpose?

What steps can you take to embrace your identity in Christ?

Prayer for the Day

Father, thank You for making me new in Christ. Help me to walk in this
new life, leaving behind the past and embracing Your purpose. Amen.

Daily Transformation Through God's Power

*"For God is working in you, giving you the desire and
the power to do what pleases him."*

— PHILIPPIANS 2:13 (NLT)

Additional Scripture References:

*Ephesians 3:20: "Now all glory to God, who is able, through his mighty power
at work within us, to accomplish infinitely more than we might ask or think."*

1 Thessalonians 5:24: "The one who calls you is faithful, and he will do it."

Devotional Thought:

God works in us every day, empowering us to grow in faith and purpose. By surrendering to His work, we experience daily transformation. Today, let God's power guide you, shaping your heart and life to please Him.

Reflection Questions ?

Are there areas where you need God's power to help you grow?

How does daily transformation bring you closer to God's purpose?

What steps can you take to surrender to God's work each day?

Prayer for the Day

Lord, continue to work in my heart, transforming me daily. Let Your power guide my thoughts, actions, and purpose, bringing me closer to You. Amen.

The Gift of Accountability

"As iron sharpens iron,
so a friend sharpens a friend."
— PROVERBS 27:17 (NLT)

Additional Scripture References:

Ecclesiastes 4:9: "Two are better than one, for they can help each other succeed."

Hebrews 10:24: "Let us think of ways to motivate one another to acts of love and good works."

Devotional Thought:

Accountability is a gift that helps us grow stronger, encouraging us to live in truth and integrity. Trusted friends help us stay on the right path, providing encouragement and guidance. Today, embrace accountability as a tool for growth, allowing others to help you become stronger in faith.

Reflection Questions

Are there people in your life who help hold you accountable?

How does having accountability strengthen your walk with God?

What steps can you take to build meaningful accountability relationships?

Prayer for the Day

Father, thank You for the gift of accountability. Help me to welcome guidance from others, allowing their support to sharpen my faith and integrity. Amen.

September 2

Building Trust Through Accountability

"The trustworthy person will get a rich reward,
but a person who wants quick riches will get into trouble."
— PROVERBS 28:20 (NLT)

Additional Scripture References:

Luke 16:10: "If you are faithful in little things, you will be faithful in large ones. But if you are dishonest in little things, you won't be honest with greater responsibilities."

1 Timothy 6:9-10: "But people who long to be rich fall into temptation and are trapped by many foolish and harmful desires that plunge them into ruin and destruction. For the love of money is the root of all kinds of evil."

Devotional Thought:

Accountability helps us become trustworthy, allowing us to build strong relationships based on honesty. When we hold ourselves accountable to God and others, we gain the respect and trust of those around us. Today, let your actions reflect integrity, honoring the accountability you have with others.

Reflection Questions

Are there areas where you can grow in trustworthiness?

How does being accountable to others build stronger relationships?

What steps can you take to practice honesty and integrity daily?

Prayer for the Day

Lord, help me to be trustworthy in all I do. Let my accountability to You and others bring strength to my relationships and integrity. Amen.

The Humility of Accountability

"Humble yourselves before the Lord,
and he will lift you up in honor."

— JAMES 4:10 (NLT)

Additional Scripture References:

1 Peter 5:6: *"So humble yourselves under the mighty power of God, and at the right time he will lift you up in honor."*

Matthew 23:12: *"But those who exalt themselves will be humbled, and those who humble themselves will be exalted."*

Devotional Thought:

Accountability requires humility, acknowledging that we all have areas in need of growth. When we're open to guidance, God can shape us into people of strength and wisdom. Today, choose humility, allowing accountability to be a tool for growth and transformation.

Reflection Questions

Are there areas where pride keeps you from embracing accountability?

How does humility strengthen your relationship with God and others?

What steps can you take to practice humility in your accountability?

Prayer for the Day

Father, give me a humble heart that's open to accountability. Let my willingness to learn and grow honor You and strengthen my faith. Amen.

September 4

Strength in Being Vulnerable

*"Confess your sins to each other and pray
for each other so that you may be healed."*

— JAMES 5:16 (NLT)

Additional Scripture References:

*1 John 1:9: "If we confess our sins to him, he is faithful and just to forgive us
our sins and to cleanse us from all wickedness."*

*Philippians 4:6: "Don't worry about anything; instead, pray about everything.
Tell God what you need, and thank him for all he has done."*

Devotional Thought:

Vulnerability builds trust, allowing us to support and pray for one another in our struggles. By sharing our weaknesses with trusted people, we invite healing and growth. Today, let vulnerability be a strength, allowing those close to you to lift you up in faith.

Reflection Questions

Are there trusted friends with whom you can be vulnerable?

How does sharing struggles bring healing and support?

What steps can you take to build trust through openness?

Prayer for the Day

Lord, help me to embrace vulnerability with trusted friends. Let my openness invite Your healing and the encouragement of others. Amen.

Accountability Brings Wisdom

"Walk with the wise and become wise;
associate with fools and get in trouble."

— PROVERBS 13:20 (NLT)

Additional Scripture References:

Psalm 1:1: *"Oh, the joys of those who do not follow the advice of the wicked, or stand around with sinners, or join in with mockers."*

1 Corinthians 15:33: *"Don't be fooled by those who say such things, for 'bad company corrupts good character.'"*

Devotional Thought:

Surrounding ourselves with wise and godly people brings growth and understanding. Accountability relationships with those who live in wisdom inspire us to make godly decisions. Today, seek the wisdom of others, letting their insights guide your journey in faith.

Reflection Questions

Are there wise people in your life who offer guidance?

How does surrounding yourself with wisdom impact your choices?

What steps can you take to learn from those who live in faith?

Prayer for the Day

Father, thank You for the wisdom of those around me. Help me to seek their guidance and grow in understanding, honoring You in all I do. Amen.

September 6

Accountability for Growth

"Let us think of ways to motivate one another
to acts of love and good works."

— HEBREWS 10:24 (NLT)

Additional Scripture References:

Galatians 6:2: *"Share each other's burdens, and in this way obey the law of Christ."*

Ephesians 4:16: *"He makes the whole body fit together perfectly. As each part does its own special work, it helps the other parts grow, so that the whole body is healthy and growing and full of love."*

Devotional Thought:

Accountability helps us grow in love and good works, motivating us to live out our faith in practical ways. When we support each other, we become stronger and more compassionate. Today, let accountability be a source of encouragement, pushing you to grow in faith and action.

Reflection Questions

Are there ways you can support others in their growth?

How does accountability help you become a better version of yourself?

What steps can you take to encourage and uplift those around you?

Prayer for the Day

Lord, help me to grow through accountability. Let my actions reflect Your love, encouraging others to live out their faith. Amen.

September 7

Accountability to God's Standards

"For we must all stand before Christ to be judged. We will each receive whatever we deserve for the good or evil we have done in this earthly body."
— 2 CORINTHIANS 5:10 (NLT)

Additional Scripture References:

Romans 14:10: *"So why do you condemn another believer? Why do you look down on another believer? Remember, we will all stand before the judgment seat of God."*

Matthew 12:36: *"And I tell you this, you must give an account on judgment day for every idle word you speak."*

Devotional Thought:

While accountability with others is essential, our ultimate accountability is to God. By living according to His standards, we honor His will in every area of life. Today, let God's truth guide you, allowing His standards to shape your decisions.

Reflection Questions

Are there areas in your life where you need to align with God's standards?

How does knowing you are accountable to God impact your actions?

What steps can you take to live more fully according to His Word?

Prayer for the Day

Father, help me to live in accountability to You above all. Let my life reflect Your truth, bringing honor to Your name in every way. Amen.

September 8

Encouragement Through Accountability

"So encourage each other and build each other up,
just as you are already doing."

— 1 THESSALONIANS 5:11 (NLT)

Additional Scripture References:

Hebrews 3:13: "You must warn each other every day, while it is still today, so that none of you will be deceived by sin and hardened against God."

Ephesians 4:29: "Don't use foul or abusive language. Let everything you say be good and helpful, so that your words will be an encouragement to those who hear them."

Devotional Thought:

Accountability isn't just about correction; it's also about encouragement. Supporting each other in faith brings joy and strength to our journeys. Today, encourage someone close to you, helping them grow in faith and confidence through your words and actions.

Reflection Questions

Are there people in your life who need encouragement today?

How does being an encourager strengthen your accountability relationships?

What steps can you take to build others up in faith?

Prayer for the Day

Lord, help me to be an encourager. Let my words bring hope and strength to those around me, reflecting Your love in every interaction. Amen.

September 9

The Strength of Unity in Accountability

*"Make every effort to keep yourselves united
in the Spirit, binding yourselves together with peace."*
— EPHESIANS 4:3 (NLT)

Additional Scripture References:

Colossians 3:14: "Above all, clothe yourselves with love, which binds us all together in perfect harmony."

Philippians 2:2: "Then make me truly happy by agreeing wholeheartedly with each other, loving one another, and working together with one mind and purpose."

Devotional Thought:

Unity is strengthened through accountability, helping us stay connected to each other and God's purpose. By working together, we grow in peace, trust, and love. Today, let unity be your goal, allowing accountability to build stronger relationships within the body of Christ.

Reflection Questions

Are there ways you can foster unity through accountability?

How does working together bring strength to your faith community?

What steps can you take to build peace and unity with others?

Prayer for the Day

Father, help me to be united with others in accountability. Let my heart be open to growth and peace, strengthening the bonds of unity in Christ. Amen.

September 10

Remaining Accountable in Temptation

*"The temptations in your life are no different from what others experience.
And God is faithful. He will not allow the temptation
to be more than you can stand."*

— 1 CORINTHIANS 10:13 (NLT)

Additional Scripture References:

*James 1:12: "God blesses those who patiently endure testing and temptation.
Afterward, they will receive the crown of life that God has promised to those
who love him."*

*2 Peter 2:9: "So you see, the Lord knows how to rescue godly people from their
trials, even while keeping the wicked under punishment until the day of final
judgment."*

Devotional Thought:

Accountability helps us face temptation with strength, knowing that
we're not alone in our struggles. By sharing our challenges with
trusted friends, we find encouragement to stand firm. Today, lean on
others for support, knowing that God is faithful in every trial.

Reflection Questions

Are there temptations where accountability can help you stand firm?

How does having others support you in challenges bring strength?

What steps can you take to invite accountability into areas of temptation?

Prayer for the Day

Lord, thank You for providing strength in temptation. Help me to rely
on accountability and Your faithfulness, standing firm in every trial.
Amen.

September 11

Finding Peace Through Accountability

"Confess your sins to each other and
pray for each other so that you may be healed."

— JAMES 5:16 (NLT)

Additional Scripture References:

1 John 1:9: "If we confess our sins to him, he is faithful and just to forgive us our sins and to cleanse us from all wickedness."

Philippians 4:6: "Don't worry about anything; instead, pray about everything. Tell God what you need, and thank him for all he has done."

Devotional Thought:

Confession and accountability bring healing, releasing burdens and inviting God's peace. When we're open with others, we find comfort and encouragement in the body of Christ. Today, let accountability be a source of peace, inviting healing and freedom.

Reflection Questions

Are there areas where confession could bring healing and peace?

How does sharing struggles with others invite God's peace into your life?

What steps can you take to practice accountability in a way that brings peace?

Prayer for the Day

Father, let my heart be open to confession and healing. Help me to embrace accountability with peace, trusting that Your grace brings freedom. Amen.

September 12

The Strength of Unity in Christ

*"For where two or three gather together as my followers,
I am there among them."*

— **MATTHEW 18:20 (NLT)**

Additional Scripture References:

Hebrews 10:25: "And let us not neglect our meeting together, as some people do, but encourage one another, especially now that the day of his return is drawing near."

Acts 2:42: "All the believers devoted themselves to the apostles' teaching, and to fellowship, and to sharing in meals and to prayer."

Devotional Thought:

Unity invites God's presence, creating a powerful bond that strengthens our faith. When we gather with others in Christ's name, we are filled with His peace and strength. Today, let unity in faith be your strength, knowing that God is present in every gathering.

Reflection Questions

Are there ways you can strengthen unity with those around you?

How does knowing that God is with you bring strength to your relationships?

What steps can you take to create unity in your family, friendships, or church?

Prayer for the Day

Lord, thank You for the gift of unity in Christ. Help me to honor this bond, inviting Your presence and peace into every relationship. Amen.

September 13

Unity Through Love and Forgiveness

"Make allowance for each other's faults, and forgive anyone who offends you.
Remember, the Lord forgave you, so you must forgive others."
— COLOSSIANS 3:13 (NLT)

Additional Scripture References:

Ephesians 4:32: *"Instead, be kind to each other, tenderhearted, forgiving one another, just as God through Christ has forgiven you."*

Matthew 6:14: *"If you forgive those who sin against you, your heavenly Father will forgive you."*

Devotional Thought:

Unity requires love and forgiveness, allowing us to look past imperfections and build strong, lasting relationships. By choosing to forgive, we reflect God's love and grace. Today, let love and forgiveness guide you, building unity with those around you.

Reflection Questions

Are there people in your life you need to forgive to strengthen unity?

How does love and forgiveness bring peace to your relationships?

What steps can you take to build unity through grace and understanding?

Prayer for the Day

Father, help me to forgive as You have forgiven me. Let love and grace guide my heart, bringing unity and peace to my relationships. Amen.

September 14

Unity in Serving One Another

"For you have been called to live in freedom, my brothers and sisters. But don't use your freedom to satisfy your sinful nature. Instead, use your freedom to serve one another in love."

— GALATIANS 5:13 (NLT)

Additional Scripture References:

1 Peter 2:16: *"For you are free, yet you are God's slaves, so don't use your freedom as an excuse to do evil."*

Mark 10:45: *"For even the Son of Man came not to be served but to serve others and to give his life as a ransom for many."*

Devotional Thought:

Unity grows when we serve each other with love and humility. By putting others first, we strengthen the bonds of fellowship and reflect Christ's compassion. Today, look for ways to serve those around you, building unity through selflessness and care.

Reflection Questions

Are there ways you can serve those in your life today?

How does serving others deepen your relationships and build unity?

What steps can you take to make service a part of your daily interactions?

Prayer for the Day

Lord, help me to serve others with a heart of love. Let my actions reflect Your compassion, building unity through selflessness and kindness. Amen.

September 15

Unity in Prayer

"They all met together and
were constantly united in prayer."

— ACTS 1:14 (NLT)

Additional Scripture References:

Philippians 1:3-5: "Every time I think of you, I give thanks to my God. Whenever I pray, I make my requests for all of you with joy, for you have been my partners in spreading the Good News about Christ from the time you first heard it until now."

1 Thessalonians 5:17: "Never stop praying."

Devotional Thought:

Prayer is a powerful way to create unity, aligning our hearts and minds with God's will. When we pray together, we are strengthened as one body, united in faith and purpose. Today, gather with others in prayer, allowing God's presence to bring unity and strength.

Reflection Questions

Are there people you can pray with to strengthen unity in faith?

How does praying together bring you closer to God and each other?

What steps can you take to make group prayer a part of your routine?

Prayer for the Day

Father, let prayer be a source of unity among us. Help us to come together in faith, seeking Your guidance and strength as one. Amen.

September 16

Unity in Diversity

"For just as each of us has one body with many members, and these members do not all have the same function."

— ROMANS 12:4 (NLT)

Additional Scripture References:

1 Corinthians 12:12"The human body has many parts, but the many parts make up one whole body. So it is with the body of Christ."

Ephesians 4:16"He makes the whole body fit together perfectly. As each part does its own special work, it helps the other parts grow, so that the whole body is healthy and growing and full of love."

Devotional Thought:

Unity doesn't mean sameness; it celebrates the diversity of gifts within the body of Christ. Each person brings unique talents, and together we fulfill God's purpose. Today, appreciate the diversity in those around you, knowing that each part is essential to the whole.

Reflection Questions ?

Are there unique gifts in others you can celebrate?

How does embracing diversity strengthen the unity of the body of Christ?

What steps can you take to value and honor each person's unique role?

Prayer for the Day

Lord, thank You for the diverse gifts You've given us. Let our differences bring us closer together, honoring each role in Your plan. Amen.

Unity Brings Peace

*"How good and pleasant it is when
God's people live together in unity!"*
— PSALM 133:1 (NLT)

Additional Scripture References:

Ephesians 4:3: "Make every effort to keep yourselves united in the Spirit, binding yourselves together with peace."

Colossians 3:14: "Above all, clothe yourselves with love, which binds us all together in perfect harmony."

Devotional Thought:

Unity creates an atmosphere of peace, making our communities places of love and harmony. By working together, we reflect the beauty of God's family. Today, let unity bring peace to your relationships, knowing that harmony pleases God and blesses those around you.

Reflection Questions

Are there ways you can foster peace and unity in your life?

How does unity bring joy and harmony to your relationships?

What steps can you take to build an environment of peace around you?

Prayer for the Day

Father, help me to create peace in my relationships. Let unity be the foundation of love and harmony in my home, church, and community. Amen.

September 18

Unity in Purpose

"I appeal to you, dear brothers and sisters, by the authority of our Lord Jesus Christ, to live in harmony with each other."

— 1 CORINTHIANS 1:10 (NLT)

Additional Scripture References:

Philippians 2:2: "Then make me truly happy by agreeing wholeheartedly with each other, loving one another, and working together with one mind and purpose."

Romans 15:5-6: "May God, who gives this patience and encouragement, help you live in complete harmony with each other, as is fitting for followers of Christ Jesus. Then all of you can join together with one voice, giving praise and glory to God, the Father of our Lord Jesus Christ."

Devotional Thought:

Unity strengthens our purpose, allowing us to work together for God's kingdom. When we live in harmony, we amplify God's love and message. Today, let unity of purpose guide your actions, working with others to fulfill God's will.

Reflection Questions

Are there shared purposes you can pursue with others?

How does having a unified purpose strengthen your walk with God?

What steps can you take to align with God's purpose as a community?

Prayer for the Day

Lord, let unity in purpose guide me. Help us to work together for Your kingdom, reflecting Your love in all we do. Amen.

September 19

Encouragement Through Unity

"Therefore encourage one another and build each other up,
just as in fact you are doing."
— 1 THESSALONIANS 5:11 (NLT)

Additional Scripture References:

Hebrews 3:13: "You must warn each other every day, while it is still today, so that none of you will be deceived by sin and hardened against God."

Ephesians 4:29: "Don't use foul or abusive language. Let everything you say be good and helpful, so that your words will be an encouragement to those who hear them."

Devotional Thought:

Unity is strengthened by encouragement, lifting each other up in faith and hope. By supporting one another, we grow stronger as a community. Today, let your words and actions bring encouragement, helping those around you feel supported and valued.

Reflection Questions

Are there people in your life who need encouragement?

How does encouragement strengthen unity and community?

What steps can you take to be an encourager today?

Prayer for the Day

Lord, help me to encourage those around me. Let my words bring strength and hope, building unity and joy within my community. Amen.

September 20

Unity in Worship

"Worship the Lord with gladness.
Come before him, singing with joy."
— PSALM 100:2 (NLT)

Additional Scripture References:

Psalm 95:1: "Come, let us sing to the LORD! Let us shout joyfully to the Rock of our salvation."

Colossians 3:23: "Work willingly at whatever you do, as though you were working for the Lord rather than for people."

Devotional Thought:

Worship brings us together, uniting us in praise and gratitude for God's goodness. By lifting our voices together, we honor God and strengthen our bonds with each other. Today, let worship be a source of joy and unity, drawing you closer to God and others.

Reflection Questions

Are there ways you can worship together with others?

How does worship bring unity and joy to your community?

What steps can you take to make worship a time of connection with others?

Prayer for the Day

Father, thank You for the gift of worship. Let our praise bring unity and joy, drawing us closer to You and each other. Amen.

September 21

Unity in Faith and Hope

"Make every effort to keep yourselves united
in the Spirit, binding yourselves together with peace."
— EPHESIANS 4:3 (NLT)

Additional Scripture References:

Colossians 3:14: "Above all, clothe yourselves with love, which binds us all together in perfect harmony."

Philippians 2:2: "Then make me truly happy by agreeing wholeheartedly with each other, loving one another, and working together with one mind and purpose."

Devotional Thought:

Unity is the foundation of a strong, hope-filled community. When we are bound by peace and love, we grow together in faith. Today, make every effort to strengthen unity, building hope and trust within your faith community.

Reflection Questions

Are there actions you can take to build unity in your relationships?

How does being united in faith and hope strengthen your community?

What steps can you take to encourage unity in your church or family?

Prayer for the Day

Lord, let Your Spirit bind us together in unity and peace. Help us to grow in faith and hope, reflecting Your love in all we do. Amen.

September 22

The Power of Persistent Prayer

"Keep on asking, and you will receive what you ask for.
Keep on seeking, and you will find."

— MATTHEW 7:7 (NLT)

Additional Scripture References:

James 1:5: "If you need wisdom, ask our generous God, and he will give it to you. He will not rebuke you for asking."

John 16:24: "You haven't done this before. Ask, using my name, and you will receive, and you will have abundant joy."

Devotional Thought:

Persistent prayer deepens our faith, reminding us to trust in God's timing and purpose. When we keep seeking Him, our hearts grow stronger and our faith more steadfast. Today, let your prayers be persistent, trusting that God hears every word.

Reflection Questions

Are there prayers you need to keep lifting up to God?

How does persistence in prayer deepen your relationship with God?

What steps can you take to make persistent prayer a habit?

Prayer for the Day

Lord, help me to pray with persistence and faith. Let my heart be steadfast, trusting that You hear every prayer and answer in Your perfect time. Amen.

The Peace That Comes Through Prayer

"Don't worry about anything; instead,
pray about everything."
— PHILIPPIANS 4:6 (NLT)

Additional Scripture References:

1 Peter 5:7: "Give all your worries and cares to God, for he cares about you."

Matthew 6:34: "So don't worry about tomorrow, for tomorrow will bring its own worries. Today's trouble is enough for today."

Devotional Thought:

Prayer replaces worry, allowing God's peace to guard our hearts and minds. By bringing our concerns to Him, we find a calm that surpasses understanding. Today, let prayer bring peace to your heart, laying every concern at God's feet.

Reflection Questions

Are there worries you need to surrender in prayer?

How does praying about everything replace anxiety with peace?

What steps can you take to make prayer your first response to worry?

Prayer for the Day

Father, help me to bring every worry to You in prayer. Let Your peace guard my heart, replacing anxiety with trust and calm. Amen.

September 24

Faith Through Prayer

"You can pray for anything, and if you have faith,
you will receive it."

— **MATTHEW 21:22 (NLT)**

Additional Scripture References:

Mark 11:24: "I tell you, you can pray for anything, and if you believe that you've received it, it will be yours."

John 14:13-14: "You can ask for anything in my name, and I will do it, so that the Son can bring glory to the Father. Yes, ask me for anything in my name, and I will do it."

Devotional Thought:

Faith-filled prayer brings us closer to God, reminding us that nothing is impossible with Him. When we pray with faith, we align our desires with His will, trusting in His power. Today, let faith be the foundation of your prayers, believing that God can do all things.

Reflection Questions

Are there prayers where you need to increase your faith?

How does faith in prayer bring you closer to God's will?

What steps can you take to strengthen your faith through prayer?

Prayer for the Day

Lord, increase my faith in prayer. Help me to trust that You can do all things, aligning my heart with Your perfect will. Amen.

Gratitude in Every Circumstance

*"Be thankful in all circumstances, for this is God's will
for you who belong to Christ Jesus."*
— 1 THESSALONIANS 5:18 (NLT)

Additional Scripture References:

Ephesians 5:20: "And give thanks for everything to God the Father in the name of our Lord Jesus Christ."

Colossians 3:17: "And whatever you do or say, do it as a representative of the Lord Jesus, giving thanks through him to God the Father."

Devotional Thought:

Gratitude transforms our perspective, helping us see God's goodness even in challenging times. By giving thanks in all things, we open our hearts to joy and peace. Today, let gratitude fill your heart, reminding you of God's faithfulness.

Reflection Questions

Are there areas where you need to cultivate gratitude?

How does being thankful in all circumstances strengthen your faith?

What steps can you take to make gratitude a daily practice?

Prayer for the Day

Father, help me to be thankful in every circumstance. Let my heart overflow with gratitude, trusting in Your goodness and faithfulness. Amen.

September 26

Gratitude for God's Blessings

"Let all that I am praise the Lord;
may I never forget the good things he does for me."

— PSALM 103:2 (NLT)

Additional Scripture References:

Psalm 105:5: "Remember the wonders he has performed, his miracles, and the rulings he has given."

Philippians 4:8: "And now, dear brothers and sisters, one final thing. Fix your thoughts on what is true, and honorable, and right, and pure, and lovely, and admirable. Think about things that are excellent and worthy of praise."

Devotional Thought:

Gratitude keeps us grounded in God's blessings, reminding us of His provision and love. By remembering His goodness, we cultivate joy and contentment. Today, take a moment to thank God for His blessings, letting gratitude shape your perspective.

Reflection Questions

Are there blessings in your life you can thank God for today?

How does remembering God's goodness bring you joy?

What steps can you take to make thankfulness a daily habit?

Prayer for the Day

Lord, thank You for Your countless blessings. Let my heart be filled with gratitude, remembering Your goodness and grace each day. Amen.

The Joy of Gratitude

*"The Lord has done great things for us,
and we are filled with joy."*

— PSALM 126:3 (NLT)

Additional Scripture References:

Psalm 40:5: "O LORD my God, you have performed many wonders for us. Your plans for us are too numerous to list. You have no equal. If I tried to recite all your wonderful deeds, I would never come to the end of them."

Psalm 30:11: "You have turned my mourning into joyful dancing. You have taken away my clothes of mourning and clothed me with joy."

Devotional Thought:

Gratitude opens the door to joy, helping us celebrate God's faithfulness. By focusing on what He has done, we experience a joy that transforms our hearts. Today, let gratitude be the source of your joy, filling your heart with praise.

Reflection Questions

Are there ways gratitude can bring more joy to your life?

How does focusing on God's faithfulness increase your happiness?

What steps can you take to cultivate joy through gratitude?

Prayer for the Day

Father, thank You for the joy that gratitude brings. Let my heart be filled with happiness as I remember Your faithfulness and love. Amen.

September 28

Finding Joy in God's Presence

"You make known to me the path of life;
in your presence there is fullness of joy."

— PSALM 16:11 (NLT)

Additional Scripture References:

John 14:6: "Jesus told him, 'I am the way, the truth, and the life. No one can come to the Father except through me.'"

Psalm 27:4: "The one thing I ask of the LORD — the thing I seek most — is to live in the house of the LORD all the days of my life, delighting in the LORD's perfections and meditating in his Temple."

Devotional Thought:

True joy is found in God's presence, filling our hearts with peace, love, and purpose. By spending time with Him, we experience a joy that surpasses all else. Today, let God's presence bring joy to your spirit, reminding you of His constant love.

Reflection Questions

Are there ways you can invite more of God's presence into your life?

How does spending time with God fill you with joy and peace?

What steps can you take to seek God's presence daily?

Prayer for the Day

Lord, let Your presence be my source of joy. Help me to seek You each day, finding happiness and peace in Your love. Amen.

September 29

The Strength of Joy

"The joy of the Lord is your strength!"
— NEHEMIAH 8:10 (NLT)

Additional Scripture References:

Psalm 19:8: "The commandments of the LORD are right, bringing joy to the heart. The commands of the LORD are clear, giving insight for living."

Philippians 4:4: "Always be full of joy in the Lord. I say it again — rejoice!"

Devotional Thought:

Joy is a source of strength, empowering us to face every challenge with hope and courage. When we lean on God's joy, we find resilience and endurance. Today, let God's joy be your strength, carrying you through every obstacle.

Reflection Questions

Are there challenges where you need God's joy as strength?

How does leaning on God's joy give you resilience and hope?

What steps can you take to let joy be a source of strength?

Prayer for the Day

Father, let Your joy fill my heart with strength. Help me to rely on You in every challenge, finding courage and peace in Your love. Amen.

September 30

Joy as a Testimony of Faith

"Always be full of joy in the Lord. I say it again – rejoice!"
— PHILIPPIANS 4:4 (NLT)

Additional Scripture References:

1 Thessalonians 5:16: *"Always be joyful."*

Nehemiah 8:10: *"Don't be dejected and sad, for the joy of the LORD is your strength!"*

Devotional Thought:

Joy is a powerful testimony of faith, showing the world the hope we have in Christ. By choosing joy, we reflect God's love and faithfulness to those around us. Today, let joy be your witness, sharing the light of Christ with everyone you meet.

Reflection Questions ?

Are there ways you can share your joy with others today?

How does choosing joy impact those around you?

What steps can you take to let joy be a part of your daily witness?

Prayer for the Day

Lord, let my life be filled with Your joy, serving as a testimony to Your love and hope. Help me to rejoice in You each day, sharing Your light with others. Amen.

An Excellent Woman

"Who can find a virtuous and capable wife?
She is more precious than rubies."

— **PROVERBS 31:10 (NLT)**

Additional Scripture References:

Ruth 3:11: *"Now, my daughter, don't be afraid. I will do for you all you ask. All the people in town know you are a virtuous woman."*

1 Peter 3:3-4: *"Don't be concerned about the outward beauty of fancy hairstyles, expensive jewelry, or beautiful clothes. You should clothe yourselves instead with the beauty that comes from within, the unfading beauty of a gentle and quiet spirit, which is so precious to God."*

Devotional Thought:

The Proverbs 31 woman embodies virtue, strength, and character, qualities that are more valuable than any earthly treasure. Her worth comes from her integrity, kindness, and devotion to God. Today, reflect on the unique strengths God has given you, knowing that your value is found in His love.

Reflection Questions

Are there virtues you feel called to cultivate in your life?

How does understanding your worth in God's eyes shape your identity?

What steps can you take to let God's love define your value?

Prayer for the Day

Lord, help me to see my worth through Your eyes. Let my heart be filled with virtue and strength, reflecting the value You place on my life. Amen.

A Heart of Trust

"Her husband can trust her, and she will
greatly enrich his life."
— PROVERBS 31:11 (NLT)

Additional Scripture References:

Proverbs 12:4: "A worthy wife is a crown for her husband, but a disgraceful woman is like cancer in his bones."

Ephesians 5:25: "For husbands, this means love your wives, just as Christ loved the church. He gave up his life for her."

Devotional Thought:

Trustworthiness is a foundation of strong relationships, allowing love and respect to flourish. The Proverbs 31 woman builds trust through her integrity and faithfulness. Today, let your actions be rooted in honesty, bringing strength to your relationships and reflecting God's faithfulness.

Reflection Questions

Are there ways you can build more trust in your relationships?

How does being trustworthy deepen your connection with others?

What steps can you take to cultivate a heart of integrity?

Prayer for the Day

Father, let my words and actions be trustworthy. Help me to enrich the lives of those around me, building relationships that honor You. Amen.

Doing Good

"She brings him good, not harm,

all the days of her life."

— **PROVERBS 31:12 (NLT)**

Additional Scripture References:

Ephesians 5:28: *"In the same way, husbands ought to love their wives as their own bodies. He who loves his wife loves himself."*

Colossians 3:18: *"Wives, submit to your husbands, as is fitting for those who belong to the Lord."*

Devotional Thought:

The Proverbs 31 woman seeks the well-being of her family and loved ones, bringing blessings and encouragement into their lives. Her actions reflect a heart dedicated to serving others with kindness. Today, look for ways to bring good to those around you, being a source of joy and comfort.

Reflection Questions

Are there actions you can take to bring more goodness into your relationships?

How does serving others with kindness reflect God's love?

What steps can you take to be a blessing in others' lives?

Prayer for the Day

Lord, help me to bring good to others, reflecting Your love and kindness. Let my heart be filled with compassion, seeking the well-being of those around me. Amen.

October 4

Working Willingly

"She finds wool and flax and busily spins it."
— **PROVERBS 31:13 (NLT)**

Additional Scripture References:

Proverbs 31:19: "In her hand, she holds the distaff and grasps the spindle with her fingers."

1 Timothy 5:10: "She is well regarded for her good deeds, such as bringing up children, showing hospitality, and washing the feet of the Lord's people, helping those in trouble and devoting herself to all kinds of good deeds."

Devotional Thought:

The Proverbs 31 woman is diligent and dedicated, working with her hands to provide for her family. Her willingness to work reflects her devotion and care. Today, approach your work with a willing heart, seeing each task as an opportunity to honor God and serve others.

Reflection Questions

Are there areas where you can approach your work with more willingness?

How does working with a joyful heart bring honor to God?

What steps can you take to cultivate a positive attitude toward your tasks?

Prayer for the Day

Father, give me a willing spirit in all I do. Let my work be a reflection of my love for You and my dedication to those around me. Amen.

Providing for Others

"She is like a merchant's ship, bringing her food from afar."
— **PROVERBS 31:14 (NLT)**

Additional Scripture References:

Proverbs 31:16: "She goes to inspect a field and buys it; with her earnings, she plants a vineyard."

Isaiah 55:2: "Why spend your money on food that does not give you strength? Why pay for food that does you no good? Listen to me, and you will eat what is good. You will enjoy the finest food."

Devotional Thought:

The Proverbs 31 woman goes above and beyond to provide for her family, ensuring their needs are met with care. Her efforts show foresight and commitment. Today, consider the ways you can provide for those you love, bringing comfort, care, and support into their lives.

Reflection Questions

Are there ways you can be more intentional in caring for your loved ones?

How does providing for others reflect God's provision in your life?

What steps can you take to ensure you're meeting the needs of those around you?

Prayer for the Day

Lord, help me to care for others as You care for me. Let my actions bring provision and peace to those I love, honoring You in every way. Amen.

October 6

Rising Early to Serve

"She gets up before dawn to prepare breakfast for her household and plan the day's work for her servant girls."

— PROVERBS 31:15 (NLT)

Additional Scripture References:

1 Timothy 5:14: "So I advise these younger widows to marry again, have children, and take care of their own homes. Then the enemy will not be able to say anything against them."

Titus 2:4-5: "Then they can urge the younger women to love their husbands and their children, to live wisely and be pure, to work in their homes, to do good, and to be submissive to their husbands. Then they will not bring shame on the word of God."

Devotional Thought:

The Proverbs 31 woman is diligent and selfless, rising early to meet the needs of her household. Her dedication shows her love and commitment to serving others. Today, reflect on how you can be more intentional in preparing and caring for those around you.

Reflection Questions

Are there ways you can serve others with more dedication?

How does starting the day with a focus on others bring joy to your routine?

What steps can you take to bring thoughtfulness and preparation into your day?

Prayer for the Day

Father, help me to serve others with love and dedication. Let my actions be a reflection of Your selfless love, preparing me to bless those around me. Amen.

Investing in Opportunity

"She goes to inspect a field and buys it;
with her earnings she plants a vineyard."

— **PROVERBS 31:16 (NLT)**

Additional Scripture References:

Matthew 25:16-17: *"The servant who received the five bags of silver began to invest the money and earned five more. The servant with two bags of silver also went to work and earned two more."*

Ecclesiastes 11:6: *"Plant your seed in the morning and keep busy all afternoon, for you don't know if profit will come from one activity or another — or maybe both."*

Devotional Thought:

The Proverbs 31 woman is resourceful and wise, using her resources to create opportunities. Her actions reflect thoughtfulness, stewardship, and foresight. Today, consider how you can use your resources, time, or skills to invest in opportunities that honor God and support others.

Reflection Questions

Are there resources or talents you can invest for God's glory?

How does wise stewardship bring blessing to your life and others?

What steps can you take to make thoughtful decisions with your resources?

Prayer for the Day

Lord, help me to be a wise steward of all You've given me. Let my actions honor You, creating opportunities for growth and blessing. Amen.

Gaining Strength for the Journey

"She is energetic and strong, a hard worker."
— **PROVERBS 31:17 (NLT)**

Additional Scripture References:

Colossians 3:23: "Work willingly at whatever you do, as though you were working for the Lord rather than for people."

Proverbs 12:24: "Work hard and become a leader; be lazy and become a slave."

Devotional Thought:

The Proverbs 31 woman demonstrates strength and energy, pouring herself into her work with dedication. Her strength is both physical and spiritual, rooted in her purpose. Today, seek God's strength in all you do, allowing Him to renew your energy and purpose each day.

Reflection Questions ?

Are there areas where you need God's strength to accomplish your tasks?

How does finding strength in God empower you in your daily life?

What steps can you take to cultivate resilience in your work and service?

Prayer for the Day

Father, let my strength come from You. Help me to approach each task with energy and purpose, knowing that You provide all I need. Amen.

October 9

Working with Purpose

"She makes sure her dealings are profitable;
her lamp burns late into the night."

— PROVERBS 31:18 (NLT)

Additional Scripture References:

Proverbs 10:4: "Lazy people are soon poor; hard workers get rich."

Ecclesiastes 3:13: "And people should eat and drink and enjoy the fruits of their labor, for these are gifts from God."

Devotional Thought:

The Proverbs 31 woman works with purpose, ensuring that her efforts are fruitful and beneficial for her family. Her diligence and commitment set an example of integrity and responsibility. Today, let your work be driven by purpose, knowing that every effort is meaningful when done for God's glory.

Reflection Questions

Are there tasks you can approach with more purpose and intention?

How does working with integrity bring joy and fulfillment?

What steps can you take to make sure your work aligns with God's purpose?

Prayer for the Day

Lord, let my work reflect Your purpose and integrity. Help me to approach each task with diligence and care, honoring You in every effort. Amen.

Caring for Others with Diligence

*"Her hands are busy spinning thread,
her fingers twisting fiber."*

— **PROVERBS 31:19 (NLT)**

Additional Scripture References:

Proverbs 31:13: *"She finds wool and flax and busily spins it."*

1 Timothy 5:10: *"She is well regarded for her good deeds, such as bringing up children, showing hospitality, and washing the feet of the Lord's people, helping those in trouble and devoting herself to all kinds of good deeds."*

Devotional Thought:

The Proverbs 31 woman is dedicated to her tasks, providing for her household with care and skill. Her diligence reflects a heart of service and responsibility. Today, approach your work with the same dedication, seeing each task as an opportunity to care for others and honor God.

Reflection Questions

Are there tasks where you can apply more care and dedication?

How does serving others with skill and attention to detail reflect God's love?

What steps can you take to bring intentionality to your daily work?

Prayer for the Day

Father, help me to serve with skill and dedication. Let my hands be diligent in caring for others, showing Your love through my actions. Amen.

Compassion for the Needy

*"She extends a helping hand to the poor and
opens her arms to the needy."*

— PROVERBS 31:20 (NLT)

Additional Scripture References:

*Proverbs 19:17: "If you help the poor, you are lending to the LORD — and he
will repay you!"*

*Isaiah 58:10: "Feed the hungry, and help those in trouble. Then your light will
shine out from the darkness, and the darkness around you will be as bright as
noon."*

Devotional Thought:

The Proverbs 31 woman is compassionate and generous, reaching
out to help those in need. Her kindness and empathy reflect God's
heart for others. Today, seek ways to show compassion, extending help
to those who are struggling, and sharing God's love in tangible ways.

Reflection Questions

Are there people in your life who need your help or compassion?

How does showing kindness to others reflect God's love in your life?

What steps can you take to make compassion a regular practice?

Prayer for the Day

Lord, help me to be generous and compassionate, reaching out to those
in need. Let my actions reflect Your love and kindness in all I do. Amen.

October 12

Facing the Future with Faith

*"She has no fear of winter for her household,
for everyone has warm clothes."*

— PROVERBS 31:21 (NLT)

Additional Scripture References:

1 Timothy 5:8: "But those who won't care for their relatives, especially those in their own household, have denied the true faith. Such people are worse than unbelievers."

Proverbs 22:3: "A prudent person foresees danger and takes precautions. The simpleton goes blindly on and suffers the consequences."

Devotional Thought:

The Proverbs 31 woman prepares for the future with confidence and foresight, trusting that God will provide for her family's needs. Her faith in God's provision allows her to face challenges without fear. Today, place your trust in God's care, knowing that He will provide for you and those you love.

Reflection Questions

Are there concerns about the future you need to surrender to God?

How does trusting in God's provision bring you peace?

What steps can you take to prepare with faith, knowing God is with you?

Prayer for the Day

Father, help me to trust in Your provision, facing the future with faith. Let my heart be at peace, knowing You are always caring for me and my family. Amen.

Clothed with Strength and Dignity

*"She is clothed with strength and
dignity, and she laughs without fear of the future."*

— PROVERBS 31:25 (NLT)

Additional Scripture References:

Isaiah 41:10: "Don't be afraid, for I am with you. Don't be discouraged, for I am your God. I will strengthen you and help you. I will hold you up with my victorious right hand."

1 Peter 3:3-4: "Don't be concerned about the outward beauty of fancy hairstyles, expensive jewelry, or beautiful clothes. You should clothe yourselves instead with the beauty that comes from within, the unfading beauty of a gentle an

Devotional Thought:

Strength and dignity define the Proverbs 31 woman, enabling her to approach life's uncertainties with confidence. Her trust in God gives her joy and peace. Today, let strength and dignity be your foundation, facing each day with confidence and joy in God's promises.

Reflection Questions

Are there areas where you can rely on God's strength more fully?

How does embracing dignity and confidence in God change your outlook?

What steps can you take to approach each day with joy and faith?

Prayer for the Day

Lord, clothe me with Your strength and dignity. Let my heart be filled with joy and confidence, knowing that You hold my future. Amen.

October 14

Speaking with Wisdom and Kindness

*"When she speaks, her words are wise, and
she gives instructions with kindness."*

— PROVERBS 31:26 (NLT)

Additional Scripture References:

Proverbs 15:1: "A gentle answer deflects anger, but harsh words make tempers flare."

James 3:17: "But the wisdom from above is first of all pure. It is also peace loving, gentle at all times, and willing to yield to others. It is full of mercy and the fruit of good deeds. It shows no favoritism and is always sincere."

Devotional Thought:

The Proverbs 31 woman speaks with wisdom and kindness, using her words to uplift and encourage others. Her speech reflects a heart of grace and compassion. Today, let your words be guided by God's wisdom, bringing comfort and encouragement to those around you.

Reflection Questions

Are there ways you can bring more wisdom and kindness into your speech?

How does speaking with grace and understanding impact your relationships?

What steps can you take to make your words a source of encouragement?

Prayer for the Day

Father, help me to speak with wisdom and kindness. Let my words be filled with grace, bringing encouragement and peace to those I meet. Amen.

Attentive to Her Responsibilities

*"She carefully watches everything in her household and
suffers nothing from laziness."*

— PROVERBS 31:27 (NLT)

Additional Scripture References:

Proverbs 14:1: "A wise woman builds her home, but a foolish woman tears it down with her own hands."

Titus 2:5: "To be self-controlled and pure, to be busy at home, to be kind, and to be subject to their husbands, so that no one will malign the word of God."

Devotional Thought:

The Proverbs 31 woman is attentive and responsible, ensuring that her household is well-cared for. Her diligence reflects her love and commitment to her family. Today, approach your responsibilities with care, knowing that attentiveness brings honor to God and blessing to those around you.

Reflection Questions

Are there responsibilities where you can be more attentive?

How does caring for your duties with diligence bring honor to God?

What steps can you take to approach your tasks with care and commitment?

Prayer for the Day

Lord, help me to be diligent in all my responsibilities. Let my actions bring honor to You and blessing to those I serve. Amen.

October 16

Her Children and Husband Praise Her

"Her children stand and bless her. Her husband praises her."
— PROVERBS 31:28 (NLT)

Additional Scripture References:

Proverbs 20:7: "The godly walk with integrity; blessed are their children who follow them."

1 Timothy 5:10: "She is well regarded for her good deeds, such as bringing up children, showing hospitality, and washing the feet of the Lord's people, helping those in trouble and devoting herself to all kinds of good deeds."

Devotional Thought:

The Proverbs 31 woman is honored by her family, who recognize and appreciate her love, dedication, and kindness. Her actions inspire gratitude and respect. Today, let your actions reflect love and selflessness, knowing that your impact reaches those closest to you.

Reflection Questions

Are there ways you can show more love and care to your family?

How does living selflessly inspire gratitude in those around you?

What steps can you take to build a legacy of love and respect?

Prayer for the Day

Father, help me to be a blessing to my family. Let my actions bring love and honor, leaving a legacy of kindness and dedication. Amen.

Exceeding All Expectations

*"There are many virtuous and capable women in the world,
but you surpass them all!"*
— **PROVERBS 31:29 (NLT)**

Additional Scripture References:

*Ruth 3:11: "Now, my daughter, don't be afraid. I will do for you all you ask.
All the people in town know you are a virtuous woman."*

*1 Peter 3:5-6: "This is how the holy women of old made themselves beautiful.
They put their trust in God and accepted the authority of their husbands. For
instance, Sarah obeyed her husband, Abraham, and called him her master.
You are her daughters when you do what is right without fear of what your
husbands might do."*

Devotional Thought:

The Proverbs 31 woman stands out for her exceptional character,
strength, and wisdom. Her life reflects the beauty of living with
purpose and integrity. Today, strive to live with excellence, allowing
God's love and wisdom to guide all you do.

Reflection Questions

Are there areas where you can go above and beyond in love and service?

How does living with excellence reflect God's character?

What steps can you take to let God's wisdom guide your actions?

Prayer for the Day

Lord, help me to live with excellence in all I do. Let my actions surpass
expectations, reflecting Your love and wisdom. Amen.

The True Source of Beauty

"Charm is deceptive, and beauty does not last;
but a woman who fears the Lord will be greatly praised."

— **PROVERBS 31:30 (NLT)**

Additional Scripture References:

1 Peter 3:3-4: *"Don't be concerned about the outward beauty of fancy hairstyles, expensive jewelry, or beautiful clothes. You should clothe yourselves instead with the beauty that comes from within, the unfading beauty of a gentle and quiet spirit, which is so precious to God."*

Psalm 147:11: *"The LORD delights in those who fear him, who put their hope in his unfailing love."*

Devotional Thought:

The Proverbs 31 woman is honored not for outward beauty but for her reverence and love for God. Her faith is the true source of her strength and dignity. Today, let your relationship with God be the foundation of your beauty, radiating His love from within.

Reflection Questions

Are there ways you can deepen your reverence and love for God?

How does focusing on inner beauty change your perspective?

What steps can you take to nurture your relationship with God?

Prayer for the Day

Father, let my beauty be found in my love for You. Help me to grow in reverence and faith, reflecting Your love and grace. Amen.

Honored for Her Faithfulness

"Reward her for all she has done.
Let her deeds publicly declare her praise."

— PROVERBS 31:31 (NLT)

Additional Scripture References:

1 Timothy 5:17: "Elders who do their work well should be respected and paid well, especially those who work hard at both preaching and teaching."

Hebrews 6:10: "For God is not unjust. He will not forget how hard you have worked for him and how you have shown your love to him by caring for other believers, as you still do."

Devotional Thought:

The Proverbs 31 woman's faithfulness and dedication are honored, and her life serves as a testimony of love and devotion. Her actions speak volumes about her character and commitment. Today, let your deeds reflect God's love, allowing your actions to speak of your faith.

Reflection Questions

Are there actions you can take to reflect God's love and grace?

How does living with faithfulness impact those around you?

What steps can you take to ensure your deeds honor God?

Prayer for the Day

Lord, let my actions be a testimony of Your love and faithfulness. Help me to live in a way that honors You, bringing light to those around me. Amen.

Embracing Diligence

*"She looks well to the ways of her household,
and does not eat the bread of idleness."*

— PROVERBS 31:27 (NKJV)

Additional Scripture References:

Proverbs 14:1: "A wise woman builds her home, but a foolish woman tears it down with her own hands."

Titus 2:5: "To be self-controlled and pure, to be busy at home, to be kind, and to be subject to their husbands, so that no one will malign the word of God."

Devotional Thought:

The Proverbs 31 woman embraces diligence, staying attentive to the needs of her household. Her faithfulness brings order and care to every aspect of her life. Today, reflect on how diligence in your own life can bring peace and strength to those around you.

Reflection Questions

Are there areas where diligence could help bring more stability?

How does being attentive to responsibilities reflect love for others?

What steps can you take to practice greater diligence?

Prayer for the Day

Father, help me to embrace diligence in my daily life. Let my actions reflect care and responsibility, honoring those I serve and love. Amen.

Prepared for the Future

*"She makes sure her dealings are profitable;
her lamp burns late into the night."*

— **PROVERBS 31:18 (NLT)**

Additional Scripture References:

Proverbs 10:4" "Lazy people are soon poor; hard workers get rich."

Ecclesiastes 3:13: "And people should eat and drink and enjoy the fruits of their labor, for these are gifts from God."

Devotional Thought:

The Proverbs 31 woman is wise and prepared, carefully managing her resources to provide for her family's future. Her foresight is grounded in faithfulness and responsibility. Today, focus on preparing wisely, allowing God's guidance to shape your plans.

Reflection Questions

Are there areas where you can prepare more thoughtfully?

How does wise planning reflect trust in God's provision?

What steps can you take to create a more purposeful future?

Prayer for the Day

Lord, help me to prepare with wisdom and care. Let my efforts reflect trust in Your provision, providing stability and peace to those around me. Amen.

October 22

Strength Through Service

"She girds herself with strength, and strengthens her arms."

— **PROVERBS 31:17 (NKJV)**

Additional Scripture References:

Colossians 3:23: "Work willingly at whatever you do, as though you were working for the Lord rather than for people."

Proverbs 12:24: "Work hard and become a leader; be lazy and become a slave."

Devotional Thought:

The Proverbs 31 woman finds strength in her purpose and devotion, serving her family with resilience and love. Her strength comes from her dedication to others. Today, seek God's strength in all you do, allowing your service to be a source of purpose and fulfillment.

Reflection Questions

Are there ways you can serve with greater strength and resilience?

How does dedicating yourself to others bring purpose to your life?

What steps can you take to serve with God's strength?

Prayer for the Day

Father, fill me with strength and resilience. Help me to serve with purpose and love, finding fulfillment in my dedication to others. Amen.

Cultivating a Spirit of Joy

*"Strength and honor are her clothing;
she shall rejoice in time to come."*

— PROVERBS 31:25 (NKJV)

Additional Scripture References:

Isaiah 41:10: "Don't be afraid, for I am with you. Don't be discouraged, for I am your God. I will strengthen you and help you. I will hold you up with my victorious right hand."

1 Peter 3:3-4: "Don't be concerned about the outward beauty of fancy hairstyles, expensive jewelry, or beautiful clothes. You should clothe yourselves instead with the beauty that comes from within, the unfading beauty of a gentle and quiet spirit, which is so precious to God."

Devotional Thought:

The Proverbs 31 woman faces life with joy and confidence, knowing that her faith brings strength and honor. Her spirit is filled with hope and peace. Today, cultivate a spirit of joy, trusting that God is with you in every step.

Reflection Questions

Are there ways you can embrace joy in your daily life?

How does trusting in God bring peace and happiness?

What steps can you take to reflect God's joy in your actions?

Prayer for the Day

Lord, fill my heart with joy and confidence. Help me to rejoice in Your faithfulness, trusting in Your plan for my life. Amen.

October 24

Bringing Light to Others

"Her lamp does not go out by night."

— **PROVERBS 31:18 (NKJV)**

Additional Scripture References:

Proverbs 10:4: "Lazy people are soon poor; hard workers get rich."

Ecclesiastes 3:13: "And people should eat and drink and enjoy the fruits of their labor, for these are gifts from God."

Devotional Thought:

The Proverbs 31 woman is a light in her household, bringing warmth, care, and security. Her presence offers comfort to those around her. Today, be a light for others, letting your kindness and love shine brightly in your home and community.

Reflection Questions

Are there people in your life who need encouragement?

How does being a source of light reflect God's love?

What steps can you take to bring comfort and hope to others?

Prayer for the Day

Father, let my life be a light to those around me. Help me to bring comfort, hope, and love, shining brightly in all I do. Amen.

October 25

Wisdom in Actions and Words

"She opens her mouth with wisdom, and
on her tongue is the law of kindness."
— PROVERBS 31:26 (NKJV)

Additional Scripture References:

Proverbs 15:1: "A gentle answer deflects anger, but harsh words make tempers flare."

James 3:17: "But the wisdom from above is first of all pure. It is also peace loving, gentle at all times, and willing to yield to others. It is full of mercy and the fruit of good deeds. It shows no favoritism and is always sincere."

Devotional Thought:

The Proverbs 31 woman speaks with wisdom and kindness, using her words to uplift and inspire. Her speech reflects her love and understanding. Today, let wisdom and kindness guide your words, using them to bless and encourage others.

Reflection Questions

Are there ways you can bring more kindness into your conversations?

How does speaking with wisdom impact those around you?

What steps can you take to make your words a blessing to others?

Prayer for the Day

Lord, let wisdom and kindness guide my words. Help me to speak with love, using my words to uplift and inspire those around me. Amen.

October 26

Preparedness and Foresight

"She has no fear of winter for her household,
for everyone has warm clothes."

— PROVERBS 31:21 (NLT)

Additional Scripture References:

Philippians 4:19 - "And this same God who takes care of me will supply all your needs from his glorious riches, which have been given to us in Christ Jesus."

Psalm 37:25 - "Once I was young, and now I am old. Yet I have never seen the godly abandoned or their children begging for bread."

Devotional Thought:

The Proverbs 31 woman is thoughtful and prepared, ensuring that her family is provided for through every season. Her preparedness reflects her love and care. Today, think about how you can plan ahead and provide comfort and security for those you care for.

Reflection Questions

Are there ways you can bring peace to your home through preparation?

How does planning for the future help you serve those you love?

What steps can you take to prepare thoughtfully?

Prayer for the Day

Father, help me to be prepared, caring for my family with love and foresight. Let my actions bring comfort and security, showing Your love through my care. Amen.

October 27

Strength and Dignity as Daily Attire

*"She is clothed with strength and
dignity, and she laughs without fear of the future."*
— **PROVERBS 31:25 (NLT)**

Additional Scripture References:

Isaiah 41:10 - "Don't be afraid, for I am with you. Don't be discouraged, for I am your God. I will strengthen you and help you. I will hold you up with my victorious right hand."

1 Peter 3:3-4 - "Don't be concerned about the outward beauty of fancy hairstyles, expensive jewelry, or beautiful clothes. You should clothe yourselves instead with the beauty that comes from within, the unfading beauty of a gentle and quiet spirit, which is so precious to God."

Devotional Thought:

The Proverbs 31 woman wears strength and dignity like clothing, ready to face life's challenges with confidence and joy. Her faith in God gives her courage and peace. Today, let your strength and dignity be evident, rooted in your relationship with God.

Reflection Questions

Are there areas where you need to rely on God's strength?

How does wearing dignity and confidence shape your outlook?

What steps can you take to approach life with faith and courage?

Prayer for the Day

Lord, let strength and dignity be my daily attire. Help me to face each day with confidence and joy, rooted in faith and trust in You. Amen.

October 28

A Heart for Teaching and Kindness

"When she speaks, her words are wise, and she gives instructions with kindness."

— PROVERBS 31:26 (NLT)

Additional Scripture References:

Proverbs 16:24 - "Kind words are like honey — sweet to the soul and healthy for the body."

Colossians 4:6 - "Let your conversation be gracious and attractive so that you will have the right response for everyone."

Devotional Thought:

The Proverbs 31 woman shares wisdom and kindness in her words, guiding others with grace. Her speech reflects her character and love for God. Today, let your words reflect wisdom, using them to encourage and uplift others.

Reflection Questions

Are there opportunities to share wisdom and kindness with others?

How does speaking kindly impact your relationships?

What steps can you take to let kindness be the foundation of your words?

Prayer for the Day

Father, fill my words with wisdom and kindness. Let my speech be a reflection of Your love, encouraging and guiding those around me. Amen.

Faithfulness to Responsibilities

*"She carefully watches everything
in her household and suffers nothing from laziness."*

— **PROVERBS 31:27 (NLT)**

Additional Scripture References:

Titus 2:5 - "To teach them to love their husbands and children, to live wisely and be pure, to work in their homes, to do good, and to be submissive to their husbands. Then they will not bring shame on the word of God."

Proverbs 10:4 - "Lazy people are soon poor; hard workers get rich."

Devotional Thought:

The Proverbs 31 woman is diligent and attentive, taking care of her household with dedication. Her faithfulness is a blessing to her family. Today, approach your responsibilities with care, seeing them as opportunities to serve and honor God.

Reflection Questions

Are there responsibilities that you can approach with more diligence?

How does faithfully caring for your duties reflect love for others?

What steps can you take to bring attentiveness to your daily tasks?

Prayer for the Day

Lord, help me to be faithful in all my responsibilities. Let my actions reflect care and dedication, bringing honor to You and blessing to my family. Amen.

Being Praised for Faithfulness

"Her children stand and bless her. Her husband praises her."

— PROVERBS 31:28 (NLT)

Additional Scripture References:

Psalm 128:3 - "Your wife will be like a fruitful grapevine, flourishing within your home. Your children will be like vigorous young olive trees as they sit around your table."

Proverbs 19:14 - "Fathers can give their sons an inheritance of houses and wealth, but only the Lord can give an understanding wife."

Devotional Thought:

The Proverbs 31 woman is celebrated by her family for her love, kindness, and faithfulness. Her impact leaves a legacy of gratitude and honor. Today, let your actions be filled with love and faithfulness, creating a legacy that inspires and blesses those around you.

Reflection Questions

Are there ways you can show love and faithfulness to your family?

How does living with integrity inspire others?

What steps can you take to cultivate a legacy of love?

Prayer for the Day

Father, let my actions be filled with love and faithfulness. Help me to live in a way that blesses those around me and brings honor to You. Amen.

October 31

A Woman Who Fears the Lord

"Charm is deceptive, and beauty does not last;
but a woman who fears the Lord will be greatly praised."

— PROVERBS 31:30 (NLT)

Additional Scripture References:

1 Samuel 16:7 - *"But the Lord said to Samuel, 'Don't judge by his appearance or height, for I have rejected him. The Lord doesn't see things the way you see them. People judge by outward appearance, but the Lord looks at the heart.'"*

1 Peter 3:4 - *"You should clothe yourselves instead with the beauty that comes from within, the unfading beauty of a gentle and quiet spirit, which is so precious to God."*

Devotional Thought:

The Proverbs 31 woman's true beauty and worth come from her reverence and love for God. Her relationship with Him is the foundation of her character. Today, seek to deepen your relationship with God, knowing that your faith in Him is what truly matters.

Reflection Questions

Are there ways you can deepen your relationship with God?

How does reverence for God shape your character and actions?

What steps can you take to let God's love be the foundation of your life?

Prayer for the Day

Lord, let my life be rooted in reverence and love for You. Help me to grow closer to You each day, allowing my faith to shape my character and actions. Amen.

Truth as a Foundation

*"Lead me by your truth and teach me,
for you are the God who saves me."*

— PSALM 25:5 (NLT)

Additional Scripture References:

Proverbs 3:5-6 - "Trust in the Lord with all your heart; do not depend on your own understanding. Seek his will in all you do, and he will show you which path to take."

Isaiah 40:31 - "But those who trust in the Lord will find new strength. They will soar high on wings like eagles. They will run and not grow weary. They will walk and not faint."

Devotional Thought:

Truth is the foundation of our walk with God. When we align our lives with His truth, we live with integrity and clarity. Today, invite God's truth to guide you, helping you live with honesty in all areas of life.

Reflection Questions

Are there areas where you need God's truth to bring clarity?

How does living by God's truth strengthen your relationships?

What steps can you take to make truth the foundation of your life?

Prayer for the Day

Lord, lead me by Your truth each day. Help me to live with integrity, reflecting Your love and faithfulness in all I do. Amen.

November 2

Walking in Integrity

*"The Lord detests lying lips, but he delights in those
who tell the truth."*

— PROVERBS 12:22 (NLT)

Additional Scripture References:

*Ephesians 4:25 - "So stop telling lies. Let us tell our neighbors the truth, for we
are all parts of the same body."*

*Psalm 51:6 - "But you desire honesty from the womb, teaching me wisdom
even there."*

Devotional Thought:

God values honesty and transparency, delighting in those who
speak truthfully. When we commit to honesty, we build trust and
honor God in our words and actions. Today, let integrity guide your
words, building trust in your relationships.

Reflection Questions

Are there areas where you need to commit to more honesty?

How does living with integrity impact your relationship with God?

What steps can you take to speak truthfully each day?

Prayer for the Day

Father, help me to speak with integrity, delighting in Your truth. Let
my words reflect Your character, building trust and honor. Amen.

Truth in Our Actions

*"Dear children, let us not merely say that we love each other;
let us show the truth by our actions."*

— 1 JOHN 3:18 (NLT)

Additional Scripture References:

James 2:17 - "So you see, faith by itself isn't enough. Unless it produces good deeds, it is dead and useless."

1 John 4:20 - "If someone says, 'I love God,' but hates a fellow believer, that person is a liar; for if we don't love people we can see, how can we love God, whom we cannot see?"

Devotional Thought:

True love is demonstrated through action, not just words. By living with honesty and compassion, we reflect God's truth and love. Today, let your actions speak of truth and integrity, showing God's love to those around you.

Reflection Questions

Are there actions that can better reflect God's truth?

How does showing love through action strengthen your faith?

What steps can you take to make your actions a testament to God's love?

Prayer for the Day

Lord, let my actions reflect Your truth and love. Help me to show others Your compassion through the way I live each day. Amen.

Truth in Our Hearts

"You desire honesty from the womb,
teaching me wisdom even there."

— PSALM 51:6 (NLT)

Additional Scripture References:

Proverbs 2:6 - "For the Lord grants wisdom! From his mouth come knowledge and understanding."

John 4:24 - "For God is Spirit, so those who worship him must worship in spirit and in truth."

Devotional Thought:

God desires honesty from the deepest part of us, shaping our hearts to reflect His wisdom. When we are honest with ourselves and God, we allow His truth to transform us. Today, invite God to bring truth into your heart, allowing His wisdom to guide you.

Reflection Questions

Are there areas in your heart where you need to embrace God's truth?

How does being honest with God bring transformation to your life?

What steps can you take to let God's wisdom shape your heart?

Prayer for the Day

Father, let Your truth fill my heart. Help me to be honest with You, allowing Your wisdom to guide my life each day. Amen.

November 5

Living in the Light of Truth

"But if we are living in the light, as God is in the light, then we have fellowship with each other."

— 1 JOHN 1:7 (NLT)

Additional Scripture References:

Ephesians 5:8 - "For once you were full of darkness, but now you have light from the Lord. So live as people of light!"

John 8:12 - "Jesus spoke to the people once more and said, 'I am the light of the world. If you follow me, you won't have to walk in darkness, because you will have the light that leads to life.'"

Devotional Thought:

Living in the light means embracing God's truth and letting it guide every part of our lives. By living transparently, we build authentic relationships with God and others. Today, choose to live in the light of truth, allowing God to lead you in all things.

Reflection Questions

Are there areas where you need to bring God's light and truth?

How does living in the light strengthen your relationships?

What steps can you take to make transparency a daily practice?

Prayer for the Day

Lord, let me live in the light of Your truth. Help me to walk in honesty and build relationships rooted in trust and authenticity. Amen.

Freedom Through Truth

"And you will know the truth, and the truth will set you free."

— JOHN 8:32 (NLT)

Additional Scripture References:

John 14:6 - "Jesus told him, 'I am the way, the truth, and the life. No one can come to the Father except through me.'"

2 Corinthians 3:17 - "For the Lord is the Spirit, and wherever the Spirit of the Lord is, there is freedom."

Devotional Thought:

Truth brings freedom, releasing us from the burdens of guilt and deception. When we embrace God's truth, we experience peace and clarity in our lives. Today, let go of anything that holds you back and embrace the freedom God's truth brings.

Reflection Questions

Are there lies or deceptions you need to release?

How does embracing God's truth bring freedom to your life?

What steps can you take to live more freely in God's truth?

Prayer for the Day

Father, thank You for the freedom that comes from Your truth. Help me to let go of anything that holds me back, embracing the peace You provide. Amen.

November 7

Honoring Truth in All Things

"You must be blameless before the Lord your God."
— **DEUTERONOMY 18:13 (NLT)**

Additional Scripture References:

Matthew 5:48 - *"But you are to be perfect, even as your Father in heaven is perfect."*

1 Peter 1:15-16 - *"But now you must be holy in everything you do, just as God who chose you is holy. For the Scriptures say, 'You must be holy because I am holy.'"*

Devotional Thought:

Living blamelessly means committing to truth and integrity in every area of life. By honoring truth, we reflect God's holiness and love. Today, let truth guide your actions, bringing honor to God and reflecting His character to others.

Reflection Questions

Are there areas where you can live more blamelessly before God?

How does committing to truth reflect God's holiness?

What steps can you take to honor truth in all areas of your life?

Prayer for the Day

Lord, help me to live blamelessly before You. Let truth and integrity be my guide, honoring You in every thought, word, and action. Amen.

God's Standard of Fairness

*"The Lord demands accurate scales and
balances; he sets the standards for fairness."*
— PROVERBS 16:11 (NLT)

Additional Scripture References:

*Leviticus 19:36 - "Use honest scales and honest weights, an honest ephah and
an honest hin. I am the Lord your God who brought you out of Egypt."*

*Micah 6:8 - "No, O people, the Lord has told you what is good, and this is what
he requires of you: to do what is right, to love mercy, and to walk humbly with
your God."*

Devotional Thought:

God calls us to live with fairness and honesty, upholding integrity in
every area of life. By honoring His standards, we reflect His justice
and love. Today, let God's standard of fairness guide your actions,
making integrity the foundation of all you do.

Reflection Questions

Are there areas where you can practice more fairness and honesty?

How does living by God's standard of fairness impact those around
you?

What steps can you take to make integrity a priority in your life?

Prayer for the Day

Lord, help me to live by Your standard of fairness and honesty. Let my
actions reflect Your justice and bring honor to Your name. Amen.

November 9

Integrity in All Dealings

"You must be honest in all you do, especially in the way you weigh and measure."

— LEVITICUS 19:36 (NLT)

Additional Scripture References:

Proverbs 11:1 - *"The Lord detests dishonest scales, but accurate weights find favor with him."*

Amos 8:5 - *"You boast, 'We will soon be rid of the religious festivals and the Sabbath days of worship. We want to trade and harvest again.'"*

Devotional Thought:

God desires honesty in every detail of our lives, even in the smallest actions. When we commit to integrity, we bring His light into the world. Today, reflect on how you can honor God through honesty in all your dealings, big and small.

Reflection Questions

Are there areas where you need to prioritize honesty?

How does committing to integrity in small actions bring glory to God?

What steps can you take to make honesty a habit?

Prayer for the Day

Father, help me to be honest in all things, reflecting Your truth and integrity in every detail. Let my life be a testimony to Your goodness. Amen.

November 10

Honest Business and Relationships

"Do not cheat your neighbor by using dishonest scales."
— DEUTERONOMY 25:13 (NLT)

Additional Scripture References:

Proverbs 11:1 - "The Lord detests dishonest scales, but accurate weights find favor with him."

Micah 6:11 - "What shall I say? Should I be pure and honest? Should I sacrifice my firstborn for my sins?"

Devotional Thought:

God values integrity in every area of life, especially in how we treat others. By being honest and fair, we show respect for those around us and honor God. Today, commit to treating others fairly, seeing honesty as a foundation for trust.

Reflection Questions

Are there ways you can be more intentional about fairness in your relationships?

How does treating others with honesty strengthen trust?

What steps can you take to ensure fairness in your actions?

Prayer for the Day

Lord, help me to treat others with honesty and respect. Let my actions reflect Your love and fairness, building trust and harmony in all my relationships. Amen.

November 11

Faithfulness in the Little Things

"If you are faithful in little things,
you will be faithful in large ones."

— LUKE 16:10 (NLT)

Additional Scripture References:

Matthew 25:21 - "The master said, 'Well done, my good and faithful servant.
You have been faithful in handling this small amount, so now I will give you
many more responsibilities. Let's celebrate together!'"

Proverbs 28:20 - "The trustworthy person will get a rich reward, but a person
who wants quick riches will get into trouble."

Devotional Thought:

Integrity begins with the small things. By being faithful in minor details, we build a character of trustworthiness and honesty. Today, let your faithfulness in small actions reflect God's character, preparing you for greater responsibilities.

Reflection Questions

Are there small areas where you can practice more faithfulness?

How does being faithful in little things prepare you for larger roles?

What steps can you take to practice integrity in everyday moments?

Prayer for the Day

Father, help me to be faithful in the little things. Let my actions, no matter how small, honor You and build a foundation of trustworthiness. Amen.

November 12

Honesty in Hidden Areas

*"The Lord detests double standards;
he is not pleased by dishonest scales."*
— **PROVERBS 20:23 (NLT)**

Additional Scripture References:

*Proverbs 11:1 - "The Lord detests dishonest scales, but accurate weights find
favor with him."*

*Micah 6:10-11 - "What shall I say? Should I be pure and honest? Should I
sacrifice my firstborn for my sins? What does the Lord require of you? To act
justly, to love mercy, and to walk humbly with your God."*

Devotional Thought:

God calls us to live honestly, even when no one is watching. Hidden
actions reveal our true character. Today, examine your heart and
actions, allowing God's truth to shape your integrity in every area, seen
and unseen.

Reflection Questions

Are there hidden areas where you need to embrace God's standard of
honesty?

How does living with integrity in unseen areas shape your character?

What steps can you take to make honesty a foundation in all things?

Prayer for the Day

Lord, help me to honor You in every area of my life, seen and unseen.
Let my heart be filled with honesty, reflecting Your truth in all I do.
Amen.

November 13

True Justice

"Judges must not twist justice. You must never show partiality;
you must always judge people fairly."
— DEUTERONOMY 16:19 (NLT)

Additional Scripture References:

Proverbs 24:23 - "These are sayings of the wise: It is wrong to show favoritism when passing judgment."

Exodus 23:8 - "Take no bribes, for a bribe blinds the clear-sighted and twists the words of the innocent."

Devotional Thought:

God calls us to uphold true justice, free from favoritism or partiality. By treating others fairly, we honor God's character and love. Today, commit to fairness and justice in your decisions, seeing others through God's eyes.

Reflection Questions

Are there areas where you need to practice more fairness?

How does treating others without partiality reflect God's justice?

What steps can you take to honor fairness and equality?

Prayer for the Day

Father, let justice guide my heart and actions. Help me to see others with love and fairness, honoring Your call to truth and integrity. Amen.

November 14

Honesty as Worship

*"To do righteousness and justice is more acceptable
to the Lord than sacrifice."*

— PROVERBS 21:3 (NKJV)

Additional Scripture References:

*Micah 6:8 - "No, O people, the Lord has told you what is good, and this is what
he requires of you: to do what is right, to love mercy, and to walk humbly with
your God."*

*Isaiah 1:17 - "Learn to do good. Seek justice. Help the oppressed. Defend the
cause of orphans. Fight for the rights of widows."*

Devotional Thought:

God values righteousness and justice as a form of worship, seeing
honesty and fairness as expressions of our devotion. Today, let
honesty be a form of worship, honoring God with integrity in all things.

Reflection Questions

Are there ways you can honor God through justice and honesty?

How does living righteously serve as an act of worship?

What steps can you take to make integrity a part of your devotion?

Prayer for the Day

Lord, let my life reflect Your righteousness. Help me to honor You in all
my actions, seeing integrity as a way to worship You. Amen.

The Command to Love

"This is my commandment:
Love each other in the same way I have loved you."

— JOHN 15:12 (NLT)

Additional Scripture References:

1 John 4:7 - "Dear friends, let us continue to love one another, for love comes from God. Anyone who loves is a child of God and knows God."

Matthew 22:39 - "A second is equally important: 'Love your neighbor as yourself.'"

Devotional Thought:

Jesus calls us to love others as He has loved us — sacrificially, selflessly, and deeply. True love reflects Christ's heart, putting others' needs before our own. Today, let your love for others be a reflection of Christ's love for you.

Reflection Questions

Are there ways you can show more selfless love to those around you?

How does loving others as Christ loves you transform your relationships?

What steps can you take to deepen your compassion for others?

Prayer for the Day

Father, help me to love others as Christ has loved me. Let my actions reflect Your heart, showing compassion and care to all I encounter. Amen.

Loving Beyond Boundaries

"Love your neighbor as yourself."
— MATTHEW 22:39 (NLT)

Additional Scripture References:

Galatians 5:14 - "For the whole law can be summed up in this one command: 'Love your neighbor as yourself.'"

Romans 13:10 - "Love does no wrong to others, so love fulfills the requirements of God's law."

Devotional Thought:

Loving our neighbors means treating others with the same respect, care, and kindness we desire for ourselves. It calls us to look beyond differences, reaching out with open hearts. Today, practice kindness and understanding, loving others with the same grace you receive from God.

Reflection Questions

Are there ways you can extend love to those who are different from you?

How does loving others without boundaries reflect God's love?

What steps can you take to show kindness in all your interactions?

Prayer for the Day

Lord, help me to love my neighbor as myself. Let my actions show compassion and grace, extending Your love to all those around me. Amen.

November 17

Serving Others with Joy

"For you have been called to live in freedom...use
your freedom to serve one another in love."

— GALATIANS 5:13 (NLT)

Additional Scripture References:

1 Peter 2:16 - "For you are free, yet you are God's slaves, so don't use your freedom as an excuse to do evil."

Romans 14:19 - "So then, let us aim for harmony in the church and try to build each other up."

Devotional Thought:

God gives us freedom so we can serve others selflessly and joyfully. By putting love into action, we build each other up and honor God. Today, look for opportunities to serve, finding joy in showing Christ's love to others.

Reflection Questions

Are there ways you can serve those around you with more joy?

How does serving others reflect Christ's love in your life?

What steps can you take to make serving others a daily habit?

Prayer for the Day

Father, let my freedom be used for Your purpose. Help me to serve others with joy, reflecting Your love through my actions. Amen.

November 18

Loving in Deed and Truth

"Let us not love with words or
speech but with actions and in truth."

— 1 JOHN 3:18 (NLT)

Additional Scripture References:

James 2:17 - *"So you see, faith by itself isn't enough. Unless it produces good deeds, it is dead and useless."*

1 John 4:20 - *"If someone says, 'I love God,' but hates a fellow believer, that person is a liar; for if we don't love people we can see, how can we love God, whom we cannot see?"*

Devotional Thought:

True love is shown through actions and sincerity, going beyond words to make a lasting impact. When we love in truth, we reflect God's love genuinely and deeply. Today, let your love be shown through kindness, serving those around you with authenticity.

Reflection Questions

Are there ways you can love others more authentically?

How does loving through actions strengthen your faith and relationships?

What steps can you take to show love in tangible ways?

Prayer for the Day

Lord, let my love be genuine, shown through actions and truth. Help me to love as You do, bringing comfort and strength to those in need. Amen.

November 19

Compassion for All

"Be kind to each other, tenderhearted, forgiving one another, just as God through Christ has forgiven you."
— Ephesians 4:32 (NLT)

Additional Scripture References:

Colossians 3:13 - "Make allowance for each other's faults, and forgive anyone who offends you. Remember, the Lord forgave you, so you must forgive others."

Matthew 6:14 - "If you forgive those who sin against you, your heavenly Father will forgive you."

Devotional Thought:

Compassion and forgiveness go hand in hand, helping us build connections rooted in love and grace. When we're tenderhearted, we reflect Christ's forgiveness and kindness. Today, let compassion guide your interactions, seeing others with the same love God has shown you.

Reflection Questions

Are there areas where you need to show more compassion and forgiveness?

How does treating others tenderheartedly reflect God's love?

What steps can you take to embrace a heart of kindness?

Prayer for the Day

Father, help me to be tenderhearted and forgiving. Let my actions show Your love and compassion, bringing peace to those around me. Amen.

Loving Without Expectation

*"Give to those who ask, and don't turn away
from those who want to borrow."*

— **MATTHEW 5:42 (NLT)**

Additional Scripture References:

Luke 6:30 - "Give to anyone who asks; and when things are taken away from you, don't try to get them back."

Proverbs 19:17 - "If you help the poor, you are lending to the Lord — and he will repay you!"

Devotional Thought:

Christ calls us to give freely, loving without expecting anything in return. When we love selflessly, we reflect God's grace. Today, practice giving with an open heart, offering kindness without expectation and trusting God to provide.

Reflection Questions

Are there areas where you can give without expecting anything in return?

How does selfless giving strengthen your faith and compassion?

What steps can you take to give generously?

Prayer for the Day

Lord, help me to love selflessly, giving freely without expecting in return. Let my actions reflect Your grace, trusting that You will provide. Amen.

Patience with Others

"Be completely humble and gentle;
be patient, bearing with one another in love."

— EPHESIANS 4:2 (NLT)

Additional Scripture References:

Colossians 3:12 - "Since God chose you to be the holy people he loves, you must clothe yourselves with tenderhearted mercy, kindness, humility, gentleness, and patience."

Philippians 2:3 - "Don't be selfish; don't try to impress others. Be humble, thinking of others as better than yourselves."

Devotional Thought:

Patience is essential in loving others, helping us to be gentle and understanding. When we bear with one another in love, we show the compassion and grace God extends to us. Today, let patience guide your interactions, responding to others with kindness and humility.

Reflection Questions

Are there areas where you need to be more patient with others?

How does patience strengthen your relationships and reflect God's love?

What steps can you take to show more patience and understanding?

Prayer for the Day

Father, fill me with patience and humility. Help me to bear with others in love, showing compassion and gentleness in all I do. Amen.

God's Justice

"The Lord loves righteousness and
justice; the earth is full of his unfailing love."

— PSALM 33:5 (NLT)

Additional Scripture References:

Psalm 37:28 - "For the Lord loves justice, and he will never abandon the godly. He will keep them safe forever, but the children of the wicked will die."

Micah 6:8 - "No, O people, the Lord has told you what is good, and this is what he requires of you: to do what is right, to love mercy, and to walk humbly with your God."

Devotional Thought:

God's love for justice reflects His righteous nature and deep compassion. By standing for justice and righteousness, we align our lives with His heart. Today, seek to honor God's justice in all you do, advocating for what is right and fair.

Reflection Questions

Are there areas where you can pursue justice on behalf of others?

How does standing for righteousness reflect God's character?

What steps can you take to live out God's justice?

Prayer for the Day

Lord, help me to seek justice and righteousness in all things. Let my actions honor Your love and reflect Your compassion for others. Amen.

November 23

God's Call to Compassionate Justice

"He has told you, O man, what is good; and
what does the Lord require of you but to do justice, to love kindness,
and to walk humbly with your God?"

— MICAH 6:8 (NLT)

Additional Scripture References:

Matthew 23:23 - "What sorrow awaits you teachers of religious law and you Pharisees. Hypocrites! For you are careful to tithe even the tiniest income from your herb gardens, but you ignore the more important aspects of the law — justice, mercy, and faith. You should tithe, yes, but do not neglect the more important things."

James 1:27 - "Pure and genuine religion in the sight of God the Father means caring for orphans and widows in their distress and refusing to let the world corrupt you."

Devotional Thought:

God's justice calls us to act with compassion, kindness, and humility. When we seek justice, we do so with love and respect for others. Today, let kindness guide your pursuit of justice, walking humbly with God in all things.

Reflection Questions

Are there ways you can balance justice with kindness and humility?

How does walking humbly with God shape your view of justice?

What steps can you take to seek justice with compassion?

Prayer for the Day

Father, help me to pursue justice with humility and love. Let my actions honor You and bring kindness and respect to those around me. Amen.

The Consequences of Sin

*"For the wages of sin is death, but
the free gift of God is eternal life through Christ Jesus our Lord."*
— ROMANS 6:23 (NLT)

Additional Scripture References:

John 3:16 - "For this is how God loved the world: He gave his one and only Son, so that everyone who believes in him will not perish but have eternal life."

Ephesians 2:8-9 - "God saved you by his grace when you believed. And you can't take credit for this; it is a gift from God. Salvation is not a reward for the good things we have done, so none of us can boast about it."

Devotional Thought:

Sin separates us from God, leading to spiritual death. Yet, in His love, God offers eternal life through Jesus Christ. Today, reflect on the cost of sin and the gift of grace, choosing to live in the freedom and forgiveness God provides.

Reflection Questions

Are there areas of sin you need to surrender to God?

How does understanding the cost of sin deepen your gratitude for grace?

What steps can you take to live in the freedom of Christ's forgiveness?

Prayer for the Day

Lord, thank You for the gift of eternal life. Help me to turn from sin and walk in the freedom and grace You offer through Jesus. Amen.

November 25

Repentance and Restoration

"If we confess our sins, he is faithful and just to forgive us our sins and to cleanse us from all unrighteousness."

— 1 JOHN 1:9 (NLT)

Additional Scripture References:

Psalm 32:5 - "Finally, I confessed all my sins to you and stopped trying to hide my guilt. I said to myself, 'I will confess my rebellion to the Lord.' And you forgave me! All my guilt is gone."

Romans 10:9 - "If you openly declare that Jesus is Lord and believe in your heart that God raised him from the dead, you will be saved."

Devotional Thought:

God is faithful to forgive and restore us when we repent. His justice and mercy bring healing and a fresh start. Today, seek God's forgiveness for any sin, trusting that His grace will cleanse and renew you.

Reflection Questions

Are there sins you need to confess to God today?

How does God's forgiveness bring freedom and peace?

What steps can you take to walk in God's restoration?

Prayer for the Day

Father, thank You for Your faithful forgiveness. Cleanse my heart, renew my spirit, and help me to live in Your grace. Amen.

November 26

Gratitude for God's Blessings

"Give thanks to the Lord, for he is good!
His faithful love endures forever."
— PSALM 107:1 (NLT)

Additional Scripture References:

1 Chronicles 16:34 - *"Give thanks to the Lord, for he is good; his love endures forever."*

Psalm 136:1 - *"Give thanks to the Lord, for he is good! His faithful love endures forever."*

Devotional Thought:

Gratitude reminds us of God's goodness and draws us closer to His heart. When we thank God for His blessings, we deepen our relationship with Him. Today, let gratitude fill your heart, remembering His faithfulness in every season.

Reflection Questions

Are there blessings you can thank God for today?

How does practicing gratitude strengthen your relationship with God?

What steps can you take to make thankfulness a daily habit?

Prayer for the Day

Lord, thank You for Your goodness and love. Let my heart be filled with gratitude, rejoicing in Your faithfulness each day. Amen.

November 27

Gratefulness for Small Blessings

*"Whatever is good and perfect is a gift coming
down to us from God our Father."*

— JAMES 1:17 (NLT)

Additional Scripture References:

Matthew 7:11 - *"So if you sinful people know how to give good gifts to your
children, how much more will your heavenly Father give good gifts to those
who ask him."*

Romans 12:6 - *"In his grace, God has given us different gifts for doing certain
things well. So if God has given you the ability to prophesy, speak out with as
much faith as God has given you."*

Devotional Thought:

Every good thing in our lives comes from God's hand, reminding
us of His constant care. By recognizing His gifts, big and small, we
cultivate a heart of gratitude. Today, thank God for the simple blessings
that fill your life with joy.

Reflection Questions

Are there small blessings you can acknowledge and thank God for?

How does noticing everyday gifts deepen your appreciation for God?

What steps can you take to make gratitude part of your routine?

Prayer for the Day

Father, thank You for the countless blessings in my life. Help me to
appreciate Your goodness, finding joy in every gift. Amen.

November 28

Jesus' Sacrifice for Us

*"But God showed his great love for us by sending
Christ to die for us while we were still sinners."*

— ROMANS 5:8 (NLT)

Additional Scripture References:

John 3:16 - *"For this is how God loved the world: He gave his one and only
Son, so that everyone who believes in him will not perish but have eternal life."*

1 John 4:9-10 - *"God showed how much he loved us by sending his one and
only Son into the world so that we might have eternal life through him. This
is real love — not that we loved God, but that he loved us and sent his Son as a
sacrifice to take away our sins."*

Devotional Thought:

Jesus' sacrifice on the cross is the ultimate expression of God's love.
Even while we were sinners, Christ gave His life to redeem us.
Today, reflect on the depth of Jesus' love for you, allowing His sacrifice
to inspire gratitude and devotion.

Reflection Questions

Are there ways you can honor Jesus' sacrifice in your life?

How does understanding His love deepen your relationship with Him?

What steps can you take to live more gratefully for His gift?

Prayer for the Day

Lord, thank You for Jesus' sacrifice. Help me to live in gratitude,
honoring His love in all I do. Amen.

The Gift of Salvation

"There is salvation in no one else! God has given no other name under heaven by which we must be saved."

— ACTS 4:12 (NLT)

Additional Scripture References:

John 14:6 - "Jesus told him, 'I am the way, the truth, and the life. No one can come to the Father except through me.'"

Romans 10:13 - "For everyone who calls on the name of the Lord will be saved."

Devotional Thought:

Salvation is a gift, given to us through Jesus Christ alone. By placing our faith in Him, we receive eternal life and forgiveness. Today, rejoice in the gift of salvation, letting gratitude fill your heart for God's amazing grace.

Reflection Questions

Are there areas in your life where you need to rest in God's grace?

How does embracing salvation bring peace to your heart?

What steps can you take to express gratitude for this gift each day?

Prayer for the Day

Father, thank You for the gift of salvation. Let my life be a reflection of gratitude and faith, honoring the love You've shown through Jesus. Amen.

November 30

God Sent Jesus for Us

"For God loved the world so much that he gave his one and only Son, so that everyone who believes in him will not perish but have eternal life."

— JOHN 3:16 (NLT)

Additional Scripture References:

Romans 5:8 - "But God showed his great love for us by sending Christ to die for us while we were still sinners."

1 John 5:11-12 - "And this is what God has testified: He has given us eternal life, and this life is in his Son. Whoever has the Son has life; whoever does not have God's Son does not have life."

Devotional Thought:

God's love for us is so great that He sent Jesus to be our Savior, offering eternal life to all who believe. This incredible gift reminds us of His unfailing love and purpose for us. Today, thank God for the gift of Jesus, reflecting on His love and promise of eternal life.

Reflection Questions

Are there ways you can share God's love with others today?

How does knowing God sent Jesus for you deepen your relationship with Him?

What steps can you take to honor God's love in your life?

Prayer for the Day

Lord, thank You for sending Jesus to save us. Help me to live in the joy of Your love, sharing the hope of eternal life with those around me. Amen.

December 1

The Love of Christ: Leaving Heaven for Us

"Though he was God, he did not think of equality with
God as something to cling to."
— PHILIPPIANS 2:6 (NLT)

Additional Scripture References:

John 1:1 - "In the beginning the Word already existed. The Word was with God, and the Word was God."

Colossians 1:16-17 - "For through him God created everything in the heavenly realms and on earth. He made the things we can see and the things we can't see — such as thrones, kingdoms, rulers, and authorities in the unseen world. Everything was created through him and for him. He existed before anything else, and he holds all creation together."

Devotional Thought:

Jesus left the glory of heaven to walk among us, choosing humility and sacrifice to bring us salvation. His love led Him to give up His divine privileges for our sake. Today, let Christ's love inspire you to serve with humility, reflecting His compassion and selflessness.

Reflection Questions

Are there ways you can serve others with humility today?

How does knowing Jesus gave up heaven for you deepen your faith?

What steps can you take to reflect Christ's selflessness?

Prayer for the Day

Lord, thank You for the love that led You to leave heaven. Help me to reflect Your humility and serve others with compassion and grace. Amen.

December 2

Christs Humility and Love

"Instead, he gave up his divine privileges; he took the humble position of a slave and was born as a human being."

— PHILIPPIANS 2:7 (NLT)

Additional Scripture References:

Matthew 20:28 - "For even the Son of Man came not to be served but to serve others and to give his life as a ransom for many."

Isaiah 53:3 - "He was despised and rejected — a man of sorrows, acquainted with deepest grief. We turned our backs on him and looked the other way. He was despised, and we did not care."

Devotional Thought:

Jesus' life on earth exemplified humility and love, showing us how to serve others selflessly. His love for us knew no bounds, leading Him to embrace our humanity. Today, let Christ's humility guide your actions, remembering His love in every choice you make.

Reflection Questions

Are there areas where you can demonstrate humility?

How does understanding Christ's love change the way you approach others?

What steps can you take to honor His love through service?

Prayer for the Day

Father, thank You for the humility of Christ. Help me to walk in His example, serving others with a heart of compassion and love. Amen.

December 3

Sacrifice of Love

*"There is no greater love than to lay down
one's life for one's friends."*

— JOHN 15:13 (NLT)

Additional Scripture References:

*Romans 5:7-8 - "Now, most people would not be willing to die for an upright
person, though someone might perhaps be willing to die for a person who is
especially good. But God showed his great love for us by sending Christ to die
for us while we were still sinners."*

*1 John 3:16 - "We know what real love is because Jesus gave up his life for us.
So we also ought to give up our lives for our brothers and sisters."*

Devotional Thought:

Jesus showed the ultimate act of love by giving His life for us. His
sacrifice demonstrates the depth of His commitment to us. Today,
reflect on His love, letting it inspire you to love sacrificially, putting
others before yourself.

Reflection Questions

Are there ways you can show sacrificial love to others?

How does reflecting on Jesus' sacrifice deepen your love for Him?

What steps can you take to live out this kind of love?

Prayer for the Day

Lord, thank You for laying down Your life for me. Help me to love
others with the same selflessness and dedication that You have shown.
Amen.

December 4

What Jesus Sacrifices for Us

"For you know the grace of our Lord Jesus Christ:
Though he was rich, yet for your sake he became poor."
— 2 CORINTHIANS 8:9 (NLT)

Additional Scripture References:

Philippians 2:7-8 - "Instead, he gave up his divine privileges; he took the humble position of a slave and was born as a human being. When he appeared in human form, he humbled himself in obedience to God and died a criminal's death on a cross."

Matthew 20:28 - "For even the Son of Man came not to be served but to serve others and to give his life as a ransom for many."

Devotional Thought:

Jesus gave up His riches, humbling Himself so that we could experience the riches of His grace. His sacrifice is a gift that opens the way to eternal life. Today, let His generosity inspire you to give freely, sharing love and kindness with those around you.

Reflection Questions

Are there areas where you can give more generously?

How does Jesus' sacrifice inspire you to be selfless?

What steps can you take to reflect His love in your generosity?

Prayer for the Day

Father, thank You for the gift of Jesus' sacrifice. Let my heart be filled with gratitude, inspiring me to give generously to others. Amen.

December 5

Living Gratefully for Christ's Sacrifice

"He gave himself for our sins to rescue us
from the present evil age."

— GALATIANS 1:4 (NLT)

Additional Scripture References:

Ephesians 1:7 - "He is so rich in kindness and grace that he purchased our freedom with the blood of his Son and forgave our sins."

1 Thessalonians 1:10 - "And they speak of how you are looking forward to the coming of God's Son from heaven – Jesus, whom God raised from the dead. He is the one who has rescued us from the terrors of the coming judgment."

Devotional Thought:

Jesus' love led Him to rescue us, giving Himself fully to bring us freedom and hope. His sacrifice reminds us of the cost of our salvation and the depth of His love. Today, let gratitude fill your heart, living each day as a reflection of His love.

Reflection Questions

Are there ways you can live more gratefully for Christ's sacrifice?

How does understanding His gift influence your choices?

What steps can you take to let gratitude shape your daily life?

Prayer for the Day

Lord, thank You for the rescue You provide through Jesus. Let my life be a reflection of my gratitude, honoring You in all I do. Amen.

December 6

Sharing My Faith

*"And then he told them, 'Go into all the world and
preach the Good News to everyone.'"*

— MARK 16:15 (NLT)

Additional Scripture References:

*Matthew 28:19-20 - "Therefore, go and make disciples of all the nations,
baptizing them in the name of the Father and the Son and the Holy Spirit.
Teach these new disciples to obey all the commands I have given you. And be
sure of this: I am with you always, even to the end of the age."*

*Acts 1:8 - "But you will receive power when the Holy Spirit comes upon
you. And you will be my witnesses, telling people about me everywhere – in
Jerusalem, throughout Judea, in Samaria, and to the ends of the earth."*

Devotional Thought:

Jesus calls us to share the hope and joy of His salvation with others. By
sharing our faith, we bring light and hope to those who are searching.
Today, let your life be a testimony, sharing the Good News with love
and enthusiasm.

Reflection Questions

Are there people in your life who need to hear about Jesus?

How does sharing your faith strengthen your own relationship with
God?

What steps can you take to share the Good News with others?

Prayer for the Day

Father, help me to share the hope of Your salvation with joy. Let my
words and actions reflect Your love, bringing others closer to You.
Amen.

December 7

Living as a Witness

*"You are the light of the world — like a city on a hilltop
that cannot be hidden."*

— MATTHEW 5:14 (NLT)

Additional Scripture References:

*Philippians 2:15 - "So that no one can criticize you. Live clean, innocent lives
as children of God, shining like bright lights in a world full of crooked and
perverse people."*

*John 8:12 - "Jesus spoke to the people once more and said, 'I am the light of the
world. If you follow me, you won't have to walk in darkness, because you will
have the light that leads to life.'"*

Devotional Thought:

Jesus calls us to be a light, shining His love and truth for others to
see. When we live as His witnesses, we reflect His grace and draw
others to Him. Today, let your life be a beacon of hope, pointing others
to Christ's love.

Reflection Questions

Are there ways you can let your light shine for others?

How does living as a witness deepen your faith?

What steps can you take to be a testimony of God's love?

Prayer for the Day

Lord, let my life be a light that reflects Your love. Help me to live as a
witness, bringing others closer to You each day. Amen.

December 8

Reaching the Lost

"The Son of Man came to seek and save those who are lost."

— LUKE 19:10 (NLT)

Additional Scripture References:

Matthew 18:11 - "For the Son of Man came to save those who are lost."

John 3:17 - "God sent his Son into the world not to judge the world, but to save the world through him."

Devotional Thought:

Jesus' mission was to seek and save the lost, showing compassion and grace to those who needed Him most. We are called to carry on this mission, sharing His love with a world in need. Today, ask God to open your eyes to those who are searching, reaching out with kindness and understanding.

Reflection Questions

Are there people in your life who are spiritually lost?

How does showing compassion help you reach others?

What steps can you take to bring the lost closer to Christ?

Prayer for the Day

Father, help me to see those who are lost and searching. Let my actions and words bring hope and guidance, leading them to You. Amen.

December 9

Compassion for the Lost

"When he saw the crowds, he had compassion on them because
they were confused and helpless, like sheep without a shepherd."
— MATTHEW 9:36 (NLT)

Additional Scripture References:

Mark 6:34 - "Jesus saw the huge crowd as he stepped from the boat, and he had
compassion on them because they were like sheep without a shepherd. So he
began teaching them many things."

Luke 10:2 - "These were his instructions to them: 'The harvest is great, but the
workers are few. So pray to the Lord who is in charge of the harvest; ask him to
send more workers into his fields.'"

Devotional Thought:

Jesus looked at the lost with compassion, understanding their
struggles and offering love. When we reach out with compassion,
we reflect His heart. Today, let compassion guide you, seeing others
through Christ's eyes.

Reflection Questions

Are there ways you can show more compassion to those who are lost?

How does understanding others' struggles help you connect with
them?

What steps can you take to reach out to those who need hope?

Prayer for the Day

Lord, fill me with compassion for the lost. Help me to see others with
Your love and understanding, reaching out to guide them toward You.
Amen.

December 10

Learning from the Parables of Christ

"He taught them by telling many stories
in the form of parables."
— MATTHEW 13:3 (NLT)

Additional Scripture References:

Mark 4:2 - "He taught them by telling many stories in the form of parables, such as this one: 'Listen! A farmer went out to plant some seed.'"

Luke 8:5 - "A farmer went out to plant his seed. As he scattered it across his field, some seed fell on a footpath, where it was stepped on, and the birds ate it."

Devotional Thought:

Jesus used parables to teach profound truths, making His message accessible and memorable. His stories reveal God's kingdom, inviting us to understand His heart. Today, seek to learn from Christ's teachings, letting His wisdom shape your life.

Reflection Questions

Are there parables of Christ that have impacted your life?

How does understanding His teachings bring you closer to God?

What steps can you take to apply Jesus' lessons in your life?

Prayer for the Day

Father, thank You for the wisdom of Jesus' teachings. Help me to learn from His words, letting His truth guide me each day. Amen.

December 11

Parables of Growth and Faith

"The Kingdom of Heaven is like a mustard seed planted in a field."
— MATTHEW 13:31 (NLT)

Additional Scripture References:

Mark 4:30-32 - "Jesus said, 'How can I describe the Kingdom of God? What story should I use to illustrate it? It is like a mustard seed planted in the ground. It is the smallest of all seeds, but it becomes the largest of all garden plants. It grows into a tree, and the birds come and make nests in its branches.'"

Luke 13:18-19 - "Then Jesus said, 'What is the Kingdom of God like? How can I illustrate it? It is like a tiny mustard seed that a man planted in a garden. It grows and becomes a tree, and the birds make nests in its branches.'"

Devotional Thought:

Jesus taught that faith, even as small as a mustard seed, can grow into something mighty. This parable reminds us that God can use even the smallest amount of faith to bring about great things. Today, trust in God's power to grow your faith, no matter how small it may feel.

Reflection Questions

Are there areas in your life where you need greater faith?

How does trusting in God's growth strengthen your relationship with Him?

What steps can you take to cultivate and nurture your faith daily?

Prayer for the Day

Father, thank You for the power of faith. Help my small beginnings grow into something beautiful and strong for Your kingdom. Amen.

December 12

The Parable of the Good Samaritan

"Yes, now go and do the same."

— LUKE 10:37 (NLT)

Additional Scripture References:

Matthew 5:7 - "God blesses those who are merciful, for they will be shown mercy."

James 2:13 - "For judgment will be merciless to those who have not shown mercy. But if you have been merciful, God will be merciful when he judges you."

Devotional Thought:

Jesus' story of the Good Samaritan teaches us to show kindness and compassion to others, regardless of differences. He calls us to actively help those in need, just as the Samaritan did. Today, look for opportunities to extend kindness and grace, following Jesus' example.

Reflection Questions

Are there people in your life who need kindness and compassion?

How does helping others strengthen your faith?

What steps can you take to live out Jesus' call to "do the same"?

Prayer for the Day

Lord, help me to see others through Your eyes and extend kindness to those in need. Let my actions reflect Your love and mercy. Amen.

December 13

The Parable of the Sower

"The seed that fell on good soil represents those
who truly hear and understand God's word."

— MATTHEW 13:23 (NLT)

Additional Scripture References:

Luke 8:15 - "And the seeds that fell on the good soil represent honest, good-hearted people who hear God's word, cling to it, and patiently produce a huge harvest."

James 1:22 - "But don't just listen to God's word. You must do what it says. Otherwise, you are only fooling yourselves."

Devotional Thought:

In the Parable of the Sower, Jesus describes the importance of a heart ready to receive His Word. When we open ourselves to God's truth, we become fertile ground for His work. Today, let your heart be "good soil," ready for God's teachings to take root and grow.

Reflection Questions

Are there areas where you need to better receive God's Word?

How does preparing your heart help you grow in faith?

What steps can you take to become more receptive to God's teachings?

Prayer for the Day

Father, prepare my heart to be good soil. Let Your Word take root in me, producing fruit for Your kingdom. Amen.

December 14

The Parable of the Lost Sheep

*"If a man has a hundred sheep and
one of them gets lost, what will he do?"*

— MATTHEW 18:12 (NLT)

Additional Scripture References:

Luke 15:4 - "If a man has a hundred sheep and one of them gets lost, what will he do? Won't he leave the ninety-nine others in the wilderness and go to search for the one that is lost until he finds it?"

John 10:11 - "I am the good shepherd. The good shepherd sacrifices his life for the sheep."

Devotional Thought:

Jesus shows God's love for each of us through the Parable of the Lost Sheep. God seeks us out, no matter how far we've wandered, and rejoices when we return to Him. Today, remember that you are deeply loved and valued by God.

Reflection Questions

Are there ways you can draw closer to God if you feel lost?

How does knowing God seeks you out deepen your faith?

What steps can you take to remind others of their value to God?

Prayer for the Day

Lord, thank You for seeking me when I wander. Help me to remember Your love and share it with others. Amen.

December 15

Preparing Goals: Seeking God's Will

*"Seek his will in all you do, and
he will show you which path to take."*

— PROVERBS 3:6 (NLT)

Additional Scripture References:

Jeremiah 29:13 - "If you look for me wholeheartedly, you will find me."

Psalm 37:5 - "Commit everything you do to the Lord. Trust him, and he will help you."

Devotional Thought:

As you begin to set goals for the new year, seek God's guidance in each area of your life. When you align your plans with His will, you'll find purpose and direction. Today, pray for clarity as you prepare for the future.

Reflection Questions

Are there goals you want to bring before God?

How does seeking God's will bring peace to your plans?

What steps can you take to align your goals with God's purpose?

Prayer for the Day

Father, guide me in setting goals that honor You. Show me the path to take, and let my life reflect Your will. Amen.

December 16

Setting Goals with Faith

"For I know the plans I have for you, says the Lord."
— **JEREMIAH 29:11 (NLT)**

Additional Scripture References:

Romans 8:28 - "And we know that God causes everything to work together for the good of those who love God and are called according to his purpose for them."

Psalm 32:8 - "The Lord says, 'I will guide you along the best pathway for your life. I will advise you and watch over you.'"

Devotional Thought:

God has plans for you that are filled with hope and purpose. When setting goals, trust that He is leading you toward a future filled with His promises. Today, let your goals reflect your faith, trusting God's plans for you.

Reflection Questions

Are there areas of your future where you need to trust God more?

How does relying on God's plan influence your goals?

What steps can you take to set goals rooted in faith?

Prayer for the Day

Lord, thank You for the plans You have for me. Help me to set goals that honor Your will, trusting in Your purpose for my life. Amen.

December 17

Planning for Spiritual Growth

*"But grow in the grace and knowledge of
our Lord and Savior Jesus Christ."*

— 2 PETER 3:18 (NLT)

Additional Scripture References:

*Colossians 1:10 - "Then the way you live will always honor and please the
Lord, and your lives will produce every kind of good fruit. All the while, you
will grow as you learn to know God better and better."*

*Ephesians 4:15 - "Instead, we will speak the truth in love, growing in every
way more and more like Christ, who is the head of his body, the church."*

Devotional Thought:

As you make plans for the coming year, include goals for spiritual
growth. Cultivating your relationship with God brings lasting
joy and fulfillment. Today, consider setting goals that deepen your
understanding of His love and truth.

Reflection Questions

Are there areas in your faith you'd like to grow in this year?

How does focusing on spiritual growth strengthen your daily life?

What steps can you take to make growth in Christ a priority?

Prayer for the Day

Father, help me to grow in Your grace and knowledge. Let my heart be
set on knowing You more deeply each day. Amen.

December 18

Goals for Serving Others

"Each of you should use whatever gift
you have received to serve others."

— 1 PETER 4:10 (NLT)

Additional Scripture References:

Romans 12:6 - "In his grace, God has given us different gifts for doing certain things well. So if God has given you the ability to prophesy, speak out with as much faith as God has given you."

Ephesians 4:11-12 - "Now these are the gifts Christ gave to the church: the apostles, the prophets, the evangelists, and the pastors and teachers. Their responsibility is to equip God's people to do his work and build up the church, the body of Christ."

Devotional Thought:

God has given you unique gifts to bless others. As you set goals, consider how you can serve those around you. Today, ask God to show you ways to use your gifts for His glory and to benefit others.

Reflection Questions

Are there ways you can serve others more intentionally this year?

How does using your gifts for others bring purpose to your life?

What steps can you take to put your gifts into action?

Prayer for the Day

Lord, show me how to use my gifts to serve others. Let my life be a blessing, reflecting Your love in all I do. Amen.

December 19

Goals for a Grateful Heart

"Be thankful in all circumstances,
for this is God's will for you."

— 1 THESSALONIANS 5:18 (NLT)

Additional Scripture References:

Colossians 3:15 - "And let the peace that comes from Christ rule in your hearts. For as members of one body you are called to live in peace. And always be thankful."

Ephesians 5:20 - "And give thanks for everything to God the Father in the name of our Lord Jesus Christ."

Devotional Thought:

A heart of gratitude transforms how we see life. When setting goals, include those that help you practice thankfulness. Today, seek ways to cultivate gratitude, remembering God's blessings in every season.

Reflection Questions

Are there ways you can practice more gratitude this year?

How does thankfulness change your perspective?

What steps can you take to live with a grateful heart?

Prayer for the Day

Father, help me to be thankful in all circumstances. Let gratitude shape my life, bringing joy and peace in every season. Amen.

December 20

Reflecting on God's Faithfulness

"Remember the Lord your God,
for it is he who gives you the ability to produce wealth."
— DEUTERONOMY 8:18 (NLT)

Additional Scripture References:

James 1:17 - *"Whatever is good and perfect is a gift coming down to us from God our Father, who created all the lights in the heavens. He never changes or casts a shifting shadow."*

Psalm 37:4 - *"Take delight in the Lord, and he will give you your heart's desires."*

Devotional Thought:

As you set goals, remember that everything comes from God's provision. Reflecting on His faithfulness gives us hope and direction for the future. Today, let gratitude for God's faithfulness inspire your plans.

Reflection Questions

Are there blessings from this year that you can thank God for?

How does remembering God's provision impact your goals?

What steps can you take to focus on His faithfulness as you plan?

Prayer for the Day

Lord, thank You for Your faithfulness. Let my goals be rooted in gratitude for all You've provided, guiding me with hope for the future. Amen.

December 21

Setting Goals with Purpose

*"Commit your actions to the Lord,
and your plans will succeed."*

— PROVERBS 16:3 (NLT)

Additional Scripture References:

Psalm 37:5 - "Commit everything you do to the Lord. Trust him, and he will help you."

Proverbs 3:5-6 - "Trust in the Lord with all your heart; do not depend on your own understanding. Seek his will in all you do, and he will show you which path to take."

Devotional Thought:

When we dedicate our goals to God, we align our desires with His purpose. By placing our plans in His hands, we invite His guidance and blessing. Today, commit your goals to God, letting Him shape them according to His will.

Reflection Questions

Are there goals you need to commit to God for His guidance?

How does aligning your plans with God's purpose change your perspective?

What steps can you take to involve God in your goal-setting process?

Prayer for the Day

Lord, help me to commit my actions to You. Let my goals reflect Your purpose, bringing honor to Your name in all I do. Amen.

December 22

Goals for Building Relationships

"Do everything in love."
— 1 CORINTHIANS 16:14 (NLT)

Additional Scripture References:

Colossians 3:14 - "Above all, clothe yourselves with love, which binds us all together in perfect harmony."

1 John 4:19 - "We love each other because he loved us first."

Devotional Thought:

Setting goals to build meaningful relationships allows us to show God's love and grace in tangible ways. When we make relationships a priority, we reflect God's heart for connection and community. Today, think about how you can deepen relationships with love and care.

Reflection Questions

Are there relationships in your life that need more attention?

How does prioritizing relationships align with God's purpose for you?

What steps can you take to build loving, supportive connections?

Prayer for the Day

Father, let my relationships be filled with Your love. Help me to invest in others, showing kindness and care that reflects Your heart. Amen.

December 23

Goals for a Healthy Mind and Spirit

"Don't copy the behavior and customs of this world, but let God transform you into a new person by changing the way you think."

— ROMANS 12:2 (NLT)

Additional Scripture References:

Ephesians 4:23-24 - "Instead, let the Spirit renew your thoughts and attitudes. Put on your new nature, created to be like God — truly righteous and holy."

Colossians 3:2 - "Think about the things of heaven, not the things of earth."

Devotional Thought:

Taking time to renew your mind and spirit through God's Word strengthens your resilience and peace. Setting goals for spiritual and mental health keeps you rooted in His truth. Today, consider ways you can focus on growth and well-being.

Reflection Questions

Are there ways you can focus on spiritual renewal this year?

How does aligning your mind with God's Word impact your life?

What steps can you take to make spiritual and mental health a priority?

Prayer for the Day

Lord, renew my mind and spirit each day. Help me to set goals that keep me close to You, rooted in peace and strength. Amen.

December 24

Goals for Generosity

"You should remember the words of the Lord Jesus:
'It is more blessed to give than to receive.'"

— ACTS 20:35 (NLT)

Additional Scripture References:

2 Corinthians 9:7 - "You must each decide in your heart how much to give. And don't give reluctantly or in response to pressure. For God loves a person who gives cheerfully."

Luke 6:38 - "Give, and you will receive. Your gift will return to you in full — pressed down, shaken together to make room for more, running over, and poured into your lap. The amount you give will determine the amount you get back."

Devotional Thought:

Generosity is a reflection of God's heart, inviting us to give with joy and kindness. When we set goals to be generous, we bring blessings to others and honor God. Today, let your plans include ways to give freely, sharing love and hope with others.

Reflection Questions

Are there ways you can practice more generosity this year?

How does giving with a joyful heart bring you closer to God?

What steps can you take to make generosity a goal?

Prayer for the Day

Father, let generosity be a defining part of my life. Help me to give freely, reflecting Your love and grace to those in need. Amen.

Celebrating Christ's Birth

"For a child is born to us, a son is given to us."

— ISAIAH 9:6 (NLT)

Additional Scripture References:

Luke 2:11 - "The Savior — yes, the Messiah, the Lord — has been born today in Bethlehem, the city of David!"

John 14:27 - "I am leaving you with a gift — peace of mind and heart. And the peace I give is a gift the world cannot give. So don't be troubled or afraid."

Devotional Thought:

Christmas celebrates the greatest gift of all — Jesus, who came to bring us hope, peace, and salvation. His birth is a reminder of God's love for us. Today, let your heart be filled with gratitude, celebrating the joy of Jesus' arrival in the world.

Reflection Questions

Are there ways you can focus on the true meaning of Christmas?

How does celebrating Jesus' birth bring hope and peace?

What steps can you take to honor Christ's gift today?

Prayer for the Day

Lord, thank You for the gift of Jesus. Let my heart be filled with joy and gratitude as I celebrate His birth and the hope He brings. Amen.

December 26

Reflecting on the Year

"Let all that I am praise the Lord;
may I never forget the good things he does for me."
— PSALM 103:2 (NLT)

Additional Scripture References:

1 Thessalonians 5:18 - "Be thankful in all circumstances, for this is God's will for you who belong to Christ Jesus."

Psalm 30:12 - "O Lord my God, I will give you thanks forever!"

Devotional Thought:

As the year draws to a close, take time to reflect on God's blessings and faithfulness. Remembering His goodness strengthens our gratitude and trust. Today, spend time in reflection, thanking God for all He has done in your life this year.

Reflection Questions

Are there blessings from this year you can remember and give thanks for?

How does reflecting on God's goodness deepen your gratitude?

What steps can you take to make reflection a habit?

Prayer for the Day

Father, thank You for Your faithfulness this year. Let my heart overflow with gratitude as I remember all the ways You've blessed me. Amen.

December 27

Seeking God's Guidance for the New Year

*"The Lord says, 'I will guide you along
the best pathway for your life.'"*

— **PSALM 32:8 (NLT)**

Additional Scripture References:

*Proverbs 3:5-6 - "Trust in the Lord with all your heart; do not depend on your
own understanding. Seek his will in all you do, and he will show you which
path to take."*

*Isaiah 30:21 - "Your own ears will hear him. Right behind you a voice will say,
'This is the way you should go,' whether to the right or to the left."*

Devotional Thought:

Trusting God's guidance gives us confidence and peace as we enter
a new year. When we seek His direction, He leads us on the best
path for our lives. Today, ask God to guide you in all things, letting His
wisdom shape your plans.

Reflection Questions

Are there areas of your life where you need God's guidance?

How does seeking God's direction bring peace to your future?

What steps can you take to follow God's lead in the new year?

Prayer for the Day

Lord, guide me along the path You have for me. Let my heart be open
to Your direction as I step into the new year with faith. Amen.

Trusting God's Plans for the Future

"Commit to the Lord whatever you do,
and he will establish your plans."

— PROVERBS 16:3 (NLT)

Additional Scripture References:

Psalm 37:5 - "Commit everything you do to the Lord. Trust him, and he will help you."

Proverbs 3:5-6 - "Trust in the Lord with all your heart; do not depend on your own understanding. Seek his will in all you do, and he will show you which path to take."

Devotional Thought:

Entrusting our plans to God brings stability and assurance, knowing He is with us every step. When we commit our future to Him, we invite His wisdom and guidance. Today, surrender your plans to God, allowing Him to shape and bless them.

Reflection Questions

Are there areas of your life where you need to commit more fully to God?

How does surrendering your plans to God bring peace and trust?

What steps can you take to commit your future to Him?

Prayer for the Day

Father, I commit my plans to You. Let Your wisdom and love guide me in every choice, leading me to Your purpose for my life. Amen.

December 29

Embracing New Beginnings

"Forget the former things; do not dwell on the past. See,
I am doing a new thing!"
— ISAIAH 43:18-19 (NLT)

Additional Scripture References:

2 Corinthians 5:17 - "This means that anyone who belongs to Christ has become a new person. The old life is gone; a new life has begun!"

Revelation 21:5 - "And the one sitting on the throne said, 'Look, I am making everything new!' And then he said to me, 'Write this down, for what I tell you is trustworthy and true.'"

Devotional Thought:

God invites us to embrace new beginnings, letting go of the past and trusting in His plan for what's ahead. When we let go, we make room for His new work in our lives. Today, prepare your heart for a fresh start, ready to embrace what God has in store.

Reflection Questions

Are there past regrets or worries you need to release?

How does trusting God with your future bring hope?

What steps can you take to embrace new beginnings with faith?

Prayer for the Day

Lord, help me to let go of the past and embrace the new things You are doing. Let my heart be filled with hope and trust in Your plans. Amen.

December 30

Looking Forward with Faith

"For I know the plans I have for you," says the Lord. "They are plans for good and not for disaster, to give you a future and a hope."

— JEREMIAH 29:11 (NLT)

Additional Scripture References:

Romans 8:28 - "And we know that God causes everything to work together for the good of those who love God and are called according to his purpose for them."

Proverbs 19:21 - "You can make many plans, but the Lord's purpose will prevail."

Devotional Thought:

God's plans for you are filled with hope and promise. Trusting in His purpose allows you to enter the new year with confidence and joy. Today, look forward with faith, knowing that God's plans for you are good.

Reflection Questions

Are there areas of your future you need to trust God with?

How does believing in God's purpose bring you hope?

What steps can you take to trust His plans for the new year?

Prayer for the Day

Father, thank You for the hope and future You promise. Help me to enter the new year with faith, trusting that You hold my future in Your hands. Amen.

December 31

A New Year of Purpose

"Teach us to realize the brevity of life,
so that we may grow in wisdom."

— **PSALM 90:12 (NLT)**

Additional Scripture References:

James 4:14 - "How do you know what your life will be like tomorrow? Your life is like the morning fog – it's here a little while and then it's gone."

Ephesians 5:15-16 - "So be careful how you live. Don't live like fools, but like those who are wise. Make the most of every opportunity in these evil days."

Devotional Thought:

As the year ends, let your heart be filled with purpose and intention. God calls us to use each day wisely, honoring Him in all we do. Today, ask God for wisdom and guidance as you enter a new year, ready to live with purpose for His glory.

Reflection Questions

Are there goals you want to dedicate to God this year?

How does seeking God's wisdom shape your perspective on life?

What steps can you take to live with purpose each day?

Prayer for the Day

Lord, as I enter a new year, teach me to live with purpose. Let each day be filled with Your wisdom and love, bringing honor to Your name. Amen.

Made in the USA
Thornton, CO
01/10/25 05:55:29